PO
Factfinder

Ann Kay

RANDOM HOUSE ⌂ NEW YORK

First American edition, 1989

Copyright © 1987 by Kingfisher Books Ltd. All rights reserved under
International and Pan-American Copyright Conventions. Published in the
United States by Random House, Inc., New York. This edition first
published in Great Britain by Kingfisher Books Limited, a Grisewood &
Dempsey Company, in 1987.

Library of Congress Cataloging-in-Publication Data:
Kay, Ann.
  Pocket factfinder.
  p. cm.
  Includes index.
  SUMMARY: An illustrated almanac including thousands of facts about
such topics as the universe, countries of the world, science and nature,
government, world history and religions, the arts, and sports.
  ISBN: 0–394–82016–9
  1. Children's encyclopedias and dictionaries. [1. Encyclopedias and
dictionaries.] I. Title. AG6.K39 1989 031—dc19 88–18353

Manufactured in Spain 1 2 3 4 5 6 7 8 9 0

Contents

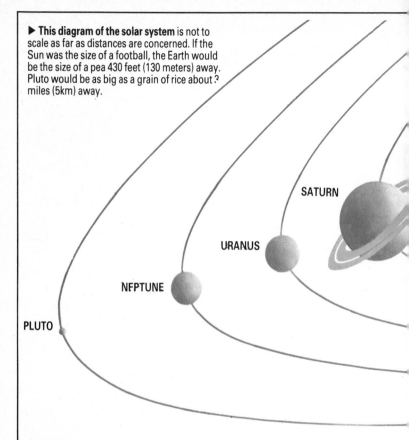

▶ **This diagram of the solar system** is not to scale as far as distances are concerned. If the Sun was the size of a football, the Earth would be the size of a pea 430 feet (130 meters) away. Pluto would be as big as a grain of rice about ? miles (5km) away.

SATURN

URANUS

NFPTUNE

PLUTO

The Universe

A few thousand years ago, people did not know whether the Earth was round or flat. A few hundred years ago they knew it was round, but thought it was at the center of the universe. Astronomers continued to observe and measure. They discovered that the Earth is one of a family of nine planets revolving around the Sun. They worked out that our solar system was born about 5 billion—5,000 million—years ago and that the atomic reactions raging at the Sun's center will go on for at least another 5 billion years. We also know that our Sun is only a very ordinary star among billions strewn throughout

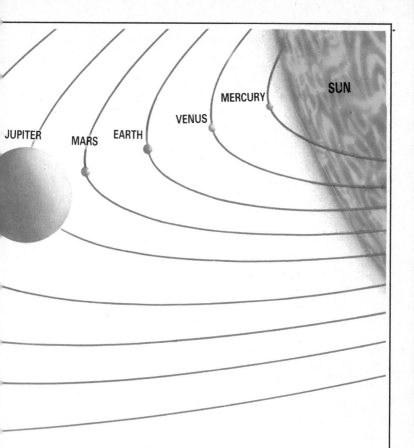

JUPITER MARS EARTH VENUS MERCURY SUN

space and forming our galaxy—the Milky Way. Farther out still, the mysterious universe contains countless other galaxies—island universes—in many shapes and sizes, with vast distances between one island and the next.

The possibility of finding intelligent life on other planets remains one of the most exciting and difficult challenges in all of science. There is evidence that most of the stars we see from Earth have their own planets. But the stars we see occupy only a tiny corner of our Milky Way galaxy. Throughout our galaxy as a whole there could be one billion planets on which intelligent beings could thrive. And our galaxy is only one of millions upon millions in the known universe. Among those countless planets there must surely be another Earth.

The Constellations

A total of 88 constellations—groups of stars—can be seen over the entire sky. Many constellations form the shape of figures from ancient mythology.

CONSTELLATIONS OF THE SOUTHERN HEMISPHERE		
1 Cetus, Sea Monster	16 Pavo, Peacock	31 Ara, Altar
2 Sculptor, Sculptor	17 Octans, Octant	32 Scorpius. Scorpion
3 Aquarius, Water Bearer	18 Dorado, Swordfish	33 Serpens, Serpent
4 Piscis Austrinus, Southern Fish	19 Pictor, Painter's Easel	34 Ophiuchus, Serpent Bearer
5 Capricornus, Sea Goat	20 Columba, Dove	35 Lupus, Wolf
6 Grus, Crane	21 Lepus, Hare	36 Centaurus, Centaur
7 Phoenix, Phoenix	22 Orion, Hunter	37 Crux, Southern Cross
8 Fornax, Furnace	23 Monoceros, Unicorn	38 Musca, Fly
9 Eridanus, River Eridanus	24 Canis Major, Great Dog	39 Vela, Sails
10 Hydrus, Water Snake	25 Puppis, Ship's Stern	40 Pyxis, Compass
11 Tucana, Toucan	26 Carina, Keel	41 Hydra, Sea Serpent
12 Indus, Indian	27 Volans, Flying Fish	42 Sextans, Sextant
13 Sagittarius, Archer	28 Chameleon, Chameleon	43 Crater, Cup
14 Aquila, Eagle	29 Apus, Bird of Paradise	44 Corvus, Crow
15 Corona Australis, Southern Crown	30 Triangulum Australe, Southern Triangle	45 Libra, Scales
		46 Virgo, Virgin

Scorpius, the Scorpion

CONSTELLATIONS OF THE NORTHERN HEMISPHERE

1 Equuleus, Colt
2 Delphinus, Dolphin
3 Pegasus, Flying Horse
4 Pisces, Fishes
5 Cetus, Sea Monster
6 Aries, Ram
7 Triangulum, Triangle
8 Andromeda, Chained Maiden
9 Lacerta, Lizard
10 Cygnus, Swan
11 Sagitta, Arrow
12 Aquila, Eagle
13 Lyra, Lyre
14 Cepheus, King
15 Cassiopeia, Lady in Chair
16 Perseus, Champion
17 Camelopardus, Giraffe
18 Auriga, Charioteer

19 Taurus, Bull
20 Orion, Hunter
21 Lynx, Lynx
22 Polaris, Pole Star
23 Ursa Minor, Little Bear
24 Draco, Dragon
25 Hercules, Kneeling Giant
26 Ophiuchus, Serpent Bearer
27 Serpens, Serpent
28 Corona Borealis, Northern Crown
29 Boötes, Herdsman
30 Ursa Major, Great Bear
31 Gemini, Twins
32 Cancer, Crab
33 Canis Minor, Little Dog
34 Hydra, Sea Serpent
35 Leo, Lion
36 Leo Minor, Little Lion

37 Canes Venatici, Hunting Dogs
38 Coma Berenices, Berenice's Hair
39 Virgo, Virgin

Taurus, the Bull

Cancer, the Crab

7

The Sun

Our Sun is about a quarter of a million times closer than the next nearest star.

SUN FACTS	
Diameter:	865,000 miles (1,392,000 km) (109 × Earth)
Mass:	328,900 × Earth
Volume:	1,300,000 × Earth
Surface temperature:	10,832°F (6000°C)
Core temperature:	about 27,000,000°F (15,000,000°C)
True rotation period:	25.38 days
Apparent rotation period	27.28 days
Mean distance from Earth:	92,960,000 miles (149,600,000 km)
Cosmic year (time to orbit Galaxy):	225 million years
Estimated age:	4.6 billion years
Distance nearest star:	4.3 light-years
Distance to center Galaxy:	30,000 light-years

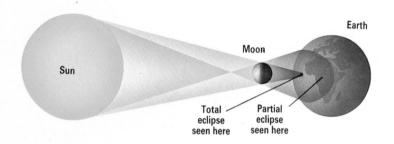

Earth

Moon

Sun

Total eclipse seen here   Partial eclipse seen here

▲ **The Moon** appears to us to be the same size as the Sun because it is much closer. When the Moon passes between the Sun and Earth a solar eclipse occurs. People in the direct shadow see a total eclipse; those farther away see a partial eclipse of the Sun.

TOTAL SOLAR ECLIPSE TABLE		
Date	Maximum duration (minutes & seconds)	Area of visibility
1988 Mar 18	3m 46s	Indian Ocean, East Indies, Pacific Ocean
1990 Jul 22	2m 33s	Finland, U.S.S.R., Pacific Ocean
1991 Jul 11	6m 54s	Pacific Ocean, Central America, Brazil
1992 Jun 30	5m 20s	South Atlantic Ocean
1994 Nov 3	4m 23s	South America, South Atlantic Ocean
1995 Oct 24	2m 05s	Iran, India, East Indies, South Pacific Ocean
1997 Mar 9	2m 50s	U.S.S.R., Arctic Ocean

The Moon

Our nearest neighbor, the Moon, is not nearly as wide as the United States.

MOON FACTS

Age: about 4.6 billion years
Diameter: 2,160 miles (3,476 km)
Surface area: 14,650,000 sq miles (37,940,600 sq km)
Mass: 0.012 × Earth
Density: 3.3 × water
Mean distance from Earth: 238,900 miles (384,400 km)
Surface temperature: 212°F (100°C) at noon, −238°F (−150°C) at night

Lunar month (new Moon to new Moon): 29 days 13 hours
Mean velocity in orbit: 0.62 miles (1.0 km) per second
Escape velocity: 1.5 miles (2.4 km) per sec
Force of gravity at surface: 0.16 of the Earth
Atmosphere: none
Rotation Period: 27 d, 7 h, 43 min
Length of day and night: about 14 Earth days each

MOON PHASES

The Sun shines on half the Moon, which is the part we see shining in the sky. As the Moon goes around the Earth, we see a different view of this sunlit half. The changing shapes are called phases. It takes 29½ days for the Moon to pass through a complete phase cycle from new Moon to new Moon—the lunar month.

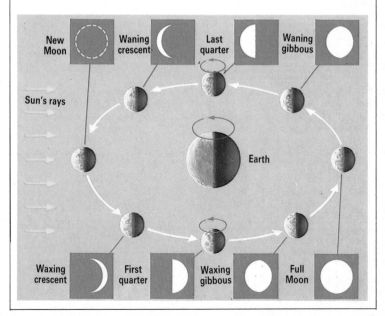

9

BRIGHTEST STARS

Star	Constellation	Apparent magnitude	Distance (light-years)
Sirius	Canis Major	−1.6	8.7
Canopus	Carina	−0.7	1,200
Alpha Centauri	Centaurus	−0.3	4.3
Arcturus	Boötes	0.0	36
Vega	Lyra	0.0	26
Capella	Auriga	+0.1	45

NEAREST STARS

Star	Distance (light-years)
Proxima Centauri	4.2
Alpha Centauri	4.3
Barnard's Star	5.9
Wolf 359	7.6
Lalande 21185	8.1
Sirius	8.7

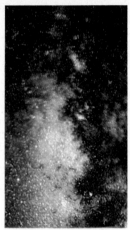

▲ **A small part** of the Milky Way and its multitude of stars.

MILKY WAY

Our galaxy, the Milky Way, is a vast spiral system of stars. It is so big that light takes about 100,000 light-years to travel from one end to the other.

Diameter:	100,000 light-years
Thickness at the center:	20,000 light-years
Thickness at the edge:	7,000 light-years
Total mass of the system:	100 billion solar masses
Density in solar neighborhood:	1,200 earth masses per cubic light-year
Absolute magnitude (from above the galactic pole):	−20.5
Total number of stars:	100 billion
Total number of globular clusters:	500
Total number of open clusters:	18,000
Total number of stellar associations:	800
Distance of Sun from galactic center:	32,000 light-years
Distance of Sun from galactic plane:	30 light-years "north"
Rotational velocity near the Sun:	155 miles/sec (250 km/sec)
Rotational period near the Sun:	225 million years
Age of Galaxy:	12 billion years

● Some stars are hundreds of times larger than our Sun. However, the material in them is spread very thinly—a million times thinner than the air we breathe.

● The Milky Way got its name from the ancients. They believed that the white band of stars that they saw in the sky was milk spilled from Juno's breast.

● If the Milky Way galaxy was the size of the continent of North America, our solar system would be the size of a football lying at one edge.

METEOR SHOWERS

Meteors are small particles that are seen as they burn up in the atmosphere. They are believed to be dust from comets. When the Earth crosses the orbit of a comet, as happens several times a year, a meteor shower is seen.

About 500 meteors strike the Earth each year. So far we do not know of anyone being killed by one. However, there have been some lucky escapes. In 1908, a meteorite that crashed into a Siberian forest knocked down trees in a 20-mile (31-kilometer) radius. Just five hours later, the meteor would have crashed into St. Petersburg, the capital of Russia at that time.

Shower	Noticeable activity	Maximum activity	Maximum number per hour
Quadrantids	Jan 1–6	Jan 3–4	50
April Lyrids	Apr 19–24	Apr 22	10
η Aquarids	May 1–8	May 5	10
δ Aquarids	Jul 15–Aug 15	Jul 27	25
Perseids	Jul 25–Aug 18	Aug 12	50
Orionids	Oct 16–26	Oct 20	20
Taurids	Oct 20–Nov 30	Nov 8	8
Leonids	Nov 15–19	Nov 17	6?
Geminids	Dec 7–15	Dec 14	50

FAMOUS COMETS

Comets are "dirty snowballs" that orbit the Sun on elongated paths.

Name	First seen	Orbital period (years)
Halley's Comet	240 B.C.	76
Encke's Comet	1786	3.3
Biela's Comet	1806	6.7
Great Comet of 1811	1811	3,000
Pons-Winnecke Comet	1819	6.0
Great Comet of 1843	1843	500
Donati's Comet	1858	2,040
Schwassmann-Wachmann Comet	1925	16.2
Arend-Roland Comet	1957	10,000
Ikeya-Seki Comet	1965	880
Comet Kohoutek*	1973	75,000
Comet West	1976	1 million

*observed from *Skylab* and *Soyuz* spacecraft

THE LARGEST ASTEROIDS

These are rocky fragments that orbit between the paths of Mars and Jupiter.

	Diameter in miles (km)	Distance from Sun in millions miles (km)
Ceres	623 (1,003)	257 (414)
Pallas	378 (608)	257 (414)
Vesta	334 (538)	219 (353)
Hygeia	280 (450)	293 (471)
Euphrosyne	230 (370)	294 (473)

▶ **Comet West** in the morning sky, 1976.

The Planets

The planets of our solar system, including the Earth, probably formed from the same huge cloud of material that made the Sun over four billion years ago.

MERCURY

Diameter, equator:	3,014 miles (4,850 km)
Volume:	0.054 Earth's volume
Mean density:	5.4 (water=1)
Mass:	0.055 Earth's mass
Gravity:	0.37 Earth's gravity
Mean distance from Sun:	36,000,000 miles (58,000,000 km)
Spins on axis in:	59 days
Orbits Sun in:	88 days
Velocity in orbit:	29.8 mi/sec (47.9 km/sec)
Escape velocity:	2.6 mi/sec (4.2 km/sec)
Satellites:	None
Surface temperature:	noon: 662°F (350°C); night: −274°F (−170°C)
Atmosphere:	None

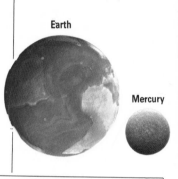

Earth

Mercury

VENUS

Diameter, equator:	7,544 miles (12,140 km)
Volume:	0.88 Earth's volume
Mean density:	5.2 (water=1)
Mass:	0.82 Earth's mass
Gravity:	0.88 Earth's gravity
Mean distance from Sun:	67,000,000 miles (108,000,000 km)
Spins on axis in:	243 days
Orbits Sun in:	225 days
Velocity in orbit:	21,7 mi/sec (35.0 km/sec)
Escape velocity:	6.4 mi/sec (10.3 km/sec)
Satellites:	None
Surface temperature:	day side: about 930°F (500°C)
Atmosphere:	Mainly carbon dioxide

Earth

Venus

MARS

Diameter, equator:	4,220 miles (6,790 km)
Volume:	0.15 Earth's volume
Mean density:	3.95 (water=1)
Mass:	0.11 Earth's mass
Gravity:	0.38 Earth's gravity
Mean distance from Sun:	142,000,000 miles (228,000,000 km)
Spins on axis in:	24 h 37 min
Orbits Sun in:	687 days
Velocity in orbit:	15.0 mi/sec (24.1 km/sec)
Escape velocity:	3.1 mi/sec (5.0 km/sec)
Satellites:	2
Surface temperature (summer):	noon: −4°F (−20°C); night: −112°F (−80°C)
Atmosphere:	Mainly carbon dioxide

Earth

Mars

JUPITER

Diameter, equator:	88,600 miles (142,600 km)
Volume:	1,316 Earth's volume
Mean density:	1.34 (water=1)
Mass:	317.8 Earth's mass
Gravity:	2.64 Earth's gravity
Mean distance from Sun:	483,000,000 miles (778,000,000 km)
Spins on axis in:	9 h 50 min
Orbits Sun in:	11.9 years
Velocity in orbit:	8.1 mi/sec (13.1 km/sec)
Escape velocity:	37 mi/sec (60 km/sec)
Satellites:	14
Cloud surface temperature:	−238°F (−150°C)
Atmosphere:	Mainly hydrogen, helium

Earth

Jupiter

Earth

Saturn

SATURN

Diameter, equator:	74,700 miles (120,200 km)
Volume:	755 Earth's volume
Mean density:	0.70 (water=1)
Mass:	95.2 Earth's mass
Gravity:	1.2 Earth's gravity
Mean distance from Sun:	887,000,000 miles (1,427,000,000 km)
Spins on axis in:	10 h 14 min
Orbits Sun in:	29.5 years
Velocity in orbit:	6.0 mi/sec (9.6 km/sec)
Escape velocity:	22 mi/sec (36 km/sec)
Satellites:	23
Cloud surface temperature:	−292°F (−180°C)
Atmosphere:	Mainly hydrogen, helium

URANUS

Diameter, equator:	32,300 miles (52,000 km)
Volume:	64 Earth's volume
Mean density:	1.25 (water=1)
Mass:	14.5 Earth's mass
Gravity:	0.9 Earth's gravity
Mean distance from Sun:	1,783,000,000 miles (2,870,000,000 km)
Spins on axis in:	16 hours
Orbits Sun in:	84 years
Velocity in orbit:	4.2 mi/sec (6.8 km/sec)
Escape velocity:	14 mi/sec (22 km/sec)
Satellites:	15
Cloud surface temperature:	−6°F (−21°C)
Atmosphere:	Mainly hydrogen, helium, methane

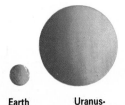

Earth   Uranus·

Neptune

Earth

NEPTUNE

Diameter, equator:	30,100 miles (48,400 km)
Volume:	54 Earth's volume
Mean density:	1.8 (water=1)
Mass:	17.2 Earth's mass
Gravity:	1.4 Earth's gravity
Mean distance from Sun:	2,794,000,000 miles (4,497,000,000 km)
Spins on axis in:	14 hours
Orbits Sun in:	164.8 years
Velocity in orbit:	3.4 mi/sec (5.4 km/sec)
Escape velocity:	16 mi/sec (25 km/sec)
Satellites:	2
Cloud surface temperature:	−364°F (−220°C)
Atmosphere:	Mainly hydrogen, helium, methane

PLUTO

(Only limited data are given because there is doubt about the planet's diameter)

Diameter, equator:	1,800 miles (3,000 km)
Mass:	0.17 Earth's mass
Mean distance from Sun:	3,670,000,000 miles (5,900,000,000 km)
Spins on axis in:	153 hours
Orbits Sun in:	247.7 years
Velocity in orbit:	2.9 mi/sec (4.7 km/sec)
Satellites:	1
Surface temperature:	−382°F (−230°C)
Atmosphere:	None

Earth

Pluto

◀ *Mariner 9* went into orbit around Mars in 1971 and sent back the first close-up pictures of another planet.

LARGEST OPTICAL TELESCOPES

Aperture	Site
20 ft. (6.0 m)	Zelenchukskaya, U.S.S.R., 1976
17 ft. (5.1 m)	Mount Palomar, U.S.A., 1948
15 ft. (4.5 m)	Mount Hopkins, U.S.A., 1979
13.8 ft. (4.2 m)	La Palma, Canary Islands, 1986
13 ft. (4.0 m)	Kitt Peak, U.S.A., 1973
13 ft. (4.0 m)	Cerro Tololo, Chile, 1976
12.8 ft. (3.9 m)	Siding Spring, Australia, 1975
12.4 ft. (3.8 m)	Mauna Kea, Hawaii, 1977
11.8 ft. (3.6 m)	La Silla, Chile, 1976
9.8 ft. (3.0 m)	Lick Observatory, U.S.A., 1958
8.8 ft. (2.7 m)	McDonald Observatory, U.S.A., 1969
8.5 ft. (2.6 m)	Crimea, U.S.S.R., 1960
8.5 ft. (2.6 m)	Byurakan, U.S.S.R., 1973
8.2 ft. (2.5 m)	Mount Wilson, U.S.A., 1917
8.2 ft. (2.5 m)	Las Campanas, Chile, 1976
8.2 ft. (2.5 m)	La Palma, Canary Islands, 1986

LARGEST RADIO TELESCOPES

Aperture	Site
1,000 ft. (305 m)	Arecibo, Puerto Rico, 1963
330 ft. (100 m)	Effelsberg, West Germany, 1976
300 ft. (91 m)	Green Bank, West Virginia, 1962
250 ft. (76 m)	Jodrell Bank, England, 1957

Famous Names in Astronomy

Aristarchus (200s B.C.), a Greek, suggested that the Earth travels around the Sun.

Brahe, Tycho (1546–1601), a Dane, was a brilliant observer of the heavens.

Copernicus, Nicolaus (1473–1543), a Polish priest, revived the idea that the Earth circles the Sun.

Einstein, Albert (1879–1955), a German physicist and mathematician, revolutionized many astronomical concepts with his theories of relativity.

Galileo (1564–1642), an Italian scientist, constructed a telescope in 1609 and became the first great observer with such an instrument.

▲ **Nicolaus Copernicus** reintroduced the idea that the Earth revolves around the Sun at a time when most people believed the opposite.

Halley, Edmund (1656–1742), the second British Astronomer Royal, is best known for his work on comets. He showed that the comet now named after him had appeared many times before at regular intervals.

Hipparchus (100s B.C.), a Greek, was the best astronomer of ancient times.

Hubble, Edwin (1899–1953), an American, founded the study of the universe beyond our own galaxy.

Kepler, Johannes (1571–1630), a German who became Tycho Brahe's assistant, developed the laws of planetary motion. The first of these states that planets travel around the Sun in elliptical orbits.

Lowell, Percival (1885–1916), an American, correctly predicted that a ninth planet exists (Pluto).

Newton, Isaac (1642–1727), a brilliant English scientist and mathematician, developed the law of gravitation, explained why the heavenly bodies move as they do, and calculated their orbits.

Ptolemy of Alexandria (A.D. 100s), a Greek, surveyed in his famous astronomical book, the *Almagest* (*The Greatest*), the work of Hipparchus.

15

An Astronomical History

B.C.

*c.*3000 Babylonian astronomical records begin.

*c.*1000 Chinese astronomical records begin.

*c.*280 Aristarchus suggests that the Earth orbits the Sun.

*c.*270 Eratosthenes makes an accurate estimate of the size of the Earth.

*c.*130 Hipparchus draws up the first star catalog.

A.D.

*c.*140 Ptolemy's *Almagest* written; his Earth-centered universe accepted.

903 Star positions measured by Al-Sufi.

1054 Supernova in Taurus recorded by Chinese astronomers.

1433 Ulugh Beigh's star catalog compiled.

1543 Nicolaus Copernicus proposes a Sun-centered system.

1572 Supernova in Cassiopeia observed by Tycho Brahe.

1600 Johannes Kepler starts analyzing Tycho's planetary observations and derives his three laws of planetary motion (1609–18).

1608 The refracting telescope invented by Hans Lippershey.

1609 Galileo and others make the first telescopic observations.

1631 Transit of Mercury across the Sun, predicted by Kepler, is observed by Gassendi.

1638 Holwarda discovers the famous variable star Mira Ceti.

1647 One of the first lunar maps is drawn by Hevelius.

1668 Isaac Newton constructs the first reflecting telescope.

1687 Newton's *Principia*, containing his theory of gravitation, is published.

1705 Edmund Halley predicts that the comet last seen in 1682 will return again in 1758.

1725 The first "modern" star catalog, based on Flamsteed's observations, published.

1758 John Dollond manufactures the first successful achromatic object-glass. Halley's Comet makes its predicted return.

▼ **This 3,000-year-old** Mesopotamian tablet shows the constellation of the Scorpion as well as the Moon and the planet Venus.

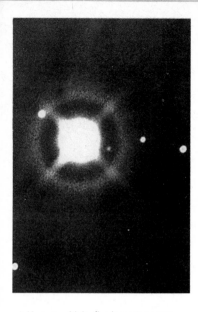

▲ **Uranus**, with its five largest moons.

1761 The first transit of Venus across the Sun observed.

1781 William Herschel discovers the new planet Uranus, and Charles Messier publishes his catalog of star clusters and nebula.

1801 Giuseppe Piazzi discovers the first asteroid, Ceres.

1838 Friedrich Wilhelm Bessel makes the first interstellar distance measurement, of 61 Cygni.

1840 The first astronomical photograph, of the Moon, taken by John William Draper.

1843 The sunspot cycle announced by Samuel Heinrich Schwabe.

1846 Neptune discovered as a result of predictions by John Couch Adams and Urbain Leverrier.

1859 Gustav Kirchhoff proves that the elements in a hot body imprint characteristic lines in its spectrum.

1870–1900 Great developments in astronomical photography and spectrum analysis. In 1891 George Ellery Hale invents spectroheliograph for photographing the Sun at a single wavelength.

1908 The Hertzsprung-Russell diagram introduces the idea of giant and dwarf stars. The first of the "giant" reflecting telescopes, the 5-foot (1.5-meter) at Mount Wilson, begins work.

1912 The Cepheid period-luminosity law announced by Henrietta Leavitt.

1920 The red shift first noticed in distant galaxies.

1923 Edwin Powell Hubble makes the first good measurement of the distance of M31 in Andromeda.

1930 Clyde Tombaugh discovers the planet Pluto.

1930–60 Many investigations into stellar energy production and the evolution of stars.

1937 The first radio waves from space detected by Grote Reber.

1948 The Mount Palomar 200-inch (5-meter) reflector completed.

1955 The Jodrell Bank 250-foot (76-meter) radio telescope completed.

1963 The great distances of quasars first established. Background radiation pervading space discovered.

1967 Pulsars discovered.

1977 The rings of Uranus discovered.

1981 The most remote known galaxies identified, at a distance of about ten billion light-years.

1987 Supernova seen in neighboring galaxy. This is the nearest supernova to be observed since 1604.

A History of Space Exploration

1804 The first high-altitude ascent made by Gay-Lussac and Biot in a hot-air balloon, reaching a height of 4.3 miles (7 kilometers).

1896 Unmanned balloons, launched by Teisserenc de Bort, analyze the atmosphere at heights of up to 9.3 miles (15 kilometers).

1903 Ziolkovsky proposes a rocket-propelled spacecraft.

1919 Goddard publishes a monograph on rocket propulsion.

1923 Oberth's book *The Rocket into Interplanetary Space* published.

1926 Goddard launches the first liquid-fuel rocket.

1942 Experiments with the V-2 rocket at Pennemunde achieve heights of 112 miles (180 kilometers).

1949 The first two-stage rocket, the WAC-Corporal, achieves a height of 250 miles (400 kilometers).

1950 Cape Canaveral first used for rocket experiments.

1955 The U.S.A. announces its intention of launching space satellites.

1957 The world's first satellite, *Sputnik 1*, launched by the U.S.S.R.

1958 *Explorer 1*, the first satellite launched by the U.S.A., discovers radiation belts around the Earth.

1959 Three lunar probes launched by the U.S.S.R.: *Luna 2* photographs the far side; *Luna 3* hits the surface.

1961 The first manned orbital flight, by U.S.S.R. astronaut Gagarin in *Vostok*.

1962 The first successful interplanetary probe, *Mariner 2*, sends back information about Venus.

1964 The first close-up pictures of the Moon obtained by *Ranger 7* (U.S.A.).

1965 *Mariner 4* (U.S.A.) passes Mars and transmits pictures and information.

1966 *Venera 3* (U.S.S.R.) lands on Venus, the first spacecraft to reach another planet. *Luna 9* (U.S.S.R.) makes the first soft landing on the Moon, followed by *Surveyor 1* (U.S.A.). The first of the *Orbiter* lunar mapping satellites launched (U.S.A.).

1967 *Venera 4* (U.S.S.R.) soft-lands on Venus and sends back information.

▼ **Robert Hutchings Goddard** launched the first true rocket vehicle in 1926.

▼ **The Soviet probe** *Luna 13* soft-landed on the Moon in December 1966.

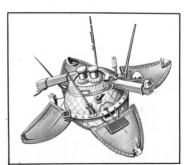

1969 *Mariner 6* and *7* (U.S.A.) pass Mars and send back pictures and information. *Apollo 11* lands the first men on the Moon (July 20).

1970 The first automatic lunar probe, *Luna 16* (U.S.S.R.), returns a sample to Earth.

1971 *Mariner 9* (U.S.A.) goes into orbit around Mars and sends back a great deal of information.

1973 The first flyby of Jupiter, by *Pioneer 10*, which becomes the first man-made artifact to escape from the solar system. *Skylab*, an orbiting astronomical laboratory, launched by the U.S.A. and visited by three different teams.

1974 *Mariner 10* (U.S.A.) passes both Venus and Mercury. *Salyut 3* and *4* (U.S.S.R.) link up to form orbiting observatory. *Pioneer 11* (U.S.A.) passes Jupiter and heads for Saturn.

1976 First successful landing on Mars by the two *Viking* craft (U.S.A.), which provide data and photographs.

1978 *Pioneer Venus* project (U.S.A.) puts two craft into orbit around Venus and lands four surface probes.

1979 *Voyagers 1* and *2* (U.S.A.) pass Jupiter and discover a faint ring around it. *Pioneer 11* passes Saturn successfully after a six-year journey.

1980 *Voyager 1* makes a successful flyby of Saturn, and then heads for outer space.

1981 The first Space Shuttle, *Columbia* (U.S.A.), completes two flights. *Voyager 2* passes Saturn and heads for Uranus.

1982 *Columbia* (U.S.A.) completes third flight. U.S.S.R. sends probes to Venus.

1984 The first "repairs" carried out in space, using the Space Shuttle to mend the Solar Max satellite. Astronauts perform the first-ever spacewalk untethered to a spacecraft.

1986 The *Challenger* tragedy (explosion soon after takeoff and death of all seven astronauts) causes a three-year delay in the Shuttle program. Space probe *Giotto* launched to study the return of Halley's Comet. *Voyager 2* sends back detailed photographs of the moons of Uranus, and heads for Neptune—arrival date 1989.

▼ **In the weightlessness** of space, dental chairs are unnecessary.

▼ *Voyager 2*, having visited Saturn and Uranus, is now on its way to Neptune.

Planet Earth

Earth—the fifth largest planet in the solar system. Scientists believe that it began as a whirling cloud of dust and gas that shrank into a fiery, semimolten mass. An outer layer formed which cooled and hardened into rock. Beneath this layer the Earth is still hot and volatile and the underground forces that gradually push up mountains and move continents also cause earthquakes and volcanic eruptions. Other forces disturb the Earth's surface too. Above us, the warm and cold air masses that make the winds blow can build up into destructive tornadoes and hurricanes. The movement of the oceans, which constantly erodes the land, sometimes produces devastating tidal waves. These are just some of the things that make the varied surface of our planet a restless place of constant change.

EARTH'S VITAL STATISTICS

Age: About 4.6 billion years
Weight: About 6,000 million million million tons
Diameter: From pole to pole through the Earth's center 7,900 miles (12,719 km);
across the equator through the Earth's center 7,927 miles (12,757 km)
Circumference: Around the poles 24,868 miles (40,020 km);
around the equator 24,912 miles (40,091 km)
Area: Land 58,701,400 sq miles (152,024,880 sq km)—29% of total surface;
Water 138,236,100 sq miles (358,003,850 sq km)—71% of total surface
Volume: 260,000 million cubic miles (1,084,000 million cubic km)
Volume of the oceans: 317 million cubic miles (1,321 million cubic km)
Average height of land: 2,756 ft. (840 m) above sea level
Average depth of ocean: 12,450 ft. (3,795 m) below sea level
Density: 5.52 times water
Mean temperature: 72°F (22°C)
Length of year: 365¼ days
Rotation period: 23 hours 56 minutes
Mean distance from the Sun: 92,960,000 miles (149,600,000 km)
Mean velocity in orbit: 18.5 miles (29.8 km) per second
Escape velocity: 6.96 miles (11.2 km) per second
Atmosphere: Main constituents are nitrogen (78.5%) and oxygen (21%)
Crust: Main constituents are oxygen (47%), silicon (28%), aluminum (8%), and iron (5%)
Known satellites: One

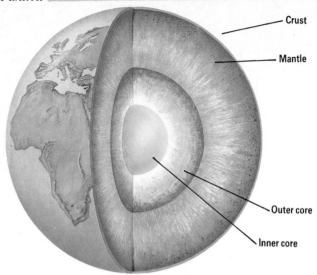

Crust

Mantle

Outer core

Inner core

▲ **Inside the Earth.** Beneath a thin outer crust of rock is a hot, partly molten layer of rock called the mantle. Under this the outer core forms a molten metal layer of iron and nickel. The inner core is a solid metal ball under great pressure.

INSIDE THE EARTH

	Density	Temp. °C	°F	State
Sial[1]	2.8	<500	<932	solid
Sima[2]	2.9	<1,100	<2,012	solid
Upper mantle	4.3	1,400	2,552	probably molten
Lower mantle	5.5	1,700	3,092	solid
Outer core	10.0	2,300	4,172	molten
Inner core	13.6	2,500	4,532	solid

Thickness of sial	0–18 miles (0–30 km)
Thickness of sima	6–30 miles (10–50 km)
Thickness of upper mantle	430 miles (700 km)
Thickness of lower mantle	1,370 miles (2,200 km)
Thickness of outer core	1,400 miles (2,250 km)
Radius of inner core	800 miles (1,300 km)

[1] Light rocks of the crust that lie underneath the continents
[2] Dense rocks under the sial that form much of the ocean bed

THE AGES OF THE EARTH

Era, Period, Epoch	Millions of years ago
Pleistocene Epoch	10,000 years –2 million
Quaternary Period	
Pliocene Epoch	2–5
Miocene Epoch	5–25
Oligocene Epoch	25–35
Eocene Epoch	35–60
Paleocene Epoch	60–65
Tertiary Period	
CENOZOIC ERA	
Cretaceous Period	65–145
Jurassic Period	145–210
Triassic Period	210–245
MESOZOIC ERA	
Permian Period	245–285
Carboniferous Period	285–360
Devonian Period	360–410
Silurian Period	410–440
Ordovician Period	440–505
Cambrian Period	505–570
PALEOZOIC ERA	

We measure the age of our planet by dating the rocks in its crust. There are three kinds of rock. **Igneous** rock forms when molten rock is pushed up from deep down. **Sedimentary** rock is hardened layers of sediment, usually under water. **Metamorphic** rocks are igneous or sedimentary rocks that have been changed by heat and pressure inside the Earth.

1. Obsidian. Igneous rock that cooled on the surface.

2. Granite. Igneous rock with large crystals that hardened underground.

3. Marble. Metamorphic rock formed from limestone.

4. Slate. Metamorphic rock formed from shale.

5. Coal. Sedimentary rock formed from crushed remains of prehistoric plants and trees.

6. Limestone. Sedimentary rock from seabed deposits of calcium carbonate.

7. Sandstone. Sedimentary rock made mostly from grains of quartz from igneous rocks.

8. Conglomerate. Stones stuck together in a sedimentary "concrete."

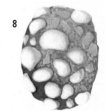

WORLD RECORD BREAKERS

FACTS ABOUT VOLCANOES

Active volcanoes: There are about 535; of these, 80 are below the sea.

Largest known eruption: Tambora, Indonesia, in 1815. The volcano threw out about about 35 cubic miles (150 cubic km) of matter and lost 4,100 ft. (1,250 m) in height.

Greatest disaster: 36,000 people were drowned by a giant wave unleashed when Krakatoa, Indonesia, exploded in 1883.

Greatest volcanic explosion: About 1470 B.C., Santorini in the Aegean Sea exploded with maybe 130 times the force of the greatest H-bomb.

FAMOUS EARTHQUAKES

Shensi Province, China, 1556: Over 800,000 people perished—more than in any other earthquake.

Lisbon, Portugal, 1755: About 60,000 people died and shocks were felt as far away as Norway.

San Francisco, CA, 1906: An earthquake and the fires it caused destroyed the city.

Kwanto Plain, Japan, 1923: Some 570,000 buildings collapsed. This was the costliest earthquake ever as measured by damage to property.

Lebu, Chile, 1977: The strongest earthquake shock ever recorded.

DEEP, LONG, AND HIGH

Greatest ocean depth: 36,197 ft. (11.033 m), Marianas trench, Pacific Ocean.
Deepest gorge: 7,900 ft. (2,408 m), Hells Canyon, Idaho, USA.
Longest gorge: 217 miles (349 km), Grand Canyon, Arizona.
Highest navigated lake: Titicaca, Peru/Bolivia, 12,500 ft. (3,810 m) above sea level.
Deepest lake: Baikal, Siberia, U.S.S.R., 5,315 ft. (1,620 m).

▼ The lava from volcanoes on the Pacific islands of Hawaii is very liquid and flows a long way. Mauna Loa, on Hawaii, is 13,765 ft. (4,196 km) high and the largest volcano in the world. It erupts every 3½ years.

LONGEST RIVERS

	miles	km
Nile (Africa)	4,160	6,690
Amazon (South America)	4,080	6,570
Mississippi-Missouri (U.S.A.)	3,860	6,212
Irtysh (U.S.S.R.)	3,461	5,570
Chang Jiang (Yangtze) (China)	3,430	5,520
Hwang Ho (Yellow) (China)	2,903	4,672
Zaire (Congo) (Africa)	2,900	4,667
Amur (Asia)	2,802	4,509
Lena (U.S.S.R.)	2,653	4,269
Mackenzie (Canada)	2,635	4,241
Mekong (Asia)	2,600	4,184
Niger (Africa)	2,590	4,168

WORLD RECORD BREAKERS

DESERTS

	sq miles	sq km
Sahara	3,500,000	9,065,000
Australian Desert	600,000	1,550,000
Arabian Desert	500,000	1,300,000
Gobi Desert	500,000	1,295,000
Kalahari	200,800	520,000

▲ About one eighth of the Earth's surface is desert. These are areas with, on average, only 10in. (25cm) of rain per year, or where the land retains too little moisture for plants to grow.

MAJOR WATERFALLS

Highest	feet	meters
Angel Falls (Venezuela)	3,212	979
Tugela Falls (South Africa)	3,110	948
Yosemite Falls (California)	2,425	739
Greatest volume	ft³/sec	m³/sec
Boyoma (Zaire)	600,300	17,000
Niagara (N. America)	212,000	6,000

LARGEST LAKES

	sq miles	sq km
Caspian Sea (U.S.S.R./Iran)	152,096	393,898
Superior (U.S.A./Canada)	31,980	82,814
Victoria Nyanza (Africa)	26,830	69,485
Aral (U.S.S.R.)	26,520	68,682
Huron (U.S.A./Canada)	23,010	59,596
Michigan (U.S.A.)	22,400	58,016
Tanganyika (Africa)	12,700	32,893
Great Bear (Canada)	12,275	31,792
Baikal (U.S.S.R.)	12,159	31,492
Great Slave (Canada)	10,980	28,438

WORLD RECORD BREAKERS

LARGEST ISLANDS

	sq miles	sq km
Greenland (Kalaallit Nunaat) (N. Atlantic)	840,000	2,175,600
New Guinea (S.W. Pacific)	306,600	794,090
Borneo (Kalimantan) (S.W. Pacific)	290,330	751,900
Madagascar (Indian Ocean)	226,670	587,041
Baffin I. (Canadian Arctic)	195,940	507,451
Sumatra (Indian Ocean)	182,870	473,607
Honshu (N.W. Pacific)	89,190	230,988
Great Britain (N. Atlantic)	88,625	229,522
Ellesmere (Canadian Arctic)	76,070	197,000
Victoria I. (Canadian Arctic)	74,405	192,695

OCEANS

	sq miles	sq km
Pacific	63,860,000	165,384,000
Atlantic	31,746,000	82,217,000
Indian	28,373,000	73,481,000
Arctic	5,427,000	14,056,000

HIGHEST MOUNTAINS

	feet	meters
ASIA		
Everest (Himalaya–Nepal/Tibet)	29,028	8,848
Godwin Austen (Pakistan/India)	28,250	8,611
Kanchenjunga (Himalaya–Nepal/Sikkim)	28,205	8,597
Makalu (Himalaya–Nepal/Tibet)	27,790	8,470
Dhaulagiri (Himalaya–Nepal)	26,810	8,172
Nanga Parbat (Himalaya–India)	26,660	8,126
Annapurna (Himalaya–Nepal)	26,492	8,075
SOUTH AMERICA		
Aconcagua (Andes–Argentina)	22,834	6,960
NORTH AMERICA		
McKinley (Alaska–U.S.A.)	20,320	6,194
AFRICA		
Kilimanjaro (Tanzania)	19,340	5,895
EUROPE		
Communism Peak (Pamir/U.S.S.R.)	24,590	7,495
Elbruz (Caucasus–U.S.S.R.)	18,510	5,642
ANTARCTICA		
Vinson Massif	16,860	5,139
AUSTRALASIA		
Wilhelm (Bismarck Range–Papua New Guinea)	14,793	4,509

▼ Mount Everest above Khumbu Glacier. In 1953 New Zealander Edmund Hillary and the Sherpa Tensing Norgay became the first people to reach the summit.

WATERY RECORD BREAKERS

TIDE AND SEA LEVEL FACTS

Greatest range of tides on Earth: Bay of Fundy, Canada. A spring high tide here can be more than 53 ft. (16 m) above a spring low tide.

Single tide: At Saint Michael in Alaska there is only one high tide and one low tide each day.

Lowest tidal range: Almost nothing, at certain places in the open oceans. There are scarcely any tides in the Baltic Sea and other seas that are almost shut off from the open ocean.

Lowest inland sea: Dead Sea. Its surface is 1,302 ft. (397 m) below the level of the Mediterranean Sea.

WAVE AND CURRENT FACTS

Highest storm wave: 112 ft. (34 m)

Fastest waves: 300–500 mph (500–800 km/h), set off by earthquakes.

Largest ocean current: Antarctic Circumpolar Current. It carries 2,200 times more water than the world's largest river pours into the sea.

Fastest ocean current: Nakwakto Rapids, off western Canada: 18 mph (30 km/h).

RIVER FACTS

The world's rivers hold about 55,000 cubic miles (230,000 cubic km) of water.

Weight of soil, rock, etc., removed by rivers: About 140 tons per year from each 0.39 square miles (square kilometer) of the Earth's crust.

Thickness of land worn away by rivers: About 1 ft. (30 cm) in 9,000 years, as estimated for the United States.

Deepest gorges cut by rivers: Gorges more than 3 miles (5 km) deep made by the rivers Indus, Brahmaputra, and Ganges.

Pacific Ocean

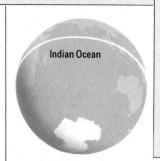

Indian Ocean

FACTS ABOUT ICE

Ice covers more than one tenth of all the land on Earth at any given time.

Largest ice sheet: Antarctic Ice Sheet, 5 million sq miles (12.7 million sq km).

Longest glacier: Lambert–Fisher Ice Passage in Antarctica. It stretches over 300 miles (500 km).

Largest iceberg: A tabular Antarctic iceberg, 12,000 sq miles (31,000 sq km). This iceberg was larger than Belgium.

The Weather

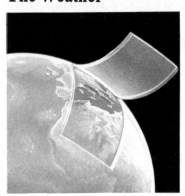

The layer of air around the Earth—the atmosphere—is constantly moving because it is unevenly heated by the Sun. As huge masses of warm air from the equator and cold air from the poles flow around the world, meeting each other, rising and falling, heating up and cooling down, they cause the weather.

◀ **The "wrapping" of atmosphere around the Earth** moderates the planet's temperature.

TYPES OF CLOUD

Clouds consist of masses of water drops or ice crystals in the atmosphere. They form when moisture in the air condenses.

Altostratus: A grayish sheet of cloud, with a hazy Sun above.
Altocumulus: Fleecy bands of cloud with blue sky between.
Cirrus: High, wispy clouds made of particles of ice.
Cirrocumulus: Thin, high lines of cloud with rippled edges.
Cirrostratus: Milky, thin, high cloud producing a halo around the Sun.

Stratus: Low, gray, sheetlike cloud covering the sky.
Nimbostratus: Low, gray, sheetlike cloud producing steady rain.
Stratocumulus: Like a low, dark, heavy kind of altocumulus.
Cumulus: A white heaped-up cloud usually seen in fair weather.
Cumulonimbus: A towering cloud that may give heavy showers.

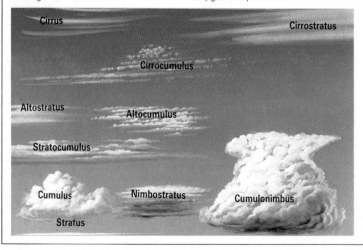

TORNADO

A tornado moves cross country only at about 40 mph (65 km/h). It measures only about 650 ft. (200 m) across, and seldom lasts much more than an hour. Yet its rapidly whirling winds can do tremendous damage. Also its air pressure is so low that houses in its path may just explode.

▶ **Lightning is a huge electric spark.** Thunder is the noise made by air heated up by lightning.

FACTS ABOUT STORMS

World's worst hurricane: A tropical cyclone that struck Bangladesh in 1970. Floods unleashed by rain and wind drowned a million people.

World's worst tornado: A tornado that struck south-central U.S.A. in 1925, killing nearly 700 people.

Most thundery area on Earth: The Tropics and nearby regions. More than 3,000 thunderstorms occur here every night of the year.

Fiercest storm winds: Those whirling around in a tornado. Meteorologists believe these can reach 500 mph (800 km/h).

Longest flash of lightning: About 20 miles (30 km), cloud to ground.

Speed of lightning: The fastest flashes move at 87,000 miles/sec (140,000 km/sec).

Strongest surface wind recorded: 231 mph (372 km/h) at Mt. Washington, N.H., in 1934.

BEAUFORT SCALE

In 1805 Admiral Sir Francis Beaufort worked out a scale for measuring wind speed. The scale is numbered from 1 to 12 and represents wind force out in the open, 33 feet (10 meters) above the ground.

No.	Wind force	mph	km/h	Observable effects
0	calm	<1	<1.6	smoke rises vertically
1	light air	1–3	1.6–4.8	direction shown by smoke
2	slight breeze	4–7	6.4–11.3	felt on face; wind vanes move
3	gentle breeze	8–12	12.9–19.3	leaves, twigs move; flags extended
4	moderate breeze	13–18	20.9–29.0	dust, paper, small branches move
5	fresh breeze	19–24	30.6–38.6	small trees sway; flags ripple
6	strong breeze	25–31	40.2–50.0	large branches move; flags beat
7	moderate gale	32–38	51.5–61.2	whole trees sway; walking difficult
8	fresh gale	39–46	62.8–74.0	twigs break off; walking hindered
9	strong gale	47–54	75.6–86.9	slight damage—chimneys, slates
10	whole gale	55–63	88.5–101.4	severe damage; trees uprooted
11	storm	64–72	103.0–115.9	widespread damage
12	hurricane	>73	>117.5	devastation

Climate and Vegetation

The map on these pages shows that climate tends to depend on latitude. Usually, warmer areas are nearer the equator, cold areas are near the poles, and temperate lands are in between. However, within these broad areas there is a huge variety of climates.

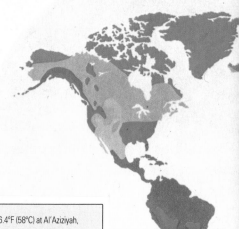

Hottest shade temperature recorded: 136.4°F (58°C) at Al'Aziziyah, Libya, on 9-13-22
Coldest temperature recorded: −128.6°F (−89.2°C) at Vostok, Antarctica, on 7-21-83
Highest annual rainfall: 463 in. (11,770 mm) at Tutunendo, Colombia
Most rain in one month: 366.14 in. (9,300 mm) at Cherrapunji, India, in July 1861
Driest place on Earth: Arica, Chile, averages 0.03 in. (0.76 mm) of rain per year
Most snow in one year: 1,224 in. (31,102 mm) on Mt. Rainier, Washington State

▼ In Svalbard, near the North Pole, there are just four months of the year when the temperature rises above freezing. During this time there are up to 24 hours of sunshine. Little rain falls, but when the snow thaws, the tundra becomes an expanse of marsh and lakes.

▼ Southern Portugal and southern Spain, including the Mediterranean coastal resort of Malaga, have hot, dry, and sunny summers. The rain falls mostly in winter, although there is still lots of sunshine—a good holiday spot all year round. Inland, there is less rain and very hot summers.

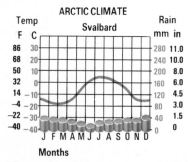

ARCTIC CLIMATE
Svalbard

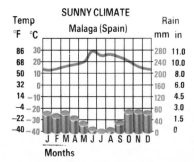

SUNNY CLIMATE
Malaga (Spain)

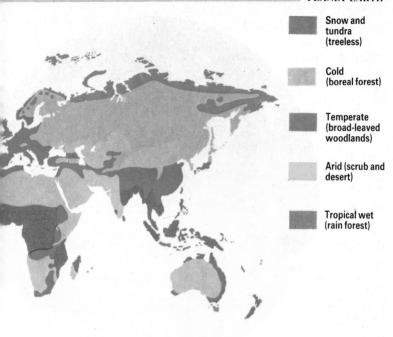

Snow and tundra (treeless)

Cold (boreal forest)

Temperate (broad-leaved woodlands)

Arid (scrub and desert)

Tropical wet (rain forest)

▶ **Most of Southeast Asia experiences** the monsoon—a wind which blows in off the warm sea and brings a season of torrential rain.

▼ **In the tropical grasslands**, 10° south of the equator, it is always hot. The year falls into a wet and a dry season.

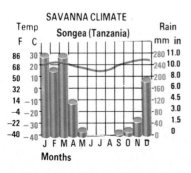

SAVANNA CLIMATE

Songea (Tanzania)

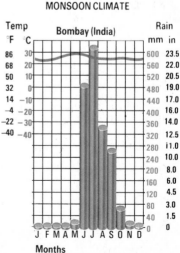

MONSOON CLIMATE

Bombay (India)

What the World Produces

Figures are based on latest available statistics for one year's production.

FOOD AND LIVESTOCK

Product	Total (leading country)[1]
Barley	167,176,000 t (U.S.A. 32.3%)
Cocoa beans	1,750,000 t (amount ground only)
Coffee beans	1,846,000 t
Cotton	81,100,000 × 480 1lb (0.4 kg) bales
Maize	344,103,000 t (U.S.A. 31%)
Millet	29,563,000 t (India 35.5%)
Oats	43,101,000 t (U.S.S.R. 37%)
Oil seeds (products)	196,700,000 t
Rice	449,827,000 t (China 38.3%)
Rye	32,194,000 t (U.S.S.R. 42%)
Sorghum	62,483,000 t (U.S.A. 19.6%)
Sugar	97,173,000 t (Brazil 9.7%)
Wheat	498,182,000 t (U.S.S.R. 16.4%)
Fisheries	76,470,600 t catch (Japan 14.7%)
Cattle	1,226,000,000 head (India 22.4%)
Horses	65,000,000 "
Pigs	764,000,000 " (China 39%)
Sheep	1,158,000,000 " (U.S.S.R. 12.5%)

[1] t = tons

▼ **France has a large perfume industry.** The flowers from these lavender bushes in Provence, southeast France, will be used to make perfume.

Wheat Production	tons
China	87,700,000
U.S.S.R.	82,000,000
U.S.A.	70,638,000
India	45,148,000
France	32,884,000
Canada	23,899,300
Australia	21,764,000

Rice Production	tons
China	172,184,000
India	59,769,000
Indonesia	37,500,000
Bangladesh	21,500,000
Thailand	19,200,000
Japan	14,848,000
Burma	14,500,000

Cattle Stock	
India	275,000,000
Brazil	132,801,000
U.S.S.R.	119,558,000
U.S.A.	114,000,000
China	58,600,000
Argentina	53,500,000
Australia	22,161,000

Pig Stock	
China	298,500,000
U.S.S.R.	78,722,000
U.S.A.	56,694,000
Brazil	33,000,000
West Germany	23,449,000
Poland	17,187,000

Sheep Stock	
U.S.S.R.	145,265,000
Australia	139,242,000
China	98,900,000
New Zealand	70,344,000
Turkey	48,707,000
India	41,700,000
Argentina	30,000,000

Natural Gas Production	billions cubic feet (billions cubic meters)	
U.S.S.R.	20,729.6	(587.0)
U.S.A.	17,240.5	(488.2)
Canada	35,872.0	(101.6)
Netherlands	2,728.1	(77.2)
Algeria	1,260.0	(35.7)
U.K.	1,236.0	(35.0)

Iron Ore Production	tons
U.S.S.R.	245,000,000
China	121,900,000
Brazil	108,160,000
Australia	88,700,000
U.S.A.	54,800,000
Canada	40,264,000

Coal	tons
U.S.A.	890,143,000
China	714,530,000
U.S.S.R.	712,000,000
Poland	242,000,000
South Africa	145,838,000
India	140,696,000
Australia	132,440,000
U.K.	119,220,000
West Germany	84,866,000

Crude Petroleum Production	barrels
U.S.S.R.	4,477,000,000
U.S.A.	3,197,000,000
Saudi Arabia	1,702,000,000
Mexico	983,000,000
U.K.	882,000,000
Iran	800,000,000
Venezuela	668,000,000
Canada	531,000,000
Nigeria	501,000,000

Electric Energy Production	1,000,000 kWh (kilowatt hours)
U.S.A.	2,367,634
U.S.S.R.	1,408,100
Japan	602,357
Canada	408,443
West Germany	373,813
France	283,400
U.K.	276,227

Nuclear Energy Production	Percentage of electricity from nuclear power
France	48.3
Sweden	37.4
U.K.	18.1
Japan	17.6
West Germany	17.6
U.S.A.	12.4
Canada	12.0
U.S.S.R.	6.0

▲ In New Zealand, sheep and cattle farming are major industries. In 1984, New Zealand produced 442,000 tons of beef, 44,000 tons of pork, and 693,000 tons of lamb.

MINERALS	Total (leading country)
Bauxite	78,800,000 t (Australia 31.7%)
Copper	8,120,000 t (Chile 16%)
Iron ore	689,000,000 t (U.S.S.R. 35.5%)
Nickel ore	697,000 t (Canada 25%)
Silver	408,300,000 troy ounces (Mexico 15.6%)
Tin ore	162,000 t (excluding communist countries)
Gold	1723 t (South Africa 48%)
Diamonds, gem	21,040,000 carats
Diamonds, industrial	36,000,000 carats } (Zaire 32.4%)

FUEL AND ENERGY	Total (leading country)
Crude petroleum	57,800,000 barrels/day (U.S.S.R. 21.7%)
Coal	3,067,000,000 t (U.S.A. 29%)
Natural gas	1,686,000,000,000 cu m (U.S.S.R. 35%)
Hydroelectric energy	485,400,000 t oil equivalent (U.S.A., exact percentage not available)
Nuclear energy	282,200,000 t oil equivalent (U.S.A., exact percentage not available)

33

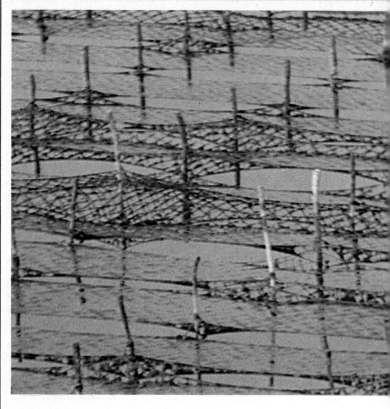

Countries of the World

You will often have heard people say that our world is shrinking every day. It takes just a few hours to fly from one side of the world to the other. Television satellites enable people in England to watch a football game live from the United States, nearly three thousand miles away. It is difficult to imagine that only 500 years ago many people believed that the Earth was flat and that it was possible to fall off the edge.

Today, around five billion people are concentrated on only about 15 percent of the Earth's land surface. The most

▲ **Harvest time for seaweed** being grown on nets off Japan, where it is a delicacy. A lot of Japan's shallow inland sea is taken up with the nets, fences, and buoys used to cultivate seaweed.

crowded areas of the globe are parts of South and East Asia and the industrialized areas of Europe and the United States. More than half of the world's population lives on the largest continent, Asia, and one third of them are Chinese or Indian. The most common language in the world is the main Chinese dialect—Mandarin. This is spoken by about 600 million people. English is the next most common language— spoken by about 360 million people—and the most widely used second language in the world. English is widespread because it is the main language of business and commerce.

Countries of the World

ARCTIC OCEAN

Greenland

ICELAND

Alaska (USA)

IRELAND

UNITED KING.

ER.

CANADA

IRELAND

SPAI

PORTUGAL

UNITED STATES OF AMERICA

ATLANTIC OCEAN

MOROCCO

PACIFIC

ALG

TROPIC OF CANCER

MEXICO

BAHAMAS

CUBA

PUERTO RICO
DOMINICA
ST LUCIA

MAURITANIA

MA

CAPE
VERDE
ISLANDS

OCEAN

46 53
48 54 55
50 56
47 52 57
49 51

26
27 29
28
30
31

EQUATOR

VENEZUELA

COLOMBIA

58
59 60

IVORY COAST

ECUADOR

PERU

BRAZIL

BOLIVIA

TROPIC OF CAPRICORN

PARAGUAY

ATLANTIC OCEAN

URUGUAY

ARGENTINA

Falkland Islands

1 DENMARK	11 YUGOSLAVIA	21 YEMEN A.R.
2 NETHERLANDS	12 ALBANIA	22 BHUTAN
3 BELGIUM	13 CYPRUS	23 BANGLADESH
4 LUXEMBOURG	14 LEBANON	24 KAMPUCHEA (CAMBODIA)
5 W. GERMANY	15 ISRAEL	25 TUNISIA
6 E. GERMANY	16 SYRIA	26 SENEGAL
7 SWITZERLAND	17 JORDAN	27 GAMBIA
8 AUSTRIA	18 KUWAIT	28 GUINEA-BISSAU
9 CZECHOSLOVAKIA	19 BAHRAIN	29 GUINEA
10 HUNGARY	20 UNITED ARAB EMIRATES	30 SIERRA LEONE

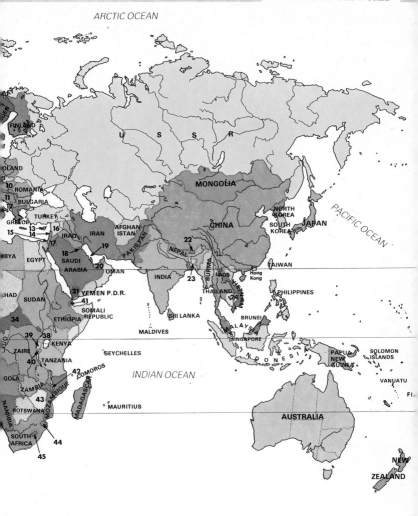

31 LIBERIA	41 DJIBOUTI	51 COSTA RICA
32 BURKINA FASO	42 MALAWI	52 PANAMA
33 TOGO	43 ZIMBABWE	53 JAMAICA
34 CENTRAL AFRICAN REPUBLIC	44 SWAZILAND	54 HAITI
35 EQUATORIAL GUINEA	45 LESOTHO	55 DOMINICAN REPUBLIC
36 GABON	46 BELIZE	56 BARBADOS
37 CAMEROON	47 GUATEMALA	57 TRINIDAD AND TOBAGO
38 UGANDA	48 HONDURAS	58 GUYANA
39 RWANDA	49 EL SALVADOR	59 SURINAME
40 BURUNDI	50 NICARAGUA	60 FRENCH GUIANA

37

Countries Checklist

About 30 percent of the Earth's surface is covered by land. The land areas are divided into seven continents: Africa, Asia, Europe, North America, South America, Oceania, and Antarctica. Oceania (Australia, New Zealand, and the Pacific islands) is often referred to as Australasia.

EUROPE

> **FACTS ABOUT EUROPE**
> **(including European U.S.S.R.)**
>
> **Area:** Europe including European U.S.S.R. is 4,053,600 sq miles (10,498,000 sq km); Total area U.S.S.R. is 8,650,170 sq miles (22,402,200 sq km).
> **Population:** Europe, 682,000,000 people; total U.S.S.R., 280,700,000 people.
> **Number of independent countries:** 33.
> **Largest country:** The U.S.S.R., which is in Europe and Asia.
> **Smallest country:** Vatican City.
> **Highest mountain:** In Europe, Mount Elbruz in Caucasus is 18,510 ft. (5,642 m); in U.S.S.R., Communism Peak is 24,590 ft. (7,495 m).
> **Largest lake:** The Caspian Sea, 152,096 sq miles (393,898 sq km).
> **Longest rivers:** In Europe, the Volga is 2,292 miles (3,688 km) and the Danube is 1,770 miles (2,848 km). In Russia (but not in Europe), the Irtysh is 3,461 miles (5,570 km) and the Lena is 2,653 miles (4,269 km).

▼ **Part of Sogne Fiord,** Norway. Fiords are steep-sided sea inlets originally worn away by glaciers.

Country	Area sq miles (sq km)	Population	Capital	Official Language
Albania	11,100 (28,748)	3,000,000	Tirane	Albanian
Andorra	175 (453)	32,700	Andorra la Vella	Catalan
Austria	32,377 (83,849)	7,500,000	Vienna	German
Belgium	11,782 (30,513)	9,900,000	Brussels	Flemish, French
Bulgaria	42,826 (110,912)	8,900,000	Sofia	Bulgarian
Czechoslovakia	49,374 (127,869)	15,500,000	Prague	Czech, Slovak
Denmark	17,403 (45,069)	5,100,000	Copenhagen	Danish
Finland	130,129 (337,009)	4,900,000	Helsinki	Finnish, Swedish
France	211,223 (547,026)	55,000,000	Paris	French
Germany, East (German Democratic Republic–DDR)	41,771 (108,178)	16,700,000	East Berlin	German
Germany, West (Federal Republic of Germany)	95,983 (248,577)	61,000,000	Bonn	German
Greece	50,948 (131,944)	10,100,000	Athens	Greek
Hungary	35,922 (93,030)	10,800,000	Budapest	Hungarian
Iceland	39,771 (103,000)	200,000	Reykjavik	Icelandic
Ireland, Republic of	27,138 (70,283)	3,600,000	Dublin	English, Irish
Italy	116,322 (301,252)	57,400,000	Rome	Italian
Liechtenstein	60.6 (157)	26,000	Vaduz	German
Luxembourg	999 (2,586)	400,000	Luxembourg City	French, Letzeburgesch (a German dialect)
Malta	122 (316)	400,000	Valletta	Maltese, English
Monaco	0.7 (1.9)	25,000	Monaco	French
Netherlands	15,771 (40,844)	14,500,000	Amsterdam; The Hague is the seat of government	Dutch
Norway	125,191 (324,219)	4,200,000	Oslo	Norwegian
Poland	120,734 (312,677)	37,300,000	Warsaw	Polish
Portugal	35,556 (92,082) (including Azores and Madeira)	10,400,000	Lisbon	Portuguese
Romania	91,706 (237,500)	22,800,000	Bucharest	Romanian
San Marino	23.5 (61)	21,000	San Marino	Italian
Spain	194,912 (504,782)	38,600,000	Madrid	Spanish

Country	Area sq miles (sq km)	Population	Capital	Official Language
Sweden	173,745 (449,964)	8,300,000	Stockholm	Swedish
Switzerland	15,943 (41,288)	6,500,000	Bern	French, German, Italian
United Kingdom	94,535 (244,828)	56,400,000	London	English
U.S.S.R.	8,650,166 (22,402,200)	280,700,000	Moscow	Russian
Vatican City State	0.17 (0.44)	1,000	Vatican City	Italian, Latin
Yugoslavia	98,774 (255,804)	23,100,000	Belgrade	Serbo-Croat, Slovene, Macedonian

ASIA

FACTS ABOUT ASIA
(excluding European U.S.S.R.)

Area: 16,815,940 sq miles (43,549,924 sq km).
Population: About 2,960,000,000 people.
Number of independent countries (excluding U.S.S.R.): 41.
Largest country: (Apart from the U.S.S.R.) China.
Smallest country: Maldive Islands.
Highest mountain: Mount Everest, 29,028 ft. (8,848 m) in the Himalayas. It is the highest mountain in the world.
Largest lake: Caspian Sea, 152,100 sq miles (393,900 sq km). It is on the border of Europe and Asia.
Longest rivers: The Yangtze (Chang Jiang) River in China is 3,430 miles (5,520 km), the Hwang Ho is 2,903 miles (4,672 km).

▼ **Since ancient times,** Hindus have believed that the Ganges is a sacred river that can wash away their sins.

Country	Area sq miles (sq km)	Population	Capital	Official Language
Afghanistan	250,018 (647,497)	14,700,000	Kabul	Pashtu, Dari
Bahrain	240 (622)	400,000	Manama	Arabic
Bangladesh	55,602 (143,998)	101,500,000	Dacca	Bengali
Bhutan	18,148 (47,000)	1,400,000	Thimphu	Dzongkha
Brunei	2,226 (5,765)	200,000	Bandar Seri Begawan	Malay
Burma	261,237 (676,552)	36,900,000	Rangoon	Burmese
Kampuchea (Cambodia)	69,903 (181,035)	6,200,000	Phnom Penh	Khmer
China	3,705,677 (9,596,961)	1,042,000,000	Beijing (Peking)	Chinese (Mandarin)
Cyprus	3,572 (9,251)	700,000	Nicosia	Greek, Turkish
Hong Kong	404 (1,045)	5,500,000	Victoria	English, Chinese (Cantonese)
India	1,269,438 (3,287,590)	762,200,000	Delhi	Hindi, English
Indonesia	782,720 (2,027,087)	168,400,000	Jakarta	Bahasa (Indonesian)
Iran	636,343 (1,648,000)	45,100,000	Tehran	Persian (Farsi)
Iraq	167,937 (434,924)	15,500,000	Baghdad	Arabic
Israel	8,020 (20,770)	4,200,000	Jerusalem	Hebrew, Arabic
Japan	143,761 (372,313)	120,800,000	Tokyo	Japanese
Jordan	37,740 (97,740)	3,600,000	Amman	Arabic
Korea, North	46,543 (120,538)	20,100,000	Pyongyang	Korean
Korea, South	38,028 (98,484)	42,700,000	Seoul	Korean
Kuwait	6,880 (17,818)	1,900,000	Kuwait	Arabic
Laos	91,436 (236,800)	3,800,000	Vientiane	Lao
Lebanon	4,016 (10,400)	2,600,000	Beirut	Arabic
Macao	6.2 (16)	300,000	Macao	Portuguese, Chinese
Malaysia	127,326 (329,749)	15,700,000	Kuala Lumpur	Malay
Maldive Islands	115 (298)	200,000	Malé	Divehi
Mongolia	604,294 (1,565,000)	1,900,000	Ulan Bator	Mongol
Nepal	54,366 (140,797)	17,000,000	Katmandu	Nepali
Oman	82,036 (212,457)	1,200,000	Muscat	Arabic
Pakistan	310,427 (803,943)	99,200,000	Islamabad	Urdu

Country	Area sq miles (sq km)	Population	Capital	Official Language
Philippines	115,839 (300,000)	56,800,000	Manila	English, Pilipino
Qatar	4,247 (11,000)	300,000	Doha	Arabic
Saudi Arabia	830,060 (2,149,690)	11,200,000	Riyadh	Arabic
Singapore	224 (581)	2,600,000	Singapore	Malay, Chinese, Tamil, English
Sri Lanka	25,334 (65,610)	16,400,000	Colombo	Sinhala
Syria	71,504 (185,180)	10,600,000	Damascus	Arabic
Taiwan	13,886 (35,961)	19,200,000	Taipei	Chinese (Mandarin)
Thailand	198,471 (514,000)	52,700,000	Bangkok	Thai
Turkey	301,404 (780,576)	52,100,000	Ankara	Turkish
United Arab Emirates	32,280 (83,600)	1,300,000	Abu Dhabi	Arabic
Vietnam	127,252 (329,556)	60,500,000	Hanoi	Vietnamese
North Yemen (Arab Republic)	75,295 (195,000)	6,100,000	San'a	Arabic
South Yemen (Peoples' Democratic Republic)	128,569 (332,968)	2,100,000	Aden	Arabic

NORTH AMERICA

FACTS ABOUT NORTH & CENTRAL AMERICA

Area: 9,363,000 sq miles (24,249,000 sq km) including North and Central America, the West Indies, and Greenland.
Population: About 400,000,000 people.
Number of independent countries: 22.
Largest country: Canada.
Smallest country: St. Kitts and Nevis.
Highest mountain: Mount McKinley in Alaska, 20,320 ft. (6,194 m).
Largest lake: Lake Superior, 31,980 sq miles (82,814 sq km).
Longest rivers: Mississippi-Missouri-Red Rock (U.S.A.) 3,860 miles (6,212 km); Mackenzie-Peace (Canada) 2,635 miles (4,241 km).

▶ **The Capitol building** on Capitol Hill in Washington, D.C. This is where the United States Congress meets. The Capitol was designed by William Thornton, who won a competition for its design in 1792.

Country	Area sq miles (sq km)	Population	Capital	Official Language
Antigua and Barbuda	171 (442)	100,000	St. John's	English
Bahamas	5,381 (13,935)	200,000	Nassau	English
Barbados	166 (431)	300,000	Bridgetown	English
Belize	8,867 (22,965)	200,000	Belmopan	English, Spanish
Canada	3,852,085 (9,976,130)	25,400,000	Ottawa	English, French
Costa Rica	19,577 (50,700)	2,600,000	San José	Spanish
Cuba	44,221 (114,524)	10,100,000	Havana	Spanish
Dominica	290 (751)	100,000	Roseau	English
Dominican Republic	18,818 (48,734)	6,200,000	Santo Domingo	Spanish
El Salvador	8,125 (21,041)	5,100,000	San Salvador	Spanish
Grenada	133 (344)	100,000	St. George's	English
Guatemala	42,045 (108,889)	8,000,000	Guatemala City	Spanish
Haiti	10,715 (27,750)	5,800,000	Port-au-Prince	French
Honduras	43,281 (112,088)	4,400,000	Tegucigalpa	Spanish
Jamaica	4,244 (10,991)	2,300,000	Kingston	English
Mexico	761,166 (1,972,547)	79,700,000	Mexico City	Spanish
Nicaragua	50,197 (130,000)	3,000,000	Managua	Spanish
Panama	29,211 (76,650)	2,000,000	Panama	Spanish
St. Christopher (St. Kitts) and Nevis	101 (262)	40,000	Basseterre	English
St. Lucia	238 (616)	100,000	Castries	English
St. Vincent and the Grenadines	150 (388)	100,000	Kingstown	English
Trinidad and Tobago	1,981 (5,130)	1,200,000	Port of Spain	English
United States	3,615,385 (9,363,123)	238,900,000	Washington, D.C.	English

43

SOUTH AMERICA

FACTS ABOUT SOUTH AMERICA

Area: 6,872,538 sq miles (17,798,500 sq km).
Population: About 276,000,000 people.
Number of independent countries: 12.
Largest country: Brazil.
Smallest country: French Guiana.
Highest mountain: Mount Aconcagua in Argentina is 22,834 ft. (6,960 m) high.
Largest lake: Lake Maracaibo in Venezuela, 5,127 sq miles (13,290 sq km).
Longest river: The Amazon River is 4,080 miles (6,570 km).

▶ **A coffee plant,** showing the beans. Brazil produces more coffee than any other country in the world. Colombia is another big grower—coffee makes up 50 percent of its exports.

Country	Area sq miles (sq km)	Population	Capital	Official Language
Argentina	1,068,379 (2,766,889)	30,600,000	Buenos Aires	Spanish
Bolivia	422,265 (1,093,581)	6,200,000	La Paz (seat of government); Sucre (legal capital)	Spanish
Brazil	3,286,727 (8,511,965)	138,400,000	Brasilia	Portuguese
Chile	295,754 (765,945)	12,000,000	Santiago	Spanish
Colombia	439,769 (1,138,914)	29,400,000	Bogota	Spanish
Ecuador	109,491 (283,561)	8,900,000	Quito	Spanish
French Guiana	35,138 (91,000)	76,000	Cayenne	French
Guyana	82,632 (214,000)	800,000	Georgetown	English
Paraguay	157,059 (406,752)	3,600,000	Asunción	Spanish
Peru	496,261 (1,285,216)	19,500,000	Lima	Spanish
Suriname	63,042 (163,265)	400,000	Paramaribo	Dutch, English
Uruguay	68,042 (176,216)	3,000,000	Montevideo	Spanish
Venezuela	352,170 (912,050)	17,300,000	Caracas	Spanish

AFRICA

▶ **A Zulu woman** in traditional beaded headdress. Zulus are the largest group of black Africans in South Africa.

FACTS ABOUT AFRICA

Area: 13,357,000 sq miles (34,592,000 sq km).
Population: About 568,000,000 people.
Number of independent countries: 53.
Largest country: Sudan.
Smallest country: Seychelles.
Highest mountain: Mount Kilimanjaro in Tanzania is 19,340 ft. (5,895 m) high.

Largest lake: Lake Victoria in Kenya, Tanzania, and Uganda covers 26,830 sq miles (69,485 sq km).
Longest rivers: The Nile River is 4,160 miles (6,690 km) long. It is the longest river in the world. The Zaire is 2,900 miles (4,667 km), and the Niger River is 2,590 miles (4,168 km) long.

Country	Area sq miles (sq km)	Population	Capital	Official Language
Algeria	919,662 (2,381,741)	22,200,000	Algiers	Arabic
Angola	481,389 (1,246,700)	7,900,000	Luanda	Portuguese
Benin	43,487 (112,622)	4,000,000	Porto Novo	French
Botswana	231,822 (600,372)	1,100,000	Gaborone	English, Setswana
Burkina Faso	105,877 (274,200)	6,900,000	Ouagadougou	French
Burundi	10,748 (27,834)	4,600,000	Bujumbura	French, Kirundi
Cameroon	183,583 (475,442)	9,700,000	Yaoundé	English, French
Cape Verde Islands	1,557 (4,033)	300,000	Praia	Portuguese
Central African Republic	240,553 (622,984)	2,700,000	Bangui	French
Chad	495,791 (1,284,000)	5,200,000	N'Djamena	French
Comoros	838 (2,171)	500,000	Moroni	French
Congo	132,057 (342,000)	1,700,000	Brazzaville	French
Djibouti	8,495 (22,000)	300,000	Djibouti	French
Egypt	386,690 (1,001,449)	48,300,000	Cairo	Arabic
Equatorial Guinea	10,831 (28,051)	300,000	Malabo	Spanish

Country	Area sq miles (sq km)	Population	Capital	Official Language
Ethiopia	471,812 (1,221,900)	36,000,000	Addis Ababa	Amharic
Gabon	103,354 (267,667)	1,000,000	Libreville	French
Gambia	4,361 (11,295)	800,000	Banjul	English
Ghana	92,106 (238,537)	14,300,000	Accra	English
Guinea	94,971 (245,957)	6,100,000	Conakry	French
Guinea-Bissau	13,949 (36,125)	900,000	Bissau	Portuguese
Ivory Coast	124,513 (322,463)	10,100,000	Abidjan	French
Kenya	224,977 (582,646)	20,200,000	Nairobi	English, Swahili
Lesotho	11,721 (30,355)	1,500,000	Maseru	English, Sesotho
Liberia	43,003 (111,369)	2,200,000	Monrovia	English
Libya	679,412 (1,759,540)	4,000,000	Tripoli	Arabic
Madagascar	226,674 (587,041)	10,000,000	Antananarivo	French, Malagasy
Malawi	45,750 (118,484)	7,100,000	Lilongwe	English, Chichewa
Mali	478,801 (1,240,000)	7,700,000	Bamako	French
Mauritania	397,984 (1,030,700)	1,900,000	Nouakchott	Arabic, French
Mauritius	805 (2,085)	1,000,000	Port Louis	English
Morocco	172,426 (446,550)	24,300,000	Rabat	Arabic
Mozambique	302,352 (783,030)	13,900,000	Maputo	Portuguese
Namibia	318,284 (824,292)	1,100,000	Windhoek	Afrikaans, English
Niger	489,227 (1,267,000)	6,500,000	Niamey	French
Nigeria	356,695 (923,768)	91,200,000	Lagos	English
Rwanda	10,170 (26,338)	6,300,000	Kigali	French, Kinyarwanda
São Tomé and Príncipe	373 (965)	100,000	Sao Tomé	Portuguese
Senegal	75,756 (196,192)	6,700,000	Dakar	French
Seychelles	108 (280)	100,000	Victoria	English, French
Sierra Leone	27,701 (71,740)	3,600,000	Freetown	English
Somali Republic	246,219 (637,657)	6,500,000	Mogadishu	Somali
South Africa	471,479 (1,221,037)	32,500,000	Pretoria (seat of government); Cape Town (legal capital)	Afrikaans, English
Sudan	967,570 (2,505,813)	21,800,000	Khartoum	Arabic
Swaziland	6,704 (17,363)	600,000	Mbabane	English

Country	Area sq miles (sq km)	Population	Capital	Official Language
Tanzania	364,927 (945,087)	21,700,000	Dodoma	English, Swahili
Togo	21,623 (56,000)	3,000,000	Lomé	French
Tunisia	63,175 (163,610)	7,200,000	Tunis	Arabic
Uganda	91,141 (236,036)	14,700,000	Kampala	English
Zaire	905,633 (2,345,409)	33,100,000	Kinshasa	French
Zambia	290,607 (752,614)	6,800,000	Lusaka	English
Zimbabwe	150,815 (390,580)	8,600,000	Harare	English

OCEANIA

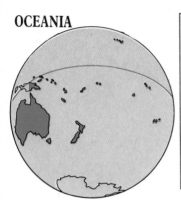

FACTS ABOUT OCEANIA

Area: 3,285,968 sq miles (8,510,000 sq km) (95% of this is Australia and New Zealand).
Population: About 24,500,000 people.
Number of independent countries: 11.
Largest country: Australia.
Smallest country: Nauru.
Highest mountain: Mount Wilhelm in Papua New Guinea, 14,793 ft. (4509 m).
Largest lake: Lake Eyre, Australia, 3,436 sq miles (8,900 sq km).
Longest rivers: The Murray in Australia is 1,597 miles (2,570 km) and its tributary, the Darling, is 1,899 miles (3,057 km).

Country	Area sq miles (sq km)	Population	Capital	Official Language
Australia	2,968,125 (7,686,849)	15,800,000	Canberra	English
Fiji	7,056 (18,274)	700,000	Suva	English, Fijian
Kiribati	359 (931)	60,000	Tarawa	English, Gilbertese
Nauru	8.1 (21)	8,000	Nauru	English, Nauruan
New Zealand	103,744 (268,676)	3,400,000	Wellington	English
Papua New Guinea	178,273 (461,691)	3,300,000	Port Moresby	English
Solomon Islands	10,984 (28,446)	300,000	Honiara	English
Tonga	270 (699)	100,000	Nuku'alofa	English
Tuvalu	9.7 (25)	8000	Fongafale	English, Tuvalu
Vanuatu	5,700 (14,763)	100,000	Port Vila	Bislama, English, French
Western Samoa	1,097 (2,842)	200,000	Apia	English, Samoan

POPULATION DENSITY

Population density means the average number of people living on a certain area of land. The numbers given here represent the number of people per square mile, with the number per square kilometer in parentheses. Macao, Hong Kong, and Puerto Rico are densely populated areas, just as Greenland and Antarctica are virtually deserted. They have not been included here because they are not independent countries.

Ten most crowded

Country	People/sq mile (sq km)	
Singapore	11,456	(4,475)
Malta	3,241	(1,266)
Bangladesh	1,851	(723)
Barbados	1,613	(630)
Taiwan	1,395	(545)
Mauritius	1,252	(489)
South Korea	1,126	(440)
Netherlands	909	(355)
Belgium	835	(326)
Japan	92	(326)

Ten least crowded

Country	People/sq mile (sq km)	
Mongolia	3.1	(1.2)
Botswana	4.6	(1.8)
Mauritania	4.6	(1.8)
Iceland	5.1	(2.0)
Australia	5.4	(2.1)
Libya	5.6	(2.2)
Suriname	6.4	(2.5)
Canada	6.6	(2.6)
Chad	9.9	(3.9)
Central African Republic	11.0	(4.3)

Subgroup	Main Languages
Slavic	Russian, Ukrainian, Byelorussian
	Polish, Czech, Slovak
	Slovenian, Bulgarian, Serbo-Croatian, Macedonian
Baltic	Lithuanian, Latvian
	Armenian
Indo-Iranian	Persian, Pashto, Kurdish
	Sanskrit, Hindi, Urdu, Bengali, Punjabi, Rajasthani, Kashmiri, Sinhalese
Germanic	English, German, Yiddish, Dutch, Flemish, Afrikaans
	Swedish, Danish, Norwegian, Icelandic
Romance	French, Spanish, Italian, Portuguese, Romanian
Celtic	Welsh, Breton
	Irish (Gaelic), Scottish (Gaelic)
Hellenic	Greek
	Albanian

MOST POPULOUS CITIES

City (country)	Population
São Paulo (Brazil)	10,036.900 (1985 est.)
Mexico City (Mexico)	8,831,079 (1980 est.)
Tokyo (Japan)	8,362,000 (1985 est.)
New York City (U.S.A.)	7,164,742 (1984 est.)
London (U.K.)	6,756,000 (1984 est.)
Shanghai (China)	6,320,872 (1982 est.)
Cairo (Egypt)	5,881,000 (1983 est.)
Los Angeles (U.S.A.)	3,096,721 (1984 est.)
Osaka (Japan)	2,631,000 (1985 est.)
Paris (France)	2,149,900 (1984 est.)

LARGEST URBAN AREAS

City (country)	Population (metropolitan area)
Tokyo (Japan)	29,002,000 (1981 est.)
New York City (U.S.A.)	17,807,100 (1984 est.)
Mexico City (Mexico)	17,321,800 (1985 est.)
Osaka (Japan)	16,224,000 (1983 est.)
São Paulo (Brazil)	15,143,000 (1985 est.)
Los Angeles (U.S.A.)	12,372,600 (1984 est.)
London (U.K.)	12,231,200 (1983 est.)
Cairo (Egypt)	12,001,000 (1983 est.)
Shanghai (China)	11,940,000 (1983 est.)
Paris (France)	10,210,059 (1982 est.)

◀ **The commonest languages** belong to various subgroups of the Indo-European family. Most of these subgroups are divided into different branches.

THE STATES OF THE U.S.A.

Each of the fifty American states has its own state bird and flower. The chickadee is Massachusetts' bird and the black-eyed Susan is Maryland's flower.

State	Area sq miles	sq km	Population (1985 est.)	Capital
Alabama	51,705	133,915	4,021,000	Montgomery
Alaska	591,004	1,530,693	521,000	Juneau
Arizona	114,000	295,259	3,187,000	Phoenix
Arkansas	53,187	137,754	2,359,000	Little Rock
California	158,706	411,047	26,365,000	Sacramento
Colorado	104,091	269,594	3,231,000	Denver
Connecticut	5,018	12,997	3,174,000	Hartford
Delaware	2,044	5,294	622,000	Dover
Florida	58,664	151,939	11,366,000	Tallahassee
Georgia	58,910	152,576	5,976,000	Atlanta
Hawaii	6,471	16,760	1,054,000	Honolulu
Idaho	83,564	216,430	1,005,000	Boise
Illinois	57,871	149,885	11,535,000	Springfield
Indiana	36,413	94,309	5,499,000	Indianapolis
Iowa	56,275	145,752	2,884,000	Des Moines
Kansas	82,277	213,096	2,450,000	Topeka
Kentucky	40,409	104,659	3,726,000	Frankfort
Louisiana	47,752	123,677	4,481,000	Baton Rouge
Maine	33,265	86,156	1,164,000	Augusta
Maryland	10,460	27,091	4,392,000	Annapolis
Massachusetts	8,284	21,455	5,822,000	Boston
Michigan	97,102	251,493	9,088,000	Lansing
Minnesota	86,614	224,329	4,193,000	St. Paul
Mississippi	47,689	123,514	2,613,000	Jackson
Missouri	69,697	180,514	5,029,000	Jefferson City
Montana	147,046	380,847	826,000	Helena
Nebraska	77,355	200,349	1,606,000	Lincoln
Nevada	110,561	286,352	936,000	Carson City
New Hampshire	9,279	24,032	998,000	Concord
New Jersey	7,787	20,168	7,562,000	Trenton
New Mexico	121,593	314,924	1,450,000	Santa Fe
New York	52,735	136,583	17,783,000	Albany
North Carolina	52,669	136,412	6,255,000	Raleigh
North Dakota	70,702	183,117	685,000	Bismarck
Ohio	44,787	115,998	10,744,000	Columbus
Oklahoma	69,956	181,185	3,301,000	Oklahoma City
Oregon	97,073	251,418	2,687,000	Salem
Pennsylvania	46,043	119,251	11,853,000	Harrisburg
Rhode Island	1,212	3,139	968,000	Providence
South Carolina	31,113	80,582	3,347,000	Columbia
South Dakota	77,116	199,730	708,000	Pierre
Tennessee	42,144	109,152	4,762,000	Nashville
Texas	266,807	691,027	16,370,000	Austin
Utah	84,899	219,887	1,645,000	Salt Lake City
Vermont	9,614	24,900	535,000	Montpelier
Virginia	40,767	105,586	5,706,000	Richmond
Washington	68,139	176,479	4,409,000	Olympia
West Virginia	24,231	62,758	1,936,000	Charlestown
Wisconsin	66,215	171,496	4,775,000	Madison
Wyoming	97,809	253,324	509,000	Cheyenne

UNITED KINGDOM ADMINISTRATIVE AREAS

England – *counties*
Avon
Bedfordshire
Berkshire
Buckinghamshire
Cambridgeshire
Cheshire
Cleveland
Cornwall
Cumbria
Derbyshire
Devon
Dorset
Durham
East Sussex
Essex
Gloucestershire
Greater London
Greater Manchester
Hampshire
Hereford & Worcester

Hertfordshire
Humberside
Isle of Wight
Isles of Scilly[1]
Kent
Lancashire
Leicestershire
Lincolnshire
Merseyside
Norfolk
Northamptonshire
Northumberland
North Yorkshire
Nottinghamshire
Oxfordshire
Shropshire
Somerset
South Yorkshire
Staffordshire
Suffolk
Surrey

Tyne & Wear
Warwickshire
West Midlands
West Sussex
West Yorkshire
Wiltshire

Wales – *counties*
Clwyd
Dyfed
Gwent
Gwynedd
Mid Glamorgan
Powys
South Glamorgan
West Glamorgan

Scotland – *regions*
Borders

Central
Dumfries & Galloway
Fife
Grampian
Highland
Lothian
Strathclyde
Tayside

Island areas
Orkney
Shetland
Western Isles

N. Ireland – *counties*[2]
Antrim
Armagh
Down
Fermanagh
Londonderry
Tyrone

[1] Separate administration, but not full county status   [2] Divided into 26 administrative districts

THE COMMONWEALTH OF AUSTRALIA

State or territory	Area		Population (1984 est.)	Capital
	sq miles	sq km		
Capital Territory	939	2,432	245,600	Canberra
New South Wales	309,450	801,428	5,405,100	Sydney
Northern Territory	520,308	1,347,519	138,900	Darwin
Queensland	667,036	1,727,522	2,505,100	Brisbane
South Australia	380,091	984,377	1,353,000	Adelaide
Tasmania	26,385	68,322	437,300	Hobart
Victoria	87,889	227,618	4,075,900	Melbourne
Western Australia	975,973	2,527,621	1,382,600	Perth

CANADIAN PROVINCES AND TERRITORIES

Province or Territory	Area		Population (1985 est.)	Capital
	sq miles	sq km		
Alberta	255,300	661,187	2,344,600	Edmonton
British Columbia	366,240	948,560	2,888,700	Victoria
Manitoba	251,014	650,089	1,067,900	Winnipeg
New Brunswick	28,356	73,437	718,400	Fredericton
Newfoundland	156,194	404,518	579,700	St. John's
Northwest Territory	1,304,978	3,379,693	50,900	Yellowknife
Nova Scotia	21,426	55,491	879,600	Halifax
Ontario	412,606	1,068,586	9,047,900	Toronto
Prince Edward Island	2,184	5,567	127,000	Charlottetown
Quebec	594,894	1,540,685	6,572,300	Quebec
Saskatchewan	251,795	651,902	1,018,200	Regina
Yukon Territory	207,088	536,326	22,800	Whitehorse

PROVINCES OF SOUTH AFRICA

Province	Area sq miles	sq km	Population	Seat of Government
Cape Province	247,638	641,379	5,374,000	Cape Town
Natal	35,272	91,355	2,842,000	Pietermaritzburg
Transvaal	101,352	262,499	8,950,000	Pretoria
Orange Free State	49,418	127,993	2,080,000	Bloemfontein

THE BLACK HOMELANDS

The Black Homelands (called National States by South Africa) are not recognized by the United Nations.

Homeland	Area sq miles	sq km	Population	People	Capital	Independence
Bophuthatswana	15,444	40,000	1,527,000	Tswana	Mmabatho	1977
Ciskei	2,080	5,386	777,000	Xhosa	Zwelitsha	1981
Transkei	16,816	43,553	2,681,000	Xhosa	Umtata	1976
Venda	2,393	6,198	424,000	Venda	—	1979

The following are stated to be self-governing, but not yet independent, with main peoples indicated in parentheses:

Basotho-Qwaqwa (South Sotho)   Kwazulu (Zulu)   Ndebele (Ndebele)
Gazankulu (Shangaan)   Lebowa (Pedi)   Swazi (Swazi)

REPUBLICS OF THE U.S.S.R.

	Area sq miles	sq km	Population (1985 est.)	Capital
Armenia	11,540	29,886	3,267,000	Yerevan
Azerbaijan	33,400	86,500	6,506,000	Baku
Byelorussia	80,000	207,200	9,978,000	Minsk
Estonia	17,300	45,000	1,518,000	Tallin
Georgia	27,700	71,700	5,167,000	Tbilisi
Kazakhstan	1,102,300	2,854,700	15,648,000	Alma-Ata
Kirghizia	76,150	197,200	3,886,000	Frunze
Latvia	24,600	63,700	2,587,000	Riga
Lithuania	25,000	64,700	3,539,000	Vilnius
Moldavia	13,000	33,700	4,080,000	Kishinev
Russian S.F.S.R.	6,569,000	17,012,400	142,117,000	Moscow
Tadzhikistan	54,600	141,400	4,365,000	Dushanbe
Turkmenistan	188,450	488,050	3,118,000	Ashkhabad
Ukraine	231,000	598,200	50,667,000	Kiev
Uzbekistan	153,000	397,300	17,498,000	Tashkent

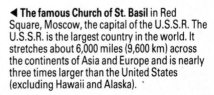

◀ **The famous Church of St. Basil** in Red Square, Moscow, the capital of the U.S.S.R. The U.S.S.R. is the largest country in the world. It stretches about 6,000 miles (9,600 km) across the continents of Asia and Europe and is nearly three times larger than the United States (excluding Hawaii and Alaska).

51

Government, Law, and Finance

Government, law, and finance together form the backbone of any country's existence. The government of a country is the method by which major decisions about that country are made by at least one person on behalf of the community. Governments make laws, control trade and the economy, and regulate industry, health, education, and housing. Subordinate local governments make local decisions. Different countries are governed in different ways.

▲ **A modern style of architecture** giving an imposing air to the new Town Hall building in Mainz, a busy center on the Rhine River in West Germany.

Governments need laws to help them to enforce their decisions and to protect members of the community. A healthy money supply is needed to carry out certain government policies and to ensure a good standard of living for members of the community. Basically, we carry on as our ancient forebears did—exchanging goods for currency and living by rules.

FORMS OF GOVERNMENT

System	Rule by
anarchy	without law
aristocracy	a privileged order
autocracy	one person, absolutely
bureaucracy	officials
democracy	the people
despotocracy	a tyrant
diarchy	two rulers or authorities
ergatocracy	the workers
ethnocracy	race or ethnic group
gerontocracy	old people
gynocracy	women
hierocracy	priests
isocracy	all—with equal power
kakistocracy	the worst
matriarchy	a mother (or mothers)
meritocracy	those in power on ability
monarchy	hereditary head of state
monocracy	one person
ochlocracy	the mob
oligarchy	small exclusive class
patriarchy	male head of family
plutocracy	the wealthy
stratocracy	the military
technocracy	technical experts
theocracy	divine guidance

SOME OTHER LAW-MAKING BODIES

Name	Country
Althing	Iceland
Bundesrat	Austria & Germany
Bundestag	West Germany
Cortes	Spain
Dail	Ireland
Folketing	Denmark
Knesset	Israel
Nationalrat	Austria & Switzerland
Parliament	United Kingdom
Riksdag	Sweden
Sobranie	Bulgaria
Soviet	U.S.S.R.
Ständerat	Switzerland
States-General	Netherlands
Storting	Norway

▼ **The Kremlin,** in Moscow, Russia's capital. Once the home of the czars, it is now the seat of the Communist government. *Bottom:* The parliament building in Ottawa, Canada.

CONGRESS

The government of the United States is divided into three branches so that no one person or group can acquire too much power. The president and the people who work with him form the *executive* branch of government. Congress makes up the *legislative* branch. The U.S. Congress is *bicameral*—it has two houses, the Senate and the House of Representatives. A member of the House of Representatives is elected for a two-year term, usually by the people of his or her home state. There are 435 members of the House. The Senate must approve a bill after the House passes it. Two members of the Senate are elected from each state, and they serve for six years. Not all senators run for election at the same time. Instead, one-third of the Senate is elected every two years.

MONARCHS OF THE WORLD

Most countries today have a parliamentary system—a council of people elected to rule. The majority of nations have at their head a president, usually elected every few years. Those which still have hereditary monarchs are:

Country	Ruler	Came to Throne
Belgium	King Baudouin I	1951
Bhutan	King Jigme Singye Wangchuk	1972
Denmark	Queen Margarethe II	1972
Great Britain	Queen Elizabeth II	1952
Japan	Emperor Hirohito	1926
Jordan	King Hussein	1952
Liechtenstein	Prince Franz Joseph II	1938
Luxembourg	Grand Duke Jean	1964
Monaco	Prince Rainier III	1949
Morocco	King Hassan II	1961
Nepal	King Mahendra Bir Bikram Shah Deva	1955
Netherlands	Queen Beatrix	1980
Norway	King Olav V	1957
Saudi Arabia	King Fahd bin Abdul Aziz	1982
Spain	King Juan Carlos I	1975
Sweden	King Carl XVI Gustav	1973
Thailand	King Bhumibol Adulaydej	1946

INTERNATIONAL ORGANIZATIONS

ASEAN	Association of Southeast Asian Nations
COMECON	Council for Mutual Economic Aid
ECSC	European Coal and Steel Community
EEC	European Economic Community
EFTA	European Free Trade Association
EURATOM	European Atomic Energy Community
NATO	North Atlantic Treaty Organization
OAS	Organization of American States
OAU	Organization of African Unity
OECD	Organization for Economic Development and Co-operation
OPEC	Organization of Petroleum-Exporting Countries
U.N.	United Nations

MEMBERS OF INTERNATIONAL ORGANIZATIONS

COMECON: Bulgaria, Czechoslovakia, East Germany, Hungary, Mongolia, Poland, Romania, U.S.S.R.

Commonwealth: Antigua & Barbuda, Australia, Bahamas, Bangladesh, Barbados, Belize, Botswana, Brunei, Canada, Cyprus, Dominica, Fiji, Gambia, Ghana, Grenada, Guyana, India, Jamaica, Kenya, Kiribati, Lesotho, Malawi, Malaysia, Maldives, Malta, Mauritius, Nauru, New Zealand, Nigeria, Papua New Guinea, St. Christopher-Nevis, St. Lucia, St. Vincent, Seychelles, Sierra Leone, Singapore, Solomon Islands, Sri Lanka, Swaziland, Tanzania, Tonga, Trinidad & Tobago, Tuvalu, Uganda, United Kingdom, Vanuatu, Western Samoa, Zambia, Zimbabwe.

EEC (Common Market): Belgium, Denmark, France, Greece, West Germany, Ireland, Italy, Luxembourg, Netherlands, Portugal (1986), Spain (1982), United Kingdom.

NATO: Belgium, Canada, Denmark, France, West Germany, Greece, Iceland, Italy, Luxembourg, Netherlands, Norway, Portugal, Spain, Turkey, United Kingdom, United States.

Warsaw Pact: Bulgaria, Czechoslovakia, East Germany, Hungary, Poland, Romania, U.S.S.R.

UNITED NATIONS: MEMBER COUNTRIES

The U.N. came into existence in 1945, when 50 nations signed its charter. In 1971 the U.N. voted for the expulsion of Nationalist China and the admittance of Communist China in its place. Today there are 159 member countries, listed below.

Country	Joined	Country	Joined	Country	Joined
Afghanistan	1946	Germany, East	1973	Panama	1945
Albania	1955	Germany, West	1973	Papua New Guinea	1975
Algeria	1962	Ghana	1957	Paraguay	1945
Angola	1976	Greece	1945	Peru	1945
Antigua and Barbuda	1981	Grenada	1974	Philippines	1945
Argentina	1945	Guatemala	1945	Poland	1945
Australia	1945	Guinea	1958	Portugal	1955
Austria	1955	Guinea-Bissau	1974	Qatar	1971
Bahamas	1973	Guyana	1966	Romania	1955
Bahrain	1971	Haiti	1945	Rwanda	1962
Bangladesh	1974	Honduras	1945	St. Lucia	1979
Barbados	1966	Hungary	1955	St. Vincent &	
Belgium	1945	Iceland	1946	the Grenadines	1980
Belize	1981	India	1945	Samoa	1976
Benin	1960	Indonesia	1950	São Tomé & Príncipe	1975
Bhutan	1971	Iran	1945	Saudi Arabia	1945
Bolivia	1945	Iraq	1945	Senegal	1960
Botswana	1966	Ireland, Rep. of	1955	Seychelles	1976
Brazil	1945	Israel	1949	Sierra Leone	1961
Brunei	1984	Italy	1955	Singapore	1965
Bulgaria	1955	Ivory Coast	1960	Solomon Islands	1978
Burkina Faso	1960	Jamaica	1962	Somali Republic	1960
(Upper Volta)		Japan	1956	South Africa	1945
Burma	1948	Jordan	1955	Spain	1955
Burundi	1962	Kampuchea (Cambodia)	1955	Sri Lanka	1955
Byelorussian S.S.R.	1945	Kenya	1963	St. Christopher-Nevis	1983
Cameroon	1960	Kuwait	1963	Sudan	1956
Canada	1945	Laos	1955	Suriname	1975
Cape Verde	1975	Lebanon	1945	Swaziland	1968
Central African Republic	1960	Lesotho	1966	Sweden	1946
Chad	1960	Liberia	1945	Syria	1945
Chile	1945	Libya	1955	Tanzania	1961
China	1945	Luxembourg	1945	Thailand	1946
Colombia	1945	Madagascar	1960	Togo	1960
Comoros	1975	Malawi	1964	Trinidad & Tobago	1962
Congo	1960	Malaysia	1957	Tunisia	1956
Costa Rica	1945	Maldive Islands	1965	Turkey	1945
Cuba	1945	Mali	1960	Uganda	1962
Cyprus	1960	Malta	1964	Ukrainian S.S.R.	1945
Czechoslovakia	1945	Mauritania	1961	U.S.S.R.	1945
Denmark	1945	Mauritius	1968	United Arab	
Djibouti	1977	Mexico	1945	Emirates	1971
Dominica	1978	Mongolia	1961	United Kingdom	1945
Dominican Republic	1945	Morocco	1956	United States	1945
Ecuador	1945	Mozambique	1975	Uruguay	1945
Egypt	1945	Nepal	1955	Vanuatu	1981
El Salvador	1945	Netherlands	1945	Venezuela	1945
Equatorial Guinea	1968	New Zealand	1945	Vietnam	1976
Ethiopia	1945	Nicaragua	1945	Yemen Arab Republic	1947
Fiji	1970	Niger	1960	Yemen P.D.R.	1967
Finland	1955	Nigeria	1960	Yugoslavia	1945
France	1945	Norway	1945	Zaire	1960
Gabon	1960	Oman	1971	Zambia	1964
Gambia	1965	Pakistan	1947	Zimbabwe	1980

UNITED NATIONS: AGENCIES

FAO	Food and Agriculture Organization
GATT	General Agreement on Tariffs and Trade
IAEA	International Atomic Energy Authority
IBRD	International Bank for Reconstruction and Development (World Bank)
ICAO	International Civil Aviation Organization
ICF	International Court of Justice
IDA	International Development Association
IFC	International Finance Corporation
ILO	International Labor Organization
IMCO	Inter-Governmental Maritime Consultative Organization
IMF	International Monetary Fund
ITU	International Telecommunications Union
UNCLOS	United Nations Conference on the Law of the Sea
UNCTAD	United Nations Conference on Trade and Development
UNEF	United Nations Emergency Fund
UNESCO	United Nations Educational, Scientific, and Cultural Organization
UNICEF	United Nations Children's Emergency Fund
UNIDO	United Nations Industrial Development Organization
UNRWA	United Nations Relief and Works Agency
UPU	Universal Postal Union
WHO	World Health Organization
WMO	World Meteorological Organization

▲ **The United Nations** can request troops from member countries to maintain peace in any area.

UNITED NATIONS: PRINCIPAL ORGANS

General Assembly consists of all members, each having one vote. Most of work done in committees: (1) Political Security, (2) Economic & Financial, (3) Social, Humanitarian & Cultural, (4) Decolonization (including Non-Self Governing Territories), (5) Administrative & Budgetary, (6) Legal.

Security Council consists of 15 members, each with 1 vote. There are 5 permanent members—China, France, U.K., U.S.A., and U.S.S.R.—the others being elected for two-year terms. Main object: maintenance of peace and security.

Economic and Social Council is responsible under General Assembly for carrying out functions of the U.N. with regard to international economic, social, cultural, educational, health, and related matters.

Trusteeship Council administers Trust Territories.

International Court of Justice is composed of 15 judges (all different nationalities) elected by U.N. Meets at The Hague.

The Secretariat is composed of the Secretary-General, who is chief administrative officer of the U.N. and is appointed by the General Assembly, and an international staff appointed by him. Secretaries-General of the U.N.:

Trygve Lie (Norway)	1946–1953
Dag Hammarskjöld (Sweden)	1953–1961
U Thant (Burma)	1961–1971
Kurt Waldheim (Austria)	1972–1981
Javier Pérez de Cuéllar (Peru)	1982–

Passing Laws

HOW A BILL BECOMES LAW IN CONGRESS

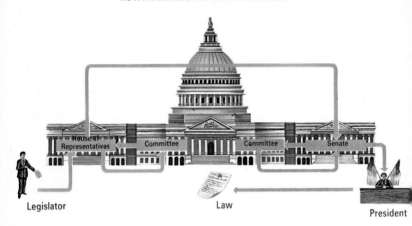

Legislator

Law

President

Laws are rules that apply to everyone in a country. Laws are made in different ways in different countries, but the basic procedure is the same. An initial proposal goes through various stages of discussion until its final form is drawn up. Once this has been approved by the highest authority, it becomes a law. In the United States, the highest authority is the president. In the U.S.S.R. it is the Supreme Soviet and in the United Kingdom it is the reigning monarch.

HOW A BILL BECOMES LAW IN U.S.S.R.

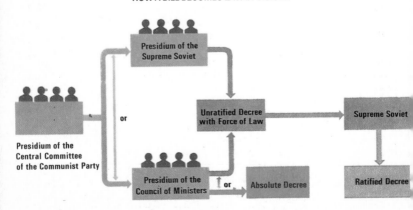

58

HOW A BILL BECOMES LAW IN PARLIAMENT

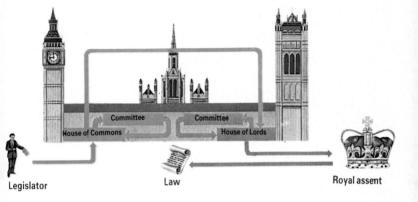

Legislator   Law   Royal assent

HOW OLD?

The age at which people are allowed by law to do certain things such as drive and vote differs form one country to another, as you can see in the table below.

Country	Drive	Military service	Marry (Male/Female)	Vote	Drink	Be executed
U.S.A.	15–21[1]	–	18/14[2]	18	21	18[3]?
Poland	16	18	21/18[4]	18	18	17/18
Japan	16	–	20/18[4]	21	20	17/18
Israel	17	18	18	18	16	18
France	18	18	18/15¼	18	15/18[5]	–
Egypt	18	21	18	18	–	18
U.K.	17	–	18[6]	18	18	–
Sweden	18	18	18	18	18	–

[1] Depends on the state
[2] With parents' consent
[3] Complicated—depends on individual state laws
[4] Girls can marry at 16 with parents' consent
[5] Depends on what is being consumed
[6] 16 with parents' consent; 16 without parents' consent in Scotland

How Money Works

◀ **The coat of arms** of the London Stock Exchange bears the words "My word is my bond."

▼ **The chart below** shows both the national debt and the GNP in different countries. GNP (**G**ross **N**ational **P**roduct) is what you get if you add up the value (in U.S. dollars) of all the goods and services produced by a country in one year (in this case 1986). The colored blocks and the numbers (millions of dollars) on top of the blocks are the GNPs. The coins inside each block and the numbers (millions of dollars) at the bottom of each block are the national debts.

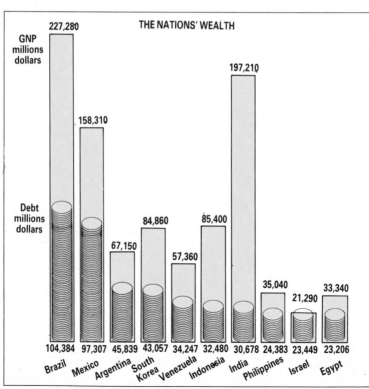

THE NATIONS' WEALTH

	GNP (millions dollars)	Debt (millions dollars)
Brazil	227,280	104,384
Mexico	158,310	97,307
Argentina	67,150	45,839
South Korea	84,860	43,057
Venezuela	57,360	34,247
Indonesia	85,400	32,480
India	197,210	30,678
Philippines	35,040	24,383
Israel	21,290	23,449
Egypt	33,340	23,206

MONEY MATTERS

● The earliest evidence of the use of paper for money was in China.

● The one kwan bill is the largest paper note ever issued. This 9 × 13 in (22.8 by 33 cm) "miniature towel" was issued in China from 1368–1399 during the Ming Dynasty.

● The largest check drawn on a bank was for $1,600 million. It was presented by the United States to the Government of India in 1974.

● The World Bank (IBRD) and its International Development Association (IDA) have now become the largest source of lending for development purposes. Lending commitments for 1986 came to $17.5 billion.

● The largest bank vault is in the Chase Manhattan building in New York City. It measures 350 × 100 ft (106 by 30 m). Just one of its doors weighs 40 tons.

● Judged by the total assets it controls, the richest commercial bank in the world is Citicorp, New York City. Its assets totaled $130 billion at the end of 1982.

● The State Bank of India has more branches than any other bank in the world. At the start of 1986 it had 10,838 branches.

▲ **This special British 50 pence piece** was minted in 1973 to commemorate the country's entry into the European Economic Community (EEC).

ECONOMICS: NOBEL PRIZE WINNERS

1969	Ragnar Frisch (Norwegian) and Jan Tinbergen (Dutch)
1970	Paul Samuelson (American)
1971	Simon Kuznets (American)
1972	Kenneth Arrow (American) and Sir John Hicks (British)
1973	Wassily Leontief (American)
1974	Gunnar Myrdal (Swedish) and Friedrich von Hayek (Austrian)
1975	Leonid Kantorovich (Russian) & Tjalling Koopmans (Dutch)
1976	Milton Friedman (American)
1977	James E. Meade (British) & Bertil Ohlin (Swedish)
1978	Herbert A. Simon (American)
1979	Theodore W. Schultz and Arthur Lewis (American)
1980	Lawrence Klein (American)
1981	James Tobin (American)
1982	George Stigler (American)
1983	Gerard Debreu (French)
1984	Sir Richard Stone (British)
1985	Franco Modigliani (American)
1986	James Buchanan (American)
1987	Robert M. Solow (American)

CALCULATING INTEREST

Simple interest $I = Prn$
Compound interest $I = P(1 + r)^n - P$

I stands for *interest*, P for *principal* (starting amount), r for *rate* (e.g. for 6% interest, $r = 6/100$ or 0.06), and n for *time* (number of years or months or whatever the unit period is).

61

CURRENCIES AROUND THE WORLD

Country	Currency
Afghanistan	afghani (100 puls)
Albania	lek (100 qindarka)
Algeria	dinar (100 centimes)
Andorra	franc (Fr) and peseta (Sp)
Angola	kwanza (100 lwei)
Antigua & Barbuda	dollar (100 cents)
Argentina	peso (100 centavos)
Australia	dollar (100 cents)
Austria	schilling (100 groschen)
Bahamas	dollar (100 cents)
Bahrain	dinar (1,000 fils)
Bangladesh	taka (100 paise)
Barbados	dollar (100 cents)
Belgium	franc (100 centimes)
Belize	dollar (100 cents)
Benin	franc
Bermuda (U.K.)	dollar (100 cents)
Bhutan	ngultrum
Bolivia	peso (100 centavos)
Botswana	pula (100 thebe)
Brazil	cruzeiro (100 centavos)
Brunei	dollar (100 sen)
Bulgaria	lev (100 stotinki)
Burkina Faso	franc
Burma	kyat (100 pyas)
Burundi	franc
Cameroon	franc
Canada	dollar (100 cents)
Cape Verde Islands	escudo
Central African Republic	franc
Chad	franc
Chile	new peso (100 old escudos)
China, People's Republic	yuan (10 chiao; 100 fen)
Colombia	peso (100 centavos)
Comoros	franc
Congo	franc
Costa Rica	colon (100 centimos)
Cuba	peso (100 centavos)
Cyprus	pound (1,000 mils)
Czechoslovakia	koruna (100 halers)
Denmark	krone (100 öre)
Djibouti	franc
Dominica	dollar (100 cents)
Dominican Republic	peso (100 centavos)
Ecuador	sucre (100 centavos)
Egypt	pound (100 piasters, 1,000 millièmes)
El Salvador	colon (100 cetavos)
Equatorial Guinea	ekuele
Ethiopia	dollar (100 cents)
Fiji	dollar (100 cents)
Finland	markka (100 pennia)
France	franc (100 centimes)
French Guiana	franc
Gabon	franc
Gambia	dalasi (100 bututs)
Germany, East	DDR mark (100 pfennigs)
Germany, West	deutsch mark (100 pfennigs)
Ghana	cedi (100 pesewas)
Gibraltar	pound (100 pence)
Greece	drachma (100 lepta)

▼ **Some of the small change** of the world of money. Most currencies have a main unit that is divided into 100 smaller units. The smaller units are often called "cents," "centavos," "centimos," or "centimes." These words come from *centum*, the Latin word for one hundred.

Grenada	dollar (100 cents)
Guatemala	quetzal (100 centavos)
Guinea	syli
Guinea-Bissau	peso
Guyana	dollar (100 cents)
Haiti	gourde (100 centimes)
Honduras	lempira (100 centavos)
Hong Kong	dollar
Hungary	forint (100 fillér)
Iceland	króna (100 aurar)
India	rupee (100 paisa)
Indonesia	rupiah (100-sen)
Iran	rial (100 dinars)
Iraq	dinar (1,000 fils)
Ireland, Rep. of	pound (punt) (100 pence)
Israel	shekel (100 agorot)
Italy	lira
Ivory Coast	franc
Jamaica	dollar (100 cents)
Japan	yen
Jordan	dinar (1,000 fils)
Kenya	shilling (100 cents)
Kiribati	dollar
Kampuchea (Cambodia)	riel (100 sen)
Korea, North	won (100 jun)
Korea, South	won (100 jun)
Kuwait	dinar (1,000 fils)
Laos	kip (100 ats)
Lebanon	pound (100 piasters)
Lesotho	loti
Liberia	dollar (100 cents)
Libya	dinar (1,000 dirhams)
Liechtenstein	franc (Swiss)
Luxembourg	franc (100 centimes)
Macao (Portugal)	pataca (100 avos)
Madagascar	franc
Malawi	kwacha (100 tambala)
Malaysia	dollar (100 cents)
Maldives, Rep. of	rupee (100 laris)
Mali	franc
Malta	pound (100 cents, 1,000 mils)
Mauritania	ouguiya (5 khoums)
Mauritius	rupee (100 cents)
Mexico	peso (100 centavos)
Monaco	franc (Fr)
Mongolian People's Republic	tugrik (100 möngö)
Morocco	dirham (100 centimes)
Mozambique	metical
Namibia	rand
Nauru	dollar (Australian) (100 cents)
Nepal	rupee (100 paisa)
Netherlands	guilder (100 cents)
New Zealand	dollar (100 cents)
Nicaragua	córdoba (100 centavos)
Niger	franc
Nigeria	naira (100 kobo)
Norway	krone (100 öre)
Oman	rial Omani (1,000 baizas)
Pakistan	rupee (100 paisa)
Panama	balboa (100 cents)
Papua New Guinea	kina

Continued on next page

Continued from previous page

Country	Currency
Paraguay	guarani (100 céntimos)
Peru	sol (100 centavos)
Philippines	peso (100 centavos)
Poland	zloti (100 groszy)
Portugal	escudo (100 centavos)
Qatar	riyal (100 dirhams)
Romania	leu (100 bani)
Rwanda	franc
St. Christopher-Nevis	dollar (100 cents)
St. Lucia	dollar (100 cents)
St. Vincent & the Grenadines	dollar (100 cents)
San Marino	lira (Italian)
São Tomé & Príncipe	dobra
Saudi Arabia	riyal (20 qursh)
Senegal	franc
Sierra Leone	leone (100 cents)
Singapore	dollar (100 cents)
Solomon Islands	dollar
Somali Democratic Republic	shilling (100 cents)
South Africa	rand (100 cents)
Spain	peseta (100 céntimos)
Sri Lanka	rupee (100 cents)
Sudan	pound (100 piasters, 1,000 milliemes)
Suriname	guilder (100 cents)
Swaziland	lilangeni (pl. emalangeni) (100 cents)
Sweden	krona (100 öre)
Switzerland	franc (100 centimes)
Syria	pound (100 piasters)
Taiwan	dollar (100 cents)
Tanzania	shilling (100 cents)
Thailand	baht (100 satang)
Togo	franc
Tonga	pa'anga (100 seniti)
Trinidad & Tobago	dollar (100 cents)
Tunisia	dinar (1,000 millimes)
Turkey	lira (100 kurus)
Tuvalu	dollar (Aust.)
Uganda	shilling (100 cents)
United Arab Emirates	dirham (100 fils)
United Kingdom	pound sterling (100 pence)
United States	dollar (100 cents)
Uruguay	peso (100 centésimos)
U.S.S.R.	ruble (100 kopecks)
Vanuatu	vatu
Vatican City State	lira
Venezuela	bolivar (100 céntimos)
Vietnam	dong (100 xu)
Western Samoa	tala (100 sene)
Yemen, North (Arab Rep.)	rial (40 bogaches)
Yemen, South (PDR)	dinar (1,000 fils)
Yugoslavia	dinar (100 paras)
Zaïre	zaire (100 makuta [sing likuta], 10,000 sengi)
Zambia	kwacha
Zimbabwe	dollar (100 cents)

► **Computers now play a huge part** in the handling of money. Here, a customer in a Hamburg bank checks the details of his bank account on a VDU (visual display unit). He can then decide how much cash to withdraw from the computerized, automatic cash dispenser that the woman in the picture is using.

STOCK EXCHANGES

These are markets where capital, issued in the form of stocks, shares, and bonds by companies or governments, is bought and sold. The world's major stock exchanges are in New York's Wall Street, in Tokyo, Japan, and in London, England. There are 138 stock exchanges throughout the world, the oldest of which is in Amsterdam. It was founded in 1602.

The record for a day's trading on the New York Stock Exchange was 236,565 shares, on August 3, 1984.

On December 12, 1984, a record for the London Stock Exchange was established when it undertook 44,106 transactions.

"LAWS" OF ECONOMICS

Over the years, certain theories about economics have been put forward by various people. These are observations of general trends and not foolproof rules.

Diminishing Returns Hypothesis that if one factor of production is increased while the others stay constant, a point is reached when the addition of one more unit of the variable quantity adds less to output than the previous unit.

Engel's Law The greater the income of a household, the lower the proportion spent on food (Ernst Engel, 1821–96).

Gresham's Law Bad money drives out good; i.e., the public tends to hoard (or even melt down) coins with greater bullion content, such as new coins (Sir Thomas Gresham, 1519–79).

Malthusian Theory Population tends to increase by geometric progression, natural resources by (slower) arithmetic progression; thus unrestricted population growth would eventually lead to universal hardship (Thomas Robert Malthus, 1766–1834).

Pareto's Law Whatever the political or tax system in a country, the distribution of income is more or less the same (Vilfredo Pareto, 1848–1923).

Parkinson's Law Work expands to fill the time available for its completion (C. Northcote Parkinson, 1955).

Peter Principle In an organization, every employee tends to rise to his or her level of incompetence, so that all important work is done by those who have not reached that level (L. J. Peter, in 1969).

Say's Law Supply creates its own demand (Jean-Baptiste Say, 1767–1832; several interpretations, but taken literally it has proved to be not strictly true).

Supply and Demand, Law of Increase in supply tends to lead to a lower price for any particular product unless there is an increase in demand, and vice versa.

What We Believe

People have always believed in some force outside their familiar world. Many different religions share certain basic principles and most of them stress a life-style and code of behavior centered on one or more gods. Ancient civilizations had elaborate religions based on stories, or myths, about many different gods. Judaism was the first religion known to have centered on one god. Both Christianity and Islam grew

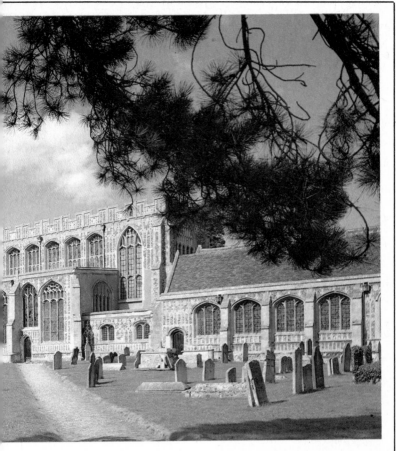

▲ **One of England's finest** parish churches—the church of the Holy Trinity at Long Melford, Suffolk.

out of Judaism. Religion has been one of the most powerful forces in our history. Many wars have been fought and millions have lost their lives or been persecuted for their beliefs.

MAJOR RELIGIONS: ESTIMATED WORLD MEMBERSHIP (millions)	
Christians	1,065
Roman Catholics	630
Eastern Orthodox	60
Protestants	375
Jews	17
Muslims	555
Shintoists	32
Taoists	20
Confucians	150
Buddhists	250
Hindus	460

DIFFERENCES IN MAJOR RELIGIONS AND BELIEFS

Bold type in the "Beliefs" text indicates a separate entry.

RELIGION	BELIEFS
ADVENTISTS	Protestants who follow the teachings of William Miller (1781–1849), who believed in the second coming of Christ. The **Seventh-day Adventists** form the largest group.
ANGLICANS	Members of churches that are in agreement with the **Church of England**.
ANGLO-CATHOLICS	Members of the **Church of England** who favor some of the ritual of the Catholic faith.
BAHA'I	A Persian (Iranian) religion, founded in the 1800s, which holds the belief that there are several true prophets, and that religion and science will establish world peace.
BAPTISTS	Protestants whose essential belief is that the adult shall be totally immersed in baptism.
BUDDHISTS	Religion that teaches that the way to salvation is through ethics and discipline as taught by Buddha (see page 70). It is a major oriental religion.
CALVINISM	Form of Protestantism. The teachings of Calvin (see page 70) are followed and the absolute sovereignty of God is preached. The churches are plain, and worship is simple and dignified.
CHRISTIANS	Followers of the teachings of Christ. The largest of the many groups are the **Roman Catholics**, the **Protestants**, and the **Eastern Orthodox Church**.
CHRISTIAN SCIENTISTS	Movement founded in the late 1800s by Mary Baker Eddy, who stressed the perfectability of God and men and women and who taught and practiced spiritual healing.
CHURCH OF ENGLAND	Church that came into being when Henry VIII broke with the pope and became head of the Church.
CONFUCIANISM	A philosophical, religious, and political system dating from about 500 B.C. in China. It spread widely in Japan and Korea.
CONGREGA-TIONALISTS	**Nonconformists** who believe that **Christians** are equal and that each local congregation is responsible only to God.
EASTERN ORTHODOX CHURCH	Members of the **Christian** Greek and Russian Orthodox churches in Eastern Europe and Egypt who follow the Creed of Constantinople.
EPISCOPALIANS	Members of any **Christian** church governed by bishops.
FRIENDS, SOCIETY OF	**Christian** group who believe that creeds, rites, and organized religion should be rejected, and spontaneous worship encouraged. Founded in 1640 by George Fox.
HINDUISM	The main religion of India. Brahman is the supreme spirit and three forms exist—*Brahma, Shiva,* and *Vishnu.*
ISLAM	Religion founded by Muhammad (see page 71) in the A.D. 600s. He taught that there was one God *(Allah)* and that he was his prophet. His followers are called *Muslims.*

RELIGION	BELIEFS
JAINISM	Founded in the A.D. 500s by a small Indian group who broke away from **Hinduism**, it teaches that salvation depends on self-effort, and a nonviolent life has to be led toward all creatures.
JEHOVAH'S WITNESSES	A religious movement founded by an American, C. T. Russell, in the late 1800s. They believe that Christ returned invisibly in 1874, and that Armageddon (a catastrophic end of the world) is near.
JUDAISM	The religion of the Jews, based on the Old Testament of the Bible and the *Talmud*.
LATTER-DAY SAINTS	See **Mormons**.
LUTHERANS	The largest group of the **Protestant** Church, founded by Martin Luther (see page 71) in 1500. The Bible is their only authority.
METHODISTS	Followers of the movement founded by John Wesley (see page 71) in the 1700s; evangelical Christianity and religious experience are stressed.
MORMONS	American religious sect, also known as Latter-day Saints. They accept the Bible, but have other scriptures, including the *Book of Mormon*. Living people may be baptized and married on behalf of the dead.
NONCONFORMISTS	Term used originally for **Protestants** separated from the **Church of England**; later applied to all dissenting groups.
PLYMOUTH BRETHREN	Group founded in 1827 by J. N. Darby and E. Cronin, who believed that the Church had fallen so far from New Testament ideals that only a direct approach to God could remedy matters.
PRESBYTERIANS	Protestants who follow John Calvin's (see page 70) system of government.
PROTESTANTS	All **Christians** except **Roman Catholics** and **Eastern Orthodox**.
QUAKERS	See **Friends, Society of**.
ROMAN CATHOLICS	**Christians** who accept the pope as their spiritual leader on Earth.
SEVENTH-DAY ADVENTISTS	See **Adventists**.
SHAKERS	Small American sect who belong to the United Society of Believers. Originally an offshoot of the **Quakers**, they got their name because of their religious fervor.
SHINTO	Japanese religion; followers worship many gods, including nature and ancestors.
SIKHISM	India's fourth-largest religion, founded by Guru Nanak (1469–1538). Sikhs reject the rigid form of both **Islam** and **Hinduism**.
TAOISM	Major Chinese religion, which shows "the way" to restore human harmony; founded by Lao Tzu (see page 71) in the 500s B.C.
UNITARIANS	Members of a church free to form their own religious beliefs. Most believe that God is one personality, not a trinity, and deny the deity of Jesus Christ, holding that all men are divine.

Religious Leaders

Booth, William (1829–1912), founder of the Salvation Army, an evangelical mission organized on military lines; he was known as General Booth. Members of his family continued his work.

Buddha, "the Enlightened One," was born about 563 B.C. in northern India. The sufferings he saw made him renounce all worldly pleasures. He became a teacher, stressing that right speech, action, living, effort, awareness, and meditation must be followed to attain perfection. He died at 80.

Calvin, John (1509–64), a French scholar, was one of the pioneers of the Protestant Reformation. He set up a Protestant Church in Geneva and wrote many books that continued to be influential after his death, particularly *Institutes of the Christian Religion.*

About a quarter of the world's Protestants are Calvinists.

Confucius (*c.* 551–479 B.C.) was a Chinese thinker and philosopher whose "system" also spread to Korea and Japan. It contained no innovations, and was based on a study of rightness which people should follow.

Eddy, Mary Baker (1821–1910), an American, founded the Christian Science movement; believed in spiritual healing.

Jesus Christ (*c.* 4 B.C.–A.D. 29) founded Christianity. He was born in Bethlehem and, growing up, he went from place to place preaching and performing miracles. He is believed to have been the son of God. He was tried by Pontius Pilate, who did not dare to run counter to popular opinion, and he was convicted and crucified. Three days later he is said to have risen from his grave.

◀ **There are certain symbols** (signs) which represent particular religions. 1. Shiva (Hindu goddess). 2. Menorah (Jewish candelabrum). 3. Christian cross 4. Shinto temple. 5. Islamic crescent moon. 6. Statue of Buddha.

Lao Tzu (*c.* 604–531 B.C.), a Chinese philosopher, is believed by many to be the founder of Taoism. He is said, in a story, to have met Confucius and ridiculed his ideas. His name is also spelled *Lao Tse*.

Luther, Martin (1483–1546), was a German theologian and Protestant leader of the Reformation. He opposed the corruption of the Church of his day in his "Ninety-five Theses," which he nailed to the door of Wittenberg church, an act said to have started the Reformation.

Muhammad (Mohammed, Mahomet) (570–632), founder of Islam, the religion of the Muslims, was born in Mecca. After a series of revelations, he preached for 13 years, but underwent persecutions resulting in his flight to Medina in 622. After much fighting, his followers defeated the Meccans in 630 and he returned to Mecca in triumph. The Koran, the sacred book of Islam, is God's message as revealed to him in his last 20 years.

Wesley, John (1703–91), founder of the Methodist Movement, was the 15th child of a family of dissenters. He trained groups of lay preachers who traveled and held classes of 12 meeting weekly for prayers, Bible study, and

▲ **The Chinese philosopher Confucius** believed that "What you do not want done to yourself, do not do to others."

discussion. Differences with the Anglican Church resulted in a separation.

Wycliffe, John (*c.* 1320–84), an English reformer, began the translation of the Bible into English, as a protest against certain accepted practices. He supported anti-papal policies, and his followers, known as Lollards, were persecuted.

71

Mythology

Myths are stories about supernatural beings. Most ancient civilizations and primitive peoples had their own myths, explaining the birth of the universe and how various customs developed.

NORSE MYTHOLOGY

Aesir Collectively, the chief Norse gods.
Asgard Home of the gods.
Balder God of summer sun; son of Odin and Frigga; killed by mistletoe twig.
Frey God of fertility and crops.
Freya (Freyja) Beautiful goddess of love and night; sister of Frey; sometimes confused with *Frigga*.
Frigga Goddess of married love; wife of Odin.
Heimdal Guardian of Asgard; he and Loki slew each other.
Hel Goddess of the dead, queen of the underworld; daughter of Loki.
Hödur (Hoth) Blind god of night; unwitting killer of twin brother, Balder.
Loki God of evil; contrived Balder's death.
Odin Supreme god, head of Aesir; god of wisdom and of the atmosphere.
Thor God of thunder; eldest son of Odin.
Valhalla Hall in Asgard where Odin welcomed souls of heroes killed in battle.
Valkyries Nine handmaidens of Odin who chose warriors to die in battle and conducted them to Valhalla.

EGYPTIAN MYTHOLOGY

Amon (Ammon, Amen) A god of Thebes, united with Ra as Amon-Ra, supreme king of the gods.
Anubis Jackal-headed son of Osiris; guided souls of the dead.
Apis Sacred bull of Memphis.
Hathor Cow-headed sky goddess of love.
Horus Hawk-headed god of light; son of Osiris and Isis.
Isis Goddess of motherhood and fertility; chief goddess of Ancient Egypt.
Osiris Supreme god, ruler of the afterlife; husband of Isis.
Ptah The creator; chief god of Memphis.
Ra Sun god; ancestor of the pharaohs.
Serapis God combining attributes of Osiris and Apis.
Set God of evil; jealous brother-son of Osiris, whom he slew and cut into pieces.
Thoth Ibis-headed god of wisdom.

▶ **The favorite household god of the ancient Egyptians** was the god of music and dancing. His name was Bes.

GODS OF GREECE AND ROME

The Greek names are listed with the Roman names in parentheses.

Aphrodite (Venus) Goddess of beauty and love; sprang from foam in sea, but also said to be daughter of Zeus; mother of Eros.
Apollo Son of Zeus and Leto; god of poetry, music, and prophecy; ideal of manly beauty.
Ares (Mars) God of war, son of Zeus and Hera; Mars said to be father of twins Romulus and Remus.
Artemis (Diana) Twin sister of Apollo; goddess of Moon and famous huntress.
Athena (Minerva) Goddess of wisdom and war, daughter of Zeus and Metis; sprang fully grown and armed from father's head.
Cronus (Saturn) A Titan, god of agriculture and harvests; father of Zeus.
Dionysus (Bacchus) God of wine and fertile crops; son of Zeus and Semele.
Hera (Juno) Queen of heaven, daughter of Cronus and Rhea, wife and sister of Zeus; guardian spirit of women.
Hermes (Mercury) Messenger of gods, son of Zeus and Maia; god of physicians, traders, and thieves.
Hestia (Vesta) Goddess of the hearth, sister of Zeus; her temple held Sacred Fire guarded by Vestal Virgins.
The Lares and Penates Gods of the household. The Penates guarded the family's larder, and the Lares the house.
Poseidon (Neptune) Chief god of sea, brother of Zeus.
Zeus (Jupiter) Chief of the Olympian gods, son of Cronus and Rhea, god of thunder and lightning.

ROMAN–GREEK EQUIVALENTS

Roman	Greek
Aesculapius	Asclepius
Apollo	Apollo
Aurora	Eos
Bacchus	Dionysus
Ceres	Demeter
Cupid	Eros
Cybele	Rhea
Diana	Artemis
Dis	Hades
Faunus	Pan
Hecate	Hecate
Hercules	Heracles
Juno	Hera
Jupiter	Zeus
Juventas	Hebe
Latona	Leto
Luna	Selene
Mars	Ares
Mercury	Hermes
Minerva	Athena
Mors	Thanatos
Neptune	Poseidon
Ops	Rhea
Pluto	Pluto
Proserpine	Persephone
Saturn	Cronus
Sol	Helios
Somnus	Hypnos
Ulysses	Odysseus
Venus	Aphrodite
Vesta	Hestia
Vulcan	Hephaestus

THE NINE MUSES

In Greek mythology, there were nine lesser goddesses, daughters of Zeus and Mnemosyne, who presided over the arts and sciences.

Name: art; symbol

Calliope: Epic poetry; tablet and stylus
Clio: History; scroll
Erato: Love poetry; lyre
Euterpe: Lyric poetry; flute
Melpomene: Tragedy; tragic mask, sword
Polyhymnia: Sacred song; none
Terpsichore: Dancing; lyre
Thalia: Comedy, pastoral poetry; comic mask, shepherd's staff
Urania: Astronomy; globe

TWELVE LABORS OF HERCULES

Heracles (Roman, Hercules), said to be the son of Zeus and Alcmene, performed 12 tasks to free himself from the imprisonment of Hera:

1 Killing Nemean lion
2 Killing Hydra (many-headed snake)
3 Capturing hind of Artemis
4 Capturing Erymanthian boar
5 Cleansing Augean stables in a day
6 Killing man-eating Stymphalian birds
7 Capturing Cretan wild bull
8 Capturing man-eating mares of Diomedes
9 Procuring girdle of Amazon Hippolyta
10 Killing the monster Geryon
11 Stealing apples from garden of Hesperides
12 Bringing Cerberus up from Hades

73

THE PROPHETS

These were the writers of the prophetic books of the Bible's Old Testament. Traditional classification according to their writings:

Major Prophets – Isaiah, Jeremiah, Ezekiel, and (except in Hebrew scriptures) Daniel

Minor Prophets – Hosea, Joel, Amos, Obadiah, Jonah, Micah, Nahum, Habakkuk, Zephaniah, Haggai, Zechariah, and Malachi

PATRON SAINTS

In the Roman Catholic faith, there are patron saints that protect certain people or places. The idea arose in the Middle Ages.

Saint	Patronage	Saint	Patronage
St. Agatha	Nurses	**St. Joseph**	Carpenters
St. Andrew	Scotland (November 30)	**St. Lawrence**	Cooks
St. Anthony	Gravediggers	**St. Luke**	Physicians
St. Augustine of Hippo	Brewers	**St. Martha**	Dieticians
		St. Matthew	Tax collectors
St. Benedict	Speleologists	**St. Michael**	Policemen and women
St. Cecilia	Musicians	**St. Nicholas**	The original Santa Claus
St. Christopher	Sailors	**St. Patrick**	Ireland (March 17)
St. Crispin	Shoemakers	**St. Paul**	Carpet weavers and tent-makers
St. David	Wales (March 1)		
St. Dunstan	Goldsmiths and silversmiths	**St. Peter**	Blacksmiths and fishermen
St. George	England (April 23)	**St. Valentine**	Sweethearts
St. Hubert	Hunters	**St. Vincent**	Wine growers
St. Jerome	Librarians	**St. Vitus**	Dancers and comedians
St. John of God	Booksellers	**St. William**	Hatters
		St. Winifred	Bakers

▶ **Saints are people** whose special virtue is recognized. Christian saints are people who have been named as saints—canonized—by the Roman Catholic or Eastern Orthodox churches. Saints are usually canonized long after their deaths. This fresco—a painting on plaster with water-based pigments—is by the Florentine artist Giotto (c. 1266–1377). It shows St. Francis preaching to the birds. The first order of friars was founded by St. Francis in 1210. The Franciscan friars lived simple lives, earning a basic living and preaching.

POPES

List of popes and their dates of accession. Antipopes and doubtful popes are not included.

St. Peter	42	Benedict I	575	Landus	913
St. Linus	67	Pelagius II	579	John X	914
St. Anacletus (Cletus)	76	St. Gregory I	590	Leo VI	928
St. Clement I	88	(the Great)		Stephen VII (VIII)	928
St. Evaristus	97	Sabinianus	604	John XI	931
St. Alexander I	105	Boniface III	607	Leo VII	936
St. Sixtus I	115	St. Boniface IV	608	Stephen VIII (IX)	939
St. Telesphorus	125	St. Deusdedit	615	Marinus II	942
St. Hyginus	136	(Adeodatus I)		Agapetus II	946
St. Pius I	140	Boniface V	619	John XII	955
St. Anicetus	155	Honorius I	625	Leo VIII	963
St. Soterus	166	Severinus	640	Benedict V	964
St. Eleutherius	175	John IV	640	John XIII	965
St. Victor I	189	Theodore I	642	Benedict VI	973
St. Zephyrinus	199	St. Martin I	649	Benedict VII	974
St. Callistus I	217	St. Eugene I	654	John XIV	983
St. Urban I	222	St. Vitalian	657	John XV	985
St. Pontian	230	Adeodatus II	672	Gregory V	996
St. Anterus	235	Donus	676	Sylvester II	999
St. Fabian	236	St. Agatho	678	John XVII	1003
St. Cornelius	251	St. Leo II	682	John XVIII	1004
St. Lucius I	253	St. Benedict II	684	Sergius IV	1009
St. Stephen I	254	John V	685	Benedict VIII	1012
St. Sixtus II	257	Conon	686	John XIX	1024
St. Dionysius	259	St. Sergius I	687	Benedict IX	1032
St. Felix I	269	John VI	701	Gregory VI	1045
St. Eutychian	275	John VII	705	Clement II	1046
St. Caius	283	Sisinnius	708	Benedict IX	1047
St. Marcellinus	296	Constantine	708	Damasus II	1048
St. Marcellus I	308	St. Gregory II	715	St. Leo IX	1049
St. Eusebius	309	St. Gregory III	731	Victor II	1055
St. Melchiades	311	St. Zachary	741	Stephen IX (X)	1057
St. Sylvester I	314	Stephen II (III)[1]	752	Nicholas II	1059
St. Marcus	336	St. Paul I	757	Alexander II	1061
St. Julius I	337	Stephen III (IV)	768	St. Gregory VII	1073
Liberius	352	Adrian I	772	Victor III	1086
St. Damasus I	366	St. Leo III	795	Urban II	1088
St. Siricius	384	Stephen IV (V)	816	Paschal II	1099
St. Anastasius I	399	St. Paschal I	817	Gelasius II	1118
St. Innocent I	401	Eugene II	824	Callistus II	1119
St. Zosimus	417	Valentine	827	Honorius II	1124
St. Boniface I	418	Gregory IV	827	Innocent II	1130
St. Celestine I	422	Sergius II	844	Celestine II	1143
St. Sixtus III	432	St. Leo IV	847	Lucius II	1144
St. Leo I (the Great)	440	Benedict III	855	Eugene III	1145
St. Hilary	461	St. Nicholas I	858	Anastasius IV	1153
St. Simplicius	468	Adrian II	867	Adrian IV	1154
St. Felix III	483	John VIII	872	Alexander III	1159
St. Gelasius I	492	Marinus I	882	Lucius III	1181
Anastasius II	496	St. Adrian III	884	Urban III	1185
St. Symmachus	498	Stephen V (VI)	885	Gregory VIII	1187
St. Hormisdas	514	Formosus	891	Clement III	1187
St. John I	523	Boniface VI	896	Celestine III	1191
St. Felix IV	526	Stephen VI (VII)	896	Innocent III	1198
Boniface II	530	Romanus	897	Honorius III	1216
John II	533	Theodore II	897	Gregory IX	1227
St. Agapetus I	535	John IX	898	Celestine IV	1241
St. Silverius	536	Benedict IV	900		
Vigilius	537	Leo V	903		
Pelagius I	556	Sergius III	904		
John III	561	Anastasius III	911		

[1] Original Stephen II died before consecration and was dropped from the list of popes in 1961. Stephen III became II and other Stephens were moved up.

Continued on next page

Continued from previous page

Innocent IV	1243	Callistus III	1455	Clement IX	1667
Alexander IV	1254	Pius II	1458	Clement X	1670
Urban IV	1261	Paul II	1464	Innocent XI	1676
Clement IV	1265	Sixtus IV	1471	Alexander VIII	1689
Gregory X	1271	Innocent VIII	1484	Innocent XII	1691
Innocent V	1276	Alexander VI	1492	Clement XI	1700
Adrian V	1276	Pius III	1503	Innocent XIII	1721
John XXI	1276	Julius II	1503	Benedict XIII	1724
Nicholas III	1277	Leo X	1513	Clement XII	1730
Martin IV	1281	Adrian VI	1522	Benedict XIV	1740
Honorius IV	1285	Clement VII	1523	Clement XIII	1758
Nicholas IV	1288	Paul III	1534	Clement XIV	1769
St. Celestine V	1294	Julius III	1550	Pius VI	1775
Boniface VIII	1294	Marcellus II	1555	Pius VII	1800
Benedict XI	1303	Paul IV	1555	Leo XII	1823
Clement V	1305	Pius IV	1559	Pius VIII	1829
John XXII	1316	St. Pius V	1566	Gregory XVI	1831
Benedict XII	1334	Gregory XIII	1572	Pius IX	1846
Clement VI	1342	Sixtus V	1585	Leo XIII	1878
Innocent VI	1352	Urban VII	1590	St. Pius X	1903
Urban V	1362	Gregory XIV	1590	Benedict XV	1914
Gregory XI	1370	Innocent IX	1591	Pius XI	1922
Urban VI	1378	Clement VIII	1592	Pius XII	1939
Boniface IX	1389	Leo XI	1605	John XXIII	1958
Innocent VII	1404	Paul V	1605	Paul VI	1963
Gregory XII	1406	Gregory XV	1621	John Paul I[1]	1978
Martin V	1417	Urban VIII	1623	John Paul II	1978
Eugene IV	1431	Innocent X	1644		
Nicholas V	1447	Alexander VII	1655		

[1] John Paul I died after only 33 days as pontiff

FACTS AND RECORDS

● The longest papal reign in history was that of Pope Pius IX, who reigned for 31 years, 236 days, from 1846 to 1878.

● The shortest papal reign lasted only two days in 752. The pope was Stephen II.

● There are more Jewish people in North America than anywhere else in the world, according to recent statistics. Two million of America's 7½ million Jewish people live in New York City.

● The oldest existing place of worship is thought to be a stone sculpture of a face in a cave in northern Spain. It dates back to around 12,000 B.C.

● The oldest existing Christian church in the world is a building in Qal'at es Salihiye in Eastern Syria. It dates back to A.D. 232.

● The largest Buddhist temple in the world dates back to the 700s. It is near Jogjakarta,
Indonesia, and measures 103×403 ft (31.5 m tall by 123 m square).

● The largest cathedral in the world is St. John the Divine in New York City. It has a floor area of 121,000 ft^2 (11,242 m^2). Building began in 1892 and the church is still not finished.

● St. Peter's in Vatican City, Rome, is the largest church in the world—inside the area is 162,990 ft^2 (15,142 m^2).

● The largest synagogue in the world is the Temple Emanu-El, New York City. The building was completed in 1927 and the whole site can hold more than 6,000 people.

● The largest mosque still in use is the Umayyad Mosque in Damascus, Syria. It covers an area of 3.8 acres (1.5 hectares).

● The tallest pagoda in the world is the Phra Pathom Chedi at Nakhon Pathom, Thailand. It is 377 ft (115 m) high.

THE TWELVE APOSTLES

These were the 12 followers—apostles—of Jesus Christ. He entrusted them with spreading his teachings. The apostles are often shown in paintings with special signs or symbols. For example, St. Peter carries keys, St. John has an eagle, St. Matthew a winged lion, and St. Andrew is shown with an X-shaped cross.

Peter (Simon)
Andrew
James the Less
John the Evangelist
Philip of Bethsaida
Bartholomew
Thomas (also known as Didymus)
Matthew (also known as Levi)
Simon the Canaanite (also known as Simon Zelotes)
Jude (also known as Judas, Thaddaeus, and Lebbaeus)
James the Greater
Judas Iscariot

Paul and Barnabus are also sometimes classed as apostles, although they were not among the original 12. Matthias took the place of Judas Iscariot.

BIBLE

The word "bible" comes from the name of an ancient town in Lebanon called Byblos, which is just north of modern Beirut. Long ago, this was one of the chief markets and export centers in the Mediterranean area for papyrus—a paper-like material made from reeds, on which early books were written. Byblos was thriving by 2500 B.C., and archaeologists believe that the first alphabet was probably developed there around 1500 B.C.

The great modern religions—**Christianity, Islam, Judaism, Hinduism, and Buddhism**—have all had amazingly long lives. The most recent of the five, Islam, is more than 1,300 years old.

◀ **Pope John Paul II** blesses children at Knock Shrine during his visit to Ireland in 1980.

World History

History is the constantly unfolding story of the human race.
Yesterday is already history and tomorrow soon will be.
Records are kept of both the everyday lives of all of us and of
the great national and international events. The first written
records date from about 3000 B.C.—the Bronze Age.
However, we know a lot about life before this date from
archaeological finds.

▲ **The three-hour battle** of Lepanto, off Greece, in 1571. A Christian fleet defeated a larger Turkish force and effectively ended Turkish dominance in the Mediterranean Sea. It was also the last major sea battle in which galleys (oared warships) took part.

Some people think that by studying the past we can understand similar situations as they arise today. Others believe that no two situations are ever similar enough in all respects to make this practical. Whatever you believe, a knowledge of the social and political events of our past certainly makes sense of many of the familiar things around us that we take for granted each day.

Chronology

This is a brief chronology of the main events from prehistory—before written records—to the present day. It is divided into four

EUROPE	
B.C.	
c. **40,000**	Last Ice Age
c. **20,000**	Cave paintings in France and Spain
c. **6500**	First farming in Greece
c. **2600**	Beginnings of Minoan civilization in Crete
c. **1600**	Beginnings of Mycenaean civilization in Greece
c. **1450**	Destruction of Minoan Crete
c. **1200**	Collapse of Mycenaean empire
c. **1100**	Phoenician supremacy in Mediterranean Sea
900–750	Rise of city-states in Greece
766	First Olympic Games
753	Foundation of Rome (traditional date)
509	Foundation of Roman Republic
477–405	Athenian supremacy in Aegean
431–404	War between Athens and Sparta
290	Roman conquest of central Italy
146	Greece comes under Roman domination
31	Battle of Actium. Octavian defeats Mark Antony

AMERICAS	
B.C.	
c. **3000**	First pottery in Mexico
c. **2000**	First metal working in Peru

▲ **Homer was one of** the greatest poets of ancient Greece. Two of his epic poems—the *Iliad* and the *Odyssey*—are literary classics. However, very little is known about him. Various Greek cities claim to have connections with him. The city of Ios issued this coin, with an imaginary portrait of Homer on it, in the 4th century B.C.

areas of the world: Europe, the Americas (North and South America), Asia, and Africa. This provides interesting comparisons between developments taking place at the same time on different parts of the globe.

ASIA	
B.C.	
c. **8000**	Agriculture develops in the Middle East
c. **6000**	Rice cultivated in Thailand
c. **4000**	Bronze casting begins in Near East
c. **3000**	Development of major cities in Sumer
c. **2750**	Growth of civilizations in Indus Valley
c. **2200**	Hsia dynasty in China
c. **1750**	Collapse of Indus Valley civilization
c. **1500**	Rise of Shang dynasty in China
c. **1200**	Beginning of Jewish religion
c. **1050**	Shang dynasty overthrown by Chou in China
c. **770**	Chou dynasty is weakening
c. **720**	Height of Assyrian power
c. **650**	First iron used in China
586	Babylonian captivity of Jews
483–221	"Warring States" period in China
202	Han dynasty reunites China

AFRICA	
B.C.	
c. **5000**	Agricultural settlements in Egypt
c. **3100**	King Menes unites Egypt
c. **2685**	Beginning of "Old Kingdom" in Egypt
c. **1570**	Beginning of "New Kingdom" in Egypt
814	Carthage founded by Phoenicians

▶ **A seal from** the Indus Valley civilization, dated about 2500–1750 B.C. It shows Pashupali, god of the animals.

81

EUROPE	
A.D.	
43	Roman invasion of Britain
116	Emperor Trajan extends Roman Empire to Euphrates
238	Beginnings of raids by Goths into Roman Empire
286	Division of Roman Empire by Diocletian
370	Huns from Asia invade Europe
410	Visigoths sack Rome
449	Angles, Saxons, and Jutes invade Britain
486	Frankish kingdom founded by Clovis
497	Franks converted to Christianity
597	St. Augustine's mission to England

Charlemagne was a religious and civilized man who reformed the administration throughout his empire. He founded the Carolingian dynasty and in the 12th century was canonized.

711	Muslim conquest of Spain
793	Viking raids begin
800	Charlemagne crowned Emperor in Rome
843	Partition of Carolingian Empire at Treaty of Verdun
874	First Viking settlers in Iceland

AMERICAS

A.D.

The **Maya Indians** built elaborate stone cities. Some of their buildings are still standing, hidden by jungle. They used stone tools for building, as they did not have any metals until a very late stage. They had no knowledge of the wheel. However, they studied astronomy and mathematics and had an advanced kind of writing.

c. **300**	Rise of Mayan civilization in Central America
c. **400**	Incas established on parts of South American Pacific coast
c. **600**	Height of Mayan civilization

▼ **The Incas** wrapped their corpses in beautiful textiles.

82

ASIA	
A.D.	
c. 0	Buddhism introduced to China from India
25	Han dynasty restored in China
45	Beginnings of St. Paul's missionary journeys
132	Jewish rebellion against Rome
220	End of Han dynasty; China splits into three states
330	Capital of Roman Empire transferred to Constantinople
350	Huns invade Persia and India
407–553	First Mongol Empire
552	Buddhism introduced to Japan
624	China reunited under T'ang dynasty
635	Muslims begin conquest of Syria and Persia
674	Muslim conquest reaches river Indus
821	Conquest of Tibet by Chinese

AFRICA	
A.D.	
30	Egypt becomes Roman province

The **Vandals** were a Germanic people. They lived between the Oder and Vistula rivers, south of the Baltic. They overran Gaul, Spain, and northern Africa in the 4th and 5th centuries A.D. and sacked Rome in A.D. 455. The Vandal kingdom in Africa lasted until A.D. 535.

429–535	Vandal kingdom in northern Africa
533–52	Justinian restores Roman power in North Africa
641	Conquest of Egypt by Muslims
c. 700	Rise of Empire of Ghana

It is thought that people lived in the now-ruined city of **Great Zimbabwe** in south-east Zimbabwe from about A.D. 300 until 200 years ago.

850	Acropolis of Zimbabwe built

EUROPE	
886	King Alfred defeats Danish King Guthrum. Danelaw established in England
911	Vikings granted duchy of Normandy by Frankish king
1016	King Cnut rules England, Denmark, and Norway
1066	William of Normandy defeats Anglo-Saxons at Hastings
1071	Normans conquer Byzantine Italy
1095	Pope summons First Crusade
1147–9	Second Crusade
1170	Murder of Thomas à Becket at Canterbury
1189–92	Third Crusade
1198	Innocent III elected pope
1202–04	Fourth Crusade leads to capture of Constantinople
1215	King John of England signs Magna Carta
1217–22	Fifth Crusade
1228–9	Sixth Crusade
1236	Mongols invade Russia
1241	Mongols invade Poland, Hungary, Bohemia, then withdraw
1248–70	Seventh Crusade
1250	Collapse of imperial power in Germany and Italy on death of Frederick II
1305	Papacy moves from Rome to Avignon
1337	Hundred Years' War begins between France and England
1346	English defeat French at Battle of Crecy

AMERICAS	
c. **990**	Expansion of Inca Empire
1100s	Inca family under Manco Capac settle in Cuzco
1151	End of Toltec Empire in Mexico
1168	Aztecs leave Chimoztoc Valley
c. **1300**	Inca Roca takes title of Sapa Inca
1325	Rise of Aztecs. Founding of Tenochtitlán

The Incas were the first people to cultivate potatoes. They even invented a way of preserving them by freezing thin slices and then extracting the water. The same basic process is used today to make "instant" mashed potato.

ASIA	
907	Last T'ang Emperor deposed in China
939	Civil wars in Japan
979	Sung dynasty reunites China
1054	Break between Greek and Latin Christian churches begins
1071	Seljuk Turks conquer most of Asia Minor
c. 1100	Polynesian Islands colonized
1156–89	Civil wars in Japan
1174	Saladin conquers Syria
1187	Saladin captures Jerusalem
1190	Temujin begins to create empire in Eastern Asia
1206	Temujin proclaimed Genghis Khan
1210	Mongols invade China
1234	Mongols destroy Chinese Empire
1261	Greek Empire restored at Constantinople
1279	Mongols conquer Southern China
1281	Mongols fail in attempt to conquer Japan
1299	Ottoman Turks begin expansion
c. 1341	Black Death begins

AFRICA	
920–1050	Height of Ghana Empire
969	Fatimids conquer Egypt and found Cairo
c. 1000	First Iron Age settlement at Zimbabwe

> **Saladin**, born Salah al-Din Yusuf ibn-Ayyub in 1138, fought to protect Egypt from the Christians. This devoted Muslim was made Sultan of Syria and Egypt in 1174.

c. 1150	Beginning of Yoruba city-states (Nigeria)
1174	Saladin conquers Egypt
c. 1200	Rise of Mali Empire in West Africa
c. 1200	Emergence of Hausa city-states (Nigeria)
1240	Collapse of Ghana Empire
c. 1300	Emergence of Ife Kingdom (West Africa)

EUROPE	
1348	Black Death reaches Europe
1356	English defeat French at Battle of Poitiers
1378–1417	Great Schism (break between Rome and Avignon); rival popes elected
1381	Peasants' Revolt in England
1385	Independence of Portugal
1415	Henry V defeats French at Battle of Agincourt
1453	England loses all French possessions except Calais
1455–85	Wars of the Roses in England
1492	Last Muslims in Spain conquered by Christians
1517	Martin Luther nails his 95 Theses to church door at Wittenberg
1519	Zwingli leads Reformation in Switzerland
1529	Reformation Parliament begins in England
1532	Calvin starts Protestant movement in France
1536	Suppression of monasteries begins in England
1545	Council of Trent marks start of Counter-Reformation
1558	England loses Calais to French
1562–98	Wars of Religion in France

AMERICAS	
1370	Expansion of Chimu kingdom
c. **1375**	Beginning of Aztec expansion
1438	Inca Empire established in Peru
1440–69	Montezuma rules Aztecs
1450	Incas conquer Chimu kingdom
1486–1502	Aztec Empire reaches sea
1493	Spanish make first settlement in New World (Hispaniola)
1502–20	Aztec conquests under Montezuma II
c. **1510**	First African slaves taken to America
1521	Cortés conquers Aztec capital, Tenochtitlán
1533	Pizarro conquers Peru
1535	Spaniards explore Chile

Two years after the Spanish commander Hernando Cortés landed on **Aztec** shores with 600 men, he had destroyed their empire. Emperor Montezuma was the last Aztec ruler. The Spanish controlled his subjects by holding him hostage soon after they arrived in the capital.

ASIA	
1363	Tamerlane begins conquest of Asia
1368	Ming dynasty founded in China
1398	Tamerlane ravages kingdom of Delhi
1401	Tamerlane conquers Damascus and Baghdad
1402	Tamerlane overruns Ottoman Empire
1421	Peking becomes capital of China
1453	Ottoman Turks capture Constantinople
1516	Ottomans overrun Syria, Egypt, and Arabia
1526	Foundation of Mughal Empire
1533	Ivan the Terrible succeeds to Russian throne
1556	Ivan the Terrible conquers Volga basin
1565	Mughal power extended

AFRICA

▲ **Built in 1469,** the Sankore Mosque in Timbuktu shows the Muslim influences in the Mali empire.

1415	Beginning of Portugal's African Empire
1450	Height of Songhai Empire in West Africa
1482	Portuguese settle Gold Coast (now Ghana)
1492	Spain begins conquest of North African coast
1505	Portuguese establish trading posts in East Africa

Huge **African empires** grew up in the Middle Ages because of trade across the Sahara. The Songhai people lived on the Niger River, around the city of Gao. The empire grew to include great Muslim centers such as Timbuktu.

1546	Destruction of Mali Empire by Songhai
1570	Bornu Empire in the Sudan flourishes

EUROPE

1571	Battle of Lepanto – end of Turkish sea power
1572	Dutch revolt against Spain
1588	Spanish Armada defeated by English
1600	English East India Company founded
1605	Gunpowder Plot
1609	Dutch win freedom from Spain
1618–48	Thirty Years' War
1642–6	English Civil War
1649	Execution of Charles I in London
1688	England's "Glorious Revolution"
1701	Act of Settlement in Britain
1701–13	War of Spanish Succession
1704	Battle of Blenheim
1707	Union of England and Scotland
1713	Treaty of Utrecht
1740–8	War of Austrian Succession
1746	Jacobites defeated at Culloden in Scotland
1756	Start of Seven Years' War
1789	French Revolution

AMERICAS

1607	First English settlement in America
1608	French colonists found Quebec
1620	Puritans land in New England
1626	Dutch settle New Amsterdam
1644	New Amsterdam seized by British and renamed New York
1654	Portuguese take Brazil from Dutch
1693	Gold discovered in Brazil

Quebec, on the St. Lawrence River, was the first permanent settlement in Canada. Its founder, the French explorer Samuel de Champlain, had explored the St. Lawrence in 1603. Also, in 1604, with a man called Sieur de Monts, Champlain had founded a colony in Acadia.

1759	British capture Quebec from French
1765	Stamp Act in American colonies
1773	Boston Tea Party
1775–83	American War of Independence
1776	Declaration of American Independence
1789	Washington becomes first U.S. president
1791	Slave revolt in Haiti

ASIA

▲ **The Taj Mahal**, at Agra, India. The Mughal Emperor Shah Jahan had this palace built between 1632 and 1653 as a tomb for his wife.

1644	Ch'ing dynasty founded in China by Manchus
1690	Foundation of Calcutta by British
1707	Breakup of Mughal Empire
1724	Hyderabad in India gains freedom from Mughals
1757	Battle of Plassey establishes British rule in India
1775	Peasant uprising in Russia
1783	India Act gives British government control of Indian affairs
1799	Napoleon invades Syria

AFRICA

1571	Portuguese begin to settle coast of Angola
1591	Moroccans destroy Songhai Empire
1652	Foundations of Cape Colony by Dutch
1686	French annex Madagascar
1705	Turks overthrown in Tunis

France abolished **slavery** in 1793. The British did not follow suit until 1833. It was Portuguese explorers who first brought African slaves to Europe in the 15th century. During the 18th century, nine to ten million slaves were transported across the Atlantic to America.

1787	British acquire Sierra Leone
1798	Napoleon attacks Egypt

EUROPE	
1804	Napoleon proclaimed emperor
1805	Battle of Trafalgar
1812	Napoleon's Russian campaign
1815	Napoleon defeated at Waterloo
1821–9	Greek War of Independence
1830	Revolutions in France, Germany, Poland, and Italy
1845	Irish potato famine
1846	Britain repeals Corn Laws
1848	Year of Revolutions
1851	Great Exhibition in London
1854–6	Crimean War
1867	North German Confederation
1871	Unification of Italy. Proclamation of German Empire
1872–1914	Triple Alliance between Germany, Austria, and Italy
1904	Anglo-French Entente
1905	First revolution in Russia
1912–13	Balkan Wars
1914–18	World War I
1917	Russian Revolution
1919	Treaty of Versailles
1919	League of Nations established
1922	Irish Free State created
1926	General Strike in Britain
1933	Hitler becomes German Chancellor

AMERICAS	
1803	Louisiana Purchase doubles size of U.S.A.
1808–28	Independence movements in South America
1819	Spain cedes Florida to U.S.A.
1836	Texas independent of Mexico
1840	Union of Upper and Lower Canada
1848	California Gold Rush begins
1861–5	American Civil War
1865	Abraham Lincoln assassinated
1867	Dominion of Canada formed
1876	Battle of Little Big Horn
1898	Spanish-American War
1903	Panama Canal Zone to U.S.A.
1911	Revolution in Mexico
1914	Panama Canal opens
1917	U.S.A. declares war on Central Powers
1920	U.S.A. refuses to join League of Nations
1929	Wall Street Crash
1933	Roosevelt introduces New Deal in America

ASIA	
1804–15	Serbs revolt against Turkey
1819	British found Singapore
1830–54	Russia conquers Kazakhstan
1842	Hong Kong ceded to Britain
1845–8	Anglo-Sikh wars in India
1850/56	Australia and New Zealand granted responsible governments
1854	Trade treaty between Japan and U.S.A.
1857	Indian Mutiny
1877	Victoria becomes Empress of India
1885	Indian National Congress formed
1886	British annex Burma
1894–5	Sino-Japanese War
1901	Unification of Australia
1906	Revolution in Persia
1910	Japan annexes Korea
1911	Chinese revolution under Sun Yat-sen
1917	Balfour Declaration promises Jewish homeland
1922	Republic proclaimed in Turkey
1926	Chiang Kai-shek unites China
1931	Japanese occupy Manchuria
1934	Mao Zedong's Long March in China

AFRICA	
1802–11	Portuguese cross Africa
1807	British abolish slave *trade* (abolish slavery in 1833)
1811	Mohammad Ali takes control in Egypt
1818	Zulu Empire founded in southern Africa
1822	Liberia founded for free slaves
1830	French begin conquest of Algeria
1835–7	Great Trek of Boers in South Africa
1860	French expansion in West Africa
1869	Opening of Suez Canal
1875	Disraeli buys Suez Canal shares
1879	Zulu War
1882	British occupy Egypt
1884	Germany acquires African colonies
1885	Belgium acquires Congo
1890	Anglo-German Agreement defines influence in East Africa
1899–1902	Anglo-Boer War
1909	Union of South Africa formed
1911	Italians conquer Libya
1914	British Protectorate in Egypt
1919	Nationalist revolt in Egypt
1922	Egypt becomes independent

EUROPE	
1936–9	Spanish Civil War
1939–45	World War II
1945	United Nations established
1949	Formation of NATO
1955	Warsaw Pact signed
1957	European Common Market set up
1961	Berlin Wall built
1963	Nuclear Test Ban Treaty
1968	Russian troops in Czechoslovakia
1973	Britain, Ireland, and Denmark join European Economic Community
1975	Monarchy restored in Spain
1978	John Paul II elected as first non-Italian pope in 450 years
1980	President Tito of Yugoslavia dies. Polish Solidarity trade union, led by Lech Walesa, confronts Communist government
1981	Greece becomes 10th member of the Common Market
1985	Mikhail Gorbachev elected new Soviet leader. Gorbachev meets Reagan in Geneva – first meeting of U.S. and Russian leaders in six years.
1986	Major accident at Chernobyl nuclear power plant in U.S.S.R.

AMERICAS	
1941	U.S.A enters World War II
1959	Cuban revolution
1962	Cuba missile crisis
1963	President Kennedy assassinated
1968	Martin Luther King, Jr., assassinated
1974	Resignation of President Nixon
1978	U.S.A. agrees to diplomatic relations with China and ends those with Taiwan
1981	U.S. hostages held in Iran released after 444 days. First flight of U.S. Space Shuttle
1982	Argentines invade Falkland Islands. British task force reoccupies islands.
1983	U.S. troops invade Caribbean island of Grenada after Marxist coup
1984	U.S. involvement in Central American politics deepens
1986	U.S./Libyan relations worsen
1987	Reagan and Gorbachev sign first pact reducing the storehouse of nuclear weapons

ASIA	
1937	Japanese capture Beijing (Peking)
1940	Japan allies with Germany
1945	First A-bombs dropped on Japan
1946–9	Civil war in China
1947	India and Pakistan independent
1950–3	Korean War
1956	Arab-Israeli War
1957	Malaysia independent
1962	Sino-Indian War
1965	United States sends troops to Vietnam
1971	East Pakistan becomes Bangladesh
1973	Arab-Israeli War
1975	Portuguese African colonies independent
1979	Shah of Iran deposed. An Islamic republic is declared
1980	Iran–Iraq War
1982	Israel invades Lebanon to drive Palestine Liberation Organization from the country
1986	Corazon Aquino becomes president of Philippines

AFRICA	
1936	Italy annexes Ethiopia
1949	Apartheid established in South Africa
1956	Suez crisis
1957	Ghana becomes independent, followed by other African states
1967–70	Nigerian civil war
1971	General Amin seizes power in Uganda
1976	Soweto race riots break out in South Africa
1979	General Amin flees from Uganda
1980	Last British colony in Africa achieves independence as Zimbabwe
1984	Start of major unrest in South Africa

◀ **Moshe Dayan** (with the black eye patch), Israeli military leader, making plans during the October War of 1973.

93

Exploration

The great age of exploration began in the 1400s, when the Turks blocked traditional trade routes and others had to be found. However, not until both poles were reached early this century did all the pieces of the jigsaw fall into place.

Place	Achievement	Explorer or discoverer	Date
World	circumnavi-gated	Ferdinand Magellan (Port. for Sp.)	1519–21
Pacific Ocean	discovered	Vasco Núñez de Balboa (Sp.)	1513
Africa			
Congo River (mouth)	discovered	Diogo Cão (Port.)	c. 1483
Cape of Good Hope	sailed around	Bartolomeu Dias (Port.)	1488
Niger River	explored	Mungo Park (Scot.)	1795
Zambezi River	discovered	David Livingstone (Scot.)	1851
Sudan	explored	Heinrich Barth (Germ. for GB)	1852–5
Victoria Falls	discovered	Livingstone	1855
Lake Tanganyika	discovered	Richard Burton & John Speke (GB)	1858
Congo River (now Zaire River)	traced	Sir Henry Stanley (GB)	1877
Asia			
China	visited	Marco Polo (Ital.)	c. 1272
India (Cape route)	visited	Vasco da Gama (Port.)	1498
Japan	visited	St. Francis Xavier (Sp.)	1549
China	explored	Ferdinand Richthofen (Germ.)	1868
North America			
North America	discovered	Leif Eriksson (Norse)	c. 1000
West Indies	discovered	Christopher Columbus (Ital. for Sp.)	1492
Newfoundland	discovered	John Cabot (Ital. for Eng.)	1497
Mexico	conquered	Hernando Cortés (Sp.)	1519–21
St. Lawrence River	explored	Jacques Cartier (Fr.)	1534–6
Mississippi River	discovered	Hernando de Soto (Sp.)	1541
Canadian interior	explored	Samuel de Champlain (Fr.)	1603–9
Hudson Bay	discovered	Henry Hudson (Eng.)	1610
Alaska	discovered	Vitus Bering (Dan. for Russ.)	1728
Mackenzie River	discovered	Sir Alexander Mackenzie (Scot.)	1789
South America			
South America	visited	Columbus	1498
Venezuela	explored	Alonso de Ojeda (Sp.)	1499
Brazil	discovered	Pedro Alvares Cabral (Port.)	1500
Rio de la Plata	discovered	Juan de Solis (Sp.)	1516
Tierra del Fuego	discovered	Magellan	1520
Peru	explored	Francisco Pizarro (Sp.)	1530–8
Amazon River	explored	Francisco de Orellana (Sp.)	1541
Cape Horn	discovered	Willem Schouten (Dut.)	1616

Australasia, polar regions, etc.

Greenland	visited	Eric the Red (Norse)	c. 982
Australia	discovered	unknown	1500s
Spitsbergen	discovered	Willem Barents (Dut.)	1596
Australia	visited	Abel Tasman (Dut.)	1642
New Zealand	sighted	Tasman	1642
New Zealand	visited	James Cook (Eng.)	1769
Antarctic Circle	crossed	Cook	1773
Antarctica	sighted	Nathaniel Palmer (U.S.)	1820
Antarctica	circumnavigated	Fabian von Bellingshausen (Russ.)	1819–21
Australian interior	explored	Charles Sturt (G.B.)	1828
Antarctica	explored	Charles Wilkes (U.S.)	1838–42
Australia	crossed (S–N)	Robert Burke (Ir.) & William Wills (Eng.)	1860–1
Greenland	explored	Fridtjof Nansen (Nor.)	1888
Arctic	explored	Abruzzi, Duke of the (Ital.)	1900
North Pole	reached	Robert Peary (U.S.)	1909
South Pole	reached	Roald Amundsen (Nor.)	1911
Antarctica	crossed	Sir Vivian Fuchs (Eng.)	1957–8

▼ **A reconstruction** of the famous *Santa Maria*. It was in this ship that Christopher Columbus first crossed the Atlantic in 1492. He was accompanied by two smaller ships called "caravels"—the *Niña* and the *Pinta*.

Major Wars

Name	Date	Won by
Abyssinian War	1935–1936	Italy
American War of Independence	1775–1783	Thirteen Colonies
Austrian Succession, War of the	1740–1748	Austria, Hungary, Britain, Holland
Boer (South African) War	1899–1902	Britain
Chinese-Japanese Wars	1894–1895	Japan
	1931–1933	Japan
	1937–1945	China
Civil War, American	1861–1865	23 Northern States (The Union)
Civil War, English	1642–1646	Parliament
Civil War, Nigerian	1967–1970	Federal government
Civil War, Pakistani	1971	East Pakistan (Bangladesh) and India
Civil War, Spanish	1936–1939	Junta de Defensa Nacional (Fascists)
Crimean War	1853–1856	Britain, France, Sardinia, Turkey
Franco-Prussian War	1870–1871	Prussia and other German states
Hundred Years' War	1337–1453	France
Korean War	1950–1953	South Korea and United Nations forces
Mexican-American War	1846–1848	United States
Napoleonic Wars	1792–1815	Austria, Britain, Prussia, Russia, Spain, Sweden
October War	1973	Ceasefire arranged by U.N.; fought by Israel against Egypt, Syria, Iraq, Sudan, Saudi Arabia, Lebanon, Jordan
Peloponnesian War	431–404 B.C.	Peloponnesian League, led by Sparta, Corinth
Punic Wars	264–146 B.C.	Rome
Russo-Japanese War	1904–1905	Japan
Seven Years' War	1756–1763	Britain, Prussia, Hanover
Six-Day War	1967	Israel
Spanish-American War	1898	United States
Spanish Succession, War of the	1701–1713	England, Austria, Prussia, the Netherlands
Thirty Years' War	1618–1648	France, Sweden, the German Protestant states
Vietnam War	1957–1975	North Vietnam
War of 1812	1812–1814	United States
Wars of the Roses	1455–1485	House of Lancaster
World War I	1914–1918	Belgium, Britain and Empire, France, Italy, Japan, Russia, Serbia, United States
World War II	1939–1945	Australia, Belgium, Britain, Canada, China, Denmark, France, Greece, Netherlands, New Zealand, Norway, Poland, Russia, South Africa, United States, Yugoslavia

Against

Abyssinia (Ethiopia)
Britain
Bavaria, France, Poland, Prussia, Sardinia,
Saxony, Spain
Boer Republics
China
China
Japan
11 Southern States (the Confederacy)
Charles I
Biafra
West Pakistan
Republican government
Russia
France
England
North Korea and Chinese forces
Mexico
France

Delian League, led by Athens

Carthage
Russia
Austria, France, Russia, Sweden
Egypt, Syria, Jordan, Iraq
Spain
France, Bavaria, Cologne, Mantua, Savoy
The Holy Roman Empire, Spain

South Vietnam, United States
Britain
House of York
Austria-Hungary, Bulgaria, Germany,
Ottoman Empire
Bulgaria, Finland, Germany, Hungary,
Italy, Japan, Romania

▲ **The darker areas** are lands in French possession around 1453—the end of the Hundred Years' War. England's success at the start of the war soon gave way and the English lost almost all their lands to the French.

▼ **American troops** during the Korean War of the 1950s. This was one of the first trouble spots in the Cold War.

Famous Battles

Marathon 490 B.C. Persian-Greek Wars. Miltiades with 10,000 Greeks routed Darius with 60,000 Persians.

Hastings 1066 Norman Conquest of England. Some 9,000 invaders under William of Normandy defeated Harold II and his Saxons.

Agincourt 1415 Hundred Years' War. Henry V and 5,700 English, mainly archers, defeated 25,000 French.

Orléans 1429 Hundred Years' War. Joan of Arc defeated an English army besieging the city.

Constantinople 1453 Fall of the Byzantine Empire. The Turks took the city of Constantinople.

Lepanto 1571 Cyprus War. Don John of Austria with 250 Spanish, Venetian, and papal ships destroyed a Turkish fleet of 270 vessels.

Blenheim 1704 War of the Spanish Succession. French and Bavarians defeated by a British-Austrian army under Prince Eugène and the Duke of Marlborough.

First battle of Ypres 1914 German forces trying to reach Calais lost 150,000 men. British and French forces held off attack, losing more than 100,000 men.

Verdun 1916 In a six-month struggle, French forces held off a major attack by German armies. French losses were 348,000; German losses 328,000.

Jutland 1916 British Grand Fleet fought German High Seas Fleet. The Germans did not again venture out to sea.

Somme 1916 In a 141-day battle following Verdun, the British and French captured 125 square miles of

▲ **The siege of Constantinople** in 1453. Its successful capture by Sultan Muhammad II's forces came when, after six weeks of battering the walls with cannon fire, he attacked the city on three sides. By 1453 the empire of Constantinople consisted of little more than the city, which was itself in decline. After Muhammad's triumph, he rebuilt the city as Istanbul, capital of the Ottoman Empire.

Battle of Waterloo, 1815 Napoleon returned from exile to be defeated at Waterloo by British, Dutch, Belgian, and Prussian troops. Wellington's 49,600 infantry outnumbered Napoleon's by about 650. But Napoleon's 15,760 cavalry and 7,230 artillerymen compared with only 12,400 cavalry and 5,650 artillerymen for Wellington. Also Napoleon had 246 guns – 90 more than Wellington. But Blücher's Prussian advance guard numbered 30,000. In dead and wounded Wellington lost 15,100; Blücher, 7,000; Napoleon, 25,000.

ground, losing 600,000 men. The German defenders lost almost 500,000 men.

Passchendaele 1917 British forces launched eight attacks over 102 days in heavy rain and through thick mud. They gained 5 miles and lost 400,000 men.

Britain 1940 A German air force of 2,500 planes launched an attack lasting 114 days to try and win air supremacy over Britain. The smaller Royal Air Force defeated the attack.

Midway 1942 A fleet of 100 Japanese ships was defeated in the Pacific by an American fleet half the size.

El Alamein 1942 Montgomery's British Eighth Army drove Rommel's German Afrika Korps out of Egypt.

Stalingrad 1942–3 Twenty-one German divisions tried to capture Stalingrad (now Volgograd), but siege was broken and more than 100,000 German troops surrendered.

Normandy 1944 Allied forces under Eisenhower invaded German-held northern France in biggest-ever seaborne attack. After a month of fighting, Germans retreated.

Leyte Gulf 1944 United States Third and Seventh fleets defeated a Japanese force, ending Japanese naval power in World War II.

Ardennes Bulge 1944–5 Last German counterattack in west through Ardennes Forest failed. Germans suffered 100,000 casualties and 110,000 Germans were taken prisoner.

▶ **After D-Day**—June 6, 1944 – hundreds of thousands of Allied troops poured into France.

Assassinations Through History

Victim	Details of assassination and date
Julius Caesar, Roman dictator	Stabbed by Brutus, Cassius, *et al.* in Senate, 44 B.C.
Thomas à Becket, English archbishop	Slain by four knights in cathedral, 12-29-1170
Lord Darnley, husband of Mary Queen of Scots	Blown up, 2-10-1567
Gustavus III of Sweden	Shot by Johan Ankarström; plot, 3-29-1792
Jean Marat, French revolutionary	Stabbed in bath by Charlotte Corday, 7-13-1793
Abraham Lincoln, U.S. president	Shot by actor, J. Wilkes Booth, in theater, 4-14-1865[1]
James Garfield, U.S. president	Shot at station by Charles Guiteau (grudge), 7-2-1881[2]
Antonio Cánovas del Castillo, Spanish premier	Shot by anarchist, 8-8-1897
Humbert I, king of Italy	By anarchist at Monza, 7-29-1900
William McKinley, U.S. president	Shot by anarchist, Leon Czolgosz, at Buffalo, 9-6-1901[3]
Pyotr Stolypin, Russian premier	Shot by revolutionary, Dmitri Bogrov, 9-14-1911[4]
George, I, king of Greece	At Salonika, 3-18-1913
Francis Ferdinand, archduke of Austria	Alleged Serbian plot: shot in car by Gavrilo Princip at Sarajevo (sparked World War I), 6-28-1914
Jean Jaurès, French socialist	By nationalist, in café, 7-31-1914
Rasputin, powerful Russian monk	By Russian noblemen, 12-31-1916
Michael Collins, Irish Sinn Fein leader	Ambushed and shot, 8-22-1922
Engelbert Dollfuss, Austrian chancellor	Shot by Nazis in chancellery, 7-25-1934
Huey Long, corrupt American politician	By Dr. Carl Austin Weiss, 9-8-1935[5]
Leon Trotsky, exiled Russian communist leader	Axed in Mexico by Ramon de Rio, 8-21-1940
Mahatma Gandhi, Indian nationalist leader	Shot by Hindu fanatic, Nathuran Godse, 1-30-1948
Count Folke Bernadotte, Swedish diplomat	Ambushed in Jerusalem by Jewish extremists, 9-17-1948
SWRD Bandaranaike, Ceylonese premier	By Buddhist monk in Columbo, 9-25-1959
Rafael Trujillo Molina, Dominican Republic dictator	Car machine-gunned, 5-30-1961
John F. Kennedy, U.S. president	Shot in car, Dallas, Texas, 11-22-1963[6]
Malcolm X (Little), U.S. Black Muslim leader	Shot at rally, 2-21-1965
Hendrike Verwoerd, South African premier	Stabbed by parliamentary messenger, Dimitri Tsafendas (later ruled mentally disordered), 9-6-1966
Rev. Martin Luther King, Jr., U.S. Black civil rights leader	Shot on hotel balcony by James Earl Ray, in Memphis, Tennessee, 4-4-1968

[1] Died next day.   [2] Died Sept. 19   [3] Died Sept. 14   [4] Died Sept. 18   [5] Died Sept. 10
[6] Accused, Lee Harvey Oswald, himself shot by Jack Ruby (Nov. 24) while awaiting trial.

Robert F. Kennedy, U.S. senator	Shot by Arab immigrant, Sirhan Sirhan, in Los Angeles (Hotel Ambassador), 6-5-1968
Christopher Ewart-Biggs, British ambassador to Republic of Ireland	Car blown up by landmine planted by IRA, 7-21-1976
Aldo Moro, president of Italy's Christian Democrats and five times prime minister of Italy	Kidnapped by Red Brigade terrorists (3-16-78) and later found dead, 5-9-1978
Airey Neave, British Conservative MP and Northern Ireland spokesman	Explosion under car while leaving House of Commons car park; IRA, 3-30-1979
Lord Mountbatten, uncle of Duke of Edinburgh	Explosion in sailing boat off coast of Ireland; IRA, 8-27-1979
Park Chung Hee, president of South Korea	Shot in restaurant by chief of Korean Central Intelligence Agency, 10-26-1979
Roman Catholic archbishop Oscar Romero y Galdamez of El Salvador	Shot by right-wing gunmen while saying mass in San Salvador, 3-24-1980
John Lennon, musician/songwriter and ex-Beatle	Shot in street in New York City by Mark David Chapman, 12-8-1980
Anwar al-Sadat, president of Egypt	Shot by rebel soldiers while reviewing military parade, 10-6-1981
Indira Gandhi, Indian prime minister	By her own Sikh bodyguards, 10-31-1984
Olof Palme, Swedish prime minister	Shot as leaving cinema in Stockholm, 2-28-86

▲ *Left:* **The Indian prime minister** Indira Gandhi, assassinated by one of her own bodyguards in 1984. *Right:* Thomas à Becket, archbishop of Canterbury and chancellor of England, quarreled with King Henry II about how much power the church should have compared with the state. He was murdered by the king's knights, but many people believe that this was not ordered by the king. Thomas à Becket was made a saint in 1173.

SEVEN WONDERS OF THE WORLD*

Pyramids of Egypt Oldest and only surviving "wonder." Built in the 2000s B.C. as royal tombs, about 80 are still standing. The largest, the Great Pyramid of Cheops, at el-Gizeh, was 482 feet high.

Hanging Gardens of Babylon Terraced gardens adjoining Nebuchadnezzar's palace, said to rise from 75 to 300 feet. Supposedly built by the king about 600 B.C. to please his wife, a princess from the mountains, but they are also associated with the Assyrian Queen Semiramis.

Statue of Zeus at Olympia Carved by Phidias, the 40-foot statue marked the site of the original Olympic Games in the 400s B.C. It was constructed of ivory and gold, and showed Zeus (Jupiter) on his throne.

Temple of Artemis (Diana) at Ephesus Constructed of Parian marble and more than 400 feet long with over 100 columns 60 feet high, it was begun about 350 B.C. and took some 120 years to build. Destroyed by the Goths in A.D. 262.

Mausoleum at Helicarnassus Erected by Queen Artemisia in memory of her husband King Mausolus of Caria (in Asia Minor), who died 353 B.C. It stood 140 feet high. All that remains are a few pieces in the British Museum and the word *mausoleum* in the English language.

Colossus of Rhodes Gigantic bronze statue of sun god Helios (or Apollo); stood about 118 feet high, dominating the harbor entrance at Rhodes. The sculptor Chares supposedly labored for 12 years before he completed it in 280 B.C. It was destroyed by an earthquake in 224 B.C.

Pharos of Alexandria Marble lighthouse and watchtower built about 270 B.C. on the island of Pharos in Alexandria's harbor. Possibly standing 400 feet high, it was destroyed by an earthquake in 1375.

▲ **The Statue of Zeus** vanished a long time ago but pictures of it have been found on ancient coins.

▼ **The Hanging Gardens** of Babylon appeared to hang in the air because they were planted on terraces laid over arches.

* Originally compiled by Antipater of Sidon, a Greek poet, in the 100s B.C.

ROMAN EMPERORS

Emperor	Reigned
Augustus (Octavian)	27 B.C.–A.D. 14
Tiberius	14–37
Caligula (Gaius)	37–41
Claudius	41–54
Nero	54–68
Galba	68–69
Otho	69
Vitellius	69
Vespasian	69–79
Titus	79–81
Domitian	81–96
Nerva	96–98
Trajan	98–117
Hadrian	117–138
Antoninus Pius	138–161
Lucius Aurelius Verus	161–169
Marcus Aurelius	161–180
Commodus	180–192
Pertinax	193
Didius Julian	193
Septimus Severus	193–211
Caracalla	211–217
Macrinus	217–218
Elagabalus	218–222
Alexander Severus	222–235
Maximinus	235–238
Gordian I	238
Gordian II	238
Pupienus	238
Balbinus	238
Gordian III	238–244
Philip "the Arab"	244–249
Decius	249–251
Gallus	251–253
Aemilian	253
Valerian	253–259
Gallienus	259–268
Claudius II	268–270
Aurelian	270–275
Tacitus	275–276
Florian	276
Probus	276–282
Carus	282–283
Numerian	283–284
Carinus	283–285
Diocletian	284–305
Maximian	286–305
Constantius I	305–306
Galerius	305–311
Constantine I, the Great	311–337
Constantine II	337–340
Constantius II	337–361
Constans	337–350

▲ **This ancient coin** shows Constantine the Great (311–337)—the first emperor of Rome to become a Christian.

Julian, the Apostate	361–363
Jovian	363–364
Valentinian I (in the West)	364–375
Valens (in the East)	364–378
Gratian (in the West)	375–383
Valentinian II (in the West)	375–392
Theodosius, the Great (in the East, and after 394, in the West)	379–395
Maximus (in the West)	383–388
Eugenius (in the West)	392–394
Arcadius (in the East)	395–408
Honorius (in the West)	395–423
Constantius III (co-emperor in the West)	421
Theodosius II (in the East)	408–450
Valentian III (in the West)	425–455
Marcian (in the East)	450–457
Petronius (in the West)	455
Avitus (in the West)	455–456
Majorian (in the West)	457–461
Leo I (in the East)	457–474
Severus (in the West)	461–465
Anthemius (in the West)	467–472
Olybrius (in the West)	472
Glycerius (in the West)	473
Julius Nepos (in the West)	473–475
Leo II (in the East)	473–474
Zeno (in the East)	474–491
Romulus Augustulus (in the West)	475–476

HOLY ROMAN EMPERORS

The Holy Roman Empire was a loose alliance of German and Italian lands under the leadership of an emperor.

FRANKISH KINGS AND EMPERORS (CAROLINGIAN)

Charlemagne	800–814
Louis I, the Pious	814–840
Lothair I	840–855
Louis II	855–875
Charles II, the Bald	875–877
Throne vacant	877–881
Charles III, the Fat	881–887
Throne vacant	887–891
Guido of Spoleto	891–894
Lambert of Spoleto (co-emperor)	892–898
Arnulf (rival)	896–901
Louis III of Provence	901–905
Berengar	905–924
Conrad I of Franconia (rival)	911–918

SAXON KINGS AND EMPERORS

Henry I, the Fowler	918–936
Otto I, the Great	936–973
Otto II	973–983
Otto III	983–1002
Henry II, the Saint	1002–1024

FRANCONIAN EMPERORS (SALIAN)

Conrad II, the Salian	1024–1039
Henry III, the Black	1039–1056
Henry IV	1056–1106
Rudolf of Swabia (rival)	1077–1080
Hermann of Luxembourg (rival)	1081–1093
Conrad of Franconia (rival)	1093–1101
Henry V	1106–1125
Lothair II	1125–1137

HOHENSTAUFEN KINGS AND EMPERORS

Conrad III	1138–1152
Frederick I Barbarossa	1152–1190
Henry VI	1190–1197
Otto IV	1198–1215
Philip of Swabia (rival)	1198–1208
Frederick II	1215–1250
Henry Raspe (rival)	1246–1247
William of Holland (rival)	1247–1256
Conrad IV	1250–1254
The Great Interregnum	1254–1273

RULERS FROM DIFFERENT HOUSES

⎰ Richard of Cornwall (rival)	1257–1272 ⎱
⎱ Alfonso X of Castile (rival)	1257–1273 ⎰
Rudolf I, of Habsburg	1273–1291
Adolf I of Nassau	1292–1298
Albert I, Habsburg	1298–1308
Henry VII, Luxembourg	1308–1313

▲ **Otto III** became Holy Roman Emperor at just 15 years of age. Otto had various disagreements with popes. Emperors of Rome claimed to control church matters in their areas and to have a final say in the choice of pope. But popes claimed total spiritual authority over all of Christian Europe. The situation erupted in 1075. Emperor Henry IV declared Pope Gregory VII deposed after the pope had forbidden Henry to control the election of bishops in Germany. The pope promptly excommunicated (banned) Henry from the church.

Louis IV of Bavaria	1314–1347
Frederick of Habsburg (co-regent)	1314–1325
Charles IV, Luxembourg	1347–1378
Wenceslas of Bohemia	1378–1400
Frederick III of Brunswick	1400
Rupert of the Palatinate	1400–1410
Sigismund, Luxembourg	1410–1437

HABSBURG EMPERORS

Albert II	1438–1439
Frederick III	1440–1493
Maximilian I	1493–1519
Charles V	1519–1558
Ferdinand I	1558–1564

Maximilian II	1564–1576
Rudolf II	1576–1612
Matthias	1612–1619
Ferdinand II	1619–1637
Ferdinand III	1637–1657
Leopold I	1658–1705
Joseph I	1705–1711
Charles VI	1711–1740
Charles VII of Bavaria	1742–1745

HABSBURG–LORRAINE EMPERORS

Francis I of Lorraine	1745–1765
Joseph II	1765–1790
Leopold II	1790–1792
Francis II	1792–1806

AMERICAN PRESIDENTS

President (party) — **Term**

1. George Washington (F) — 1789–1797
2. John Adams (F) — 1797–1801
3. Thomas Jefferson (DR) — 1801–1809
4. James Madison (DR) — 1809–1817
5. James Monroe (DR) — 1817–1825
6. John Quincy Adams (DR) — 1825–1829
7. Andrew Jackson (D) — 1829–1837
8. Martin Van Buren (D) — 1837–1841
9. William H. Harrison* (W) — 1841
10. John Tyler (W) — 1841–1845
11. James K. Polk (D) — 1845–1849
12. Zachary Taylor* (W) — 1849–1850
13. Millard Fillmore (W) — 1850–1853
14. Franklin Pierce (D) — 1853–1857
15. James Buchanan (D) — 1857–1861
16. Abraham Lincoln† (R) — 1861–1865
17. Andrew Johnson (U) — 1865–1869
18. Ulysses S. Grant (R) — 1869–1877
19. Rutherford B. Hayes (R) — 1877–1881
20. James A. Garfield† (R) — 1881
21. Chester A. Arthur (R) — 1881–1885
22. Grover Cleveland (D) — 1885–1889
23. Benjamin Harrison (R) — 1889–1893
24. Grover Cleveland (D) — 1893–1897
25. William McKinley† (R) — 1897–1901
26. Theodore Roosevelt (R) — 1901–1909
27. William H. Taft (R) — 1909–1913
28. Woodrow Wilson (D) — 1913–1921
29. Warren G. Harding* (R) — 1921–1923
30. Calvin Coolidge (R) — 1923–1929
31. Herbert C. Hoover (R) — 1929–1933
32. Franklin D. Roosevelt* (D) — 1933–1945
33. Harry S. Truman (D) — 1945–1953
34. Dwight D. Eisenhower (R) — 1953–1961
35. John F. Kennedy† (D) — 1961–1963
36. Lyndon B. Johnson (D) — 1963–1969
37. Richard M. Nixon (R) — 1969–1974
38. Gerald R. Ford (R) — 1974–1977
39. James E. Carter (D) — 1977–1980
40. Ronald Reagan (R) — 1980–1988

* Died in office † Assassinated in office
F=Federalist DR=Democratic-Republican
D=Democratic W=Whig R=Republican U=Union

▼ **President** John F. Kennedy. He was shot by Lee Harvey Oswald while being driven in an open-topped car through cheering crowds in Dallas.

RULERS OF ENGLAND

Saxons

Egbert	827–839
Ethelwulf	839–858
Ethelbald	858–860
Ethelbert	860–865
Ethelred I	865–871
Alfred the Great	871–899
Edward the Elder	899–924
Athelstan	924–939
Edmund	939–946
Edred	946–955
Edwy	955–959
Edgar	959–975
Edward the Martyr	975–978
Ethelred I the Unready	978–1016
Edmund Ironside	1016

Danes

Canute	1016–1035
Harold I Harefoot	1035–1040
Hardicanute	1040–1042

Saxons

Edward the Confessor	1042–1066
Harold II	1066

House of Normandy

William I the Conqueror	1066–1087
William II	1087–1100
Henry I	1100–1135
Stephen	1135–1154

House of Plantagenet

Henry II	1154–1189
Richard I	1189–1199
John	1199–1216
Henry III	1216–1272
Edward I	1272–1307
Edward II	1307–1327
Edward III	1327–1377
Richard II	1377–1399

House of Lancaster

Henry IV	1399–1413
Henry V	1413–1422
Henry VI	1422–1461

House of York

Edward IV	1461–1483
Edward V	1483
Richard III	1483–1485

House of Tudor

Henry VII	1485–1509
Henry VIII	1509–1547
Edward VI	1547–1553
Mary I	1553–1558
Elizabeth I	1558–1603

RULERS OF SCOTLAND

Malcolm II	1005–1034
Duncan I	1034–1040
Macbeth (usurper)	1040–1057
Malcolm III Canmore	1057–1093
Donald Bane	1093–1094
Duncan II	1094
Donald Bane (restored)	1094–1097
Edgar	1097–1107
Alexander I	1107–1124
David I	1124–1153
Malcolm IV	1153–1165
William the Lion	1165–1214
Alexander II	1214–1249
Alexander III	1249–1286
Margaret of Norway	1286–1290
Interregnum 1290–1292	
John Balliol	1292–1296
Interregnum 1296–1306	
Robert I (Bruce)	1306–1329
David II	1329–1371

House of Stuart

Robert II	1371–1390
Robert III	1390–1406
James I	1406–1437
James II	1437–1460
James III	1460–1488
James IV	1488–1513
James V	1513–1542
Mary	1542–1567
James VI (of Great Britain)	1567–1625

▼ **Robert I** (the Bruce), king of Scotland. He won independence for Scotland and made sure that succession of the monarchy in that country was undisputed.

RULERS OF GREAT BRITAIN

House of Stuart
James I	1603–1625
Charles I	1625–1649

Commonwealth 1649–1659

Charles II	1660–1685
James II	1685–1688
William III ⎤ jointly	1689–1702
Mary II ⎦	1689–1694
Anne	1702–1714

House of Hanover
George I	1714–1727
George II	1727–1760
George III	1760–1820
George IV	1820–1830
William IV	1830–1837
Victoria	1837–1901

House of Saxe-Coburg
Edward VII	1901–1910

House of Windsor
George V	1910–1936
Edward VIII	1936
George VI	1936–1952
Elizabeth II	1952–

BRITISH PRIME MINISTERS

W=Whig. T=Tory. Cln=Coalition. P=Peelite.
L=Liberal. C=Conservative. Lab=Labor.

Sir Robert Walpole (W)	1721–1742
Earl of Wilmington (W)	1742–1743
Henry Pelham (W)	1743–1754
Duke of Newcastle (W)	1754–1756
Duke of Devonshire (W)	1756–1757
Duke of Newcastle (W)	1757–1762
Earl of Bute (T)	1762–1763
George Grenville (W)	1763–1765
Marquess of Rockingham (W)	1765–1766
Earl of Chatham (W)	1766–1767
Duke of Grafton (W)	1767–1770
Lord North (T)	1770–1782
Marquess of Rockingham (W)	1782
Earl of Shelbourne (W)	1782–1783
Duke of Portland (Cln)	1783
William Pitt (T)	1783–1801
Henry Addington (T)	1801–1804
William Pitt (T)	1804–1806
Lord Grenville (W)	1806–1807
Duke of Portland (T)	1807–1809
Spencer Perceval (T)	1809–1812
Earl of Liverpool (T)	1812–1827
George Canning (T)	1827
Viscount Goderich (T)	1827–1828
Duke of Wellington (T)	1828–1830
Earl Grey (W)	1830–1834
Viscount Melbourne (W)	1834
Sir Robert Peel (T)	1834–1835
Viscount Melbourne (W)	1835–1841
Sir Robert Peel (T)	1841–1846
Lord John Russell (W)	1846–1852
Earl of Derby (T)	1852
Earl of Aberdeen (P)	1852–1855
Viscount Palmerston (L)	1855–1858
Earl of Derby (C)	1858–1859
Viscount Palmerston (L)	1859–1865
Earl Russell (L)	1865–1866
Earl of Derby (C)	1866–1868
Benjamin Disraeli (C)	1868
William Gladstone (L)	1868–1874
Benjamin Disraeli (C)	1874–1880
William Gladstone (L)	1880–1885
Marquess of Salisbury (C)	1885–1886
William Gladstone (L)	1886
Marquess of Salisbury (C)	1886–1892
William Gladstone (L)	1892–1894
Earl of Rosebery (L)	1894–1895
Marquess of Salisbury (C)	1895–1902
Arthur Balfour (C)	1902–1905
Sir Henry Campbell-Bannerman (L)	1905–1908
Herbert Asquith (L)	1908–1915
Herbert Asquith (Cln)	1915–1916
David Lloyd-George (Cln)	1916–1922
Andrew Bonar Law (C)	1922–1923
Stanley Baldwin (C)	1923–1924
James Ramsay MacDonald (Lab)	1924
Stanley Baldwin (C)	1924–1929
James Ramsay MacDonald (Lab)	1929–1931
James Ramsay MacDonald (Lab)	1931–1935
Stanley Baldwin (Cln)	1935–1937
Neville Chamberlain (Cln)	1937–1940
Winston Churchill (Cln)	1940–1945
Winston Churchill (C)	1945
Clement Atlee (Lab)	1945–1951
Sir Winston Churchill (C)	1951–1955
Sir Anthony Eden (C)	1955–1957
Harold Macmillan (C)	1957–1963
Sir Alec Douglas-Home (C)	1963–1964
Harold Wilson (Lab)	1964–1970
Edward Heath (C)	1970–1974
Harold Wilson (Lab)	1974–1976
James Callaghan (Lab)	1976–1979
Margaret Thatcher (C)	1979–

RULERS OF FRANCE

Capetian

Hugh Capet	987–996
Robert II, the Pious	996–1031
Henry I	1031–1060
Philip I	1060–1108
Louis VI	1108–1137
Louis VII	1137–1180
Philip II, Augustus	1180–1223
Louis VIII	1223–1226
Louis IX, the Saint	1226–1270
Philip III	1270–1285
Philip IV	1285–1314
Louis X	1314–1316
John I	1316
Philip V	1316–1322
Charles IV	1322–1328

House of Valois

Philip VI	1328–1350
John	1350–1364
Charles V	1364–1380
Charles VI	1380–1422
Charles VII	1422–1461
Louis XI	1461–1483
Charles VIII	1483–1498
Louis XII	1498–1515
Francis I	1515–1547
Henry II	1547–1559
Francis II	1559–1560
Charles IX	1560–1574
Henry III	1574–1589

House of Bourbon

Henry IV	1589–1610
Louis XIII	1610–1643
Louis XIV	1643–1715
Louis XV	1715–1774
Louis XVI	1774–1792

FIRST REPUBLIC
1792–1804

FIRST EMPIRE
House of Bonaparte

Napoleon I[1]	1804–1814

MONARCHY
House of Bourbon (restored)

Louis XVIII	1814–1824
Charles X[1]	1824–1830

House of Bourbon–Orléans

Louis Philippe[1]	1830–1848

SECOND REPUBLIC
President

Louis Napoleon Bonaparte	1848–1852

SECOND EMPIRE
House of Bonaparte (restored)

Napoleon III[1]	1852–1870

THIRD REPUBLIC
Presidents

Adolphe Thiers	1871–1873
Marshal MacMahon	1873–1879
Jules Grévy	1879–1887
Sadi Carnot[2]	1887–1894
Jean Casimir-Périer	1894–1895
François Félix Faure	1895–1899
Émile Loubet	1899–1906
Armand Fallières	1906–1913
Raymond Poincaré	1913–1920
Paul Deschanel	1920
Alexandre Millerand	1920–1924
Gaston Doumergue	1924–1931
Paul Doumer[3]	1931–1932
Albert Lebrun[4]	1932–1940

FRENCH STATE
Chief of State

Marshal Pétain	1940–1944

FRENCH RESISTANCE
Leader

Charles de Gaulle	1940–1946

FOURTH REPUBLIC
Presidents

Vincent-Auriol	1947–1954
René Coty	1954–1958

FIFTH REPUBLIC
Presidents

Charles de Gaulle	1958–1969
Georges Pompidou	1969–1974
Valéry Giscard d'Estaing	1974–1981
François Mitterand	1981–

[1] Abdicated
[2] Assassinated 1894
[3] Assassinated 1932
[4] Reelected 1939, deposed 1940

▲ **Emperor Napoleon I,** shown in a chalk drawing by Andrea Appiani. Napoleon made Appiani painter to the kingdom of Italy.

CZARS OF RUSSIA

Ivan III the Great	1462–1505
Basil III	1505–1533
Ivan IV the Terrible	1533–1584
Fёdor I	1584–1598
Boris Godunov	1598–1605
Fёdor II	1605
Demetrius	1605–1606
Basil (IV) Shuiski	1606–1610

Interregnum 1610–1613

Michael Romanov	1613–1645
Alexis	1645–1676
Fёdor III	1676–1682
Ivan V and	
Peter the Great	1682–1689
Peter the Great (alone)	1689–1725
Catherine I	1725–1727
Peter II	1727–1730
Anna	1730–1740
Ivan VI	1740–1741
Elizabeth	1741–1762
Peter III	1762
Catherine II the Great	1762–1796
Paul I	1796–1801
Alexander I	1801–1825
Nicholas I	1825–1855
Alexander II	1855–1881
Alexander III	1881–1894
Nicholas II	1894–1917

LEADERS OF THE SOVIET UNION

Vladimir I. Lenin	
(Prime Minister)	1917–1924
Joseph Stalin (General Secretary)	1924–1953
(Prime Minister)	1941–1953
Georgi Malenkov (Prime Minister)	1953–1955
Nikolai A. Bulganin (Prime Minister)	1955–1958
Nikita S. Khrushchev	
(First Secretary)	1953–1964
(Prime Minister)	1958–1964
Aleksei N. Kosygin (Prime Minister)	1964–1977
Leonid I. Brezhnev (First Secretary)	1964–1982
(President)	1977–1982
Yuri V. Andropov (President)	1982–1984
Konstantin U. Chernenko	
(General Secretary)	1984–1985
Mikhail S. Gorbachev	
(General Secretary)	1985–

CHINESE DYNASTIES

Han	206 B.C.–A.D. 220
Three Kingdoms	220–265
Six Dynasties	265–588
Sui	589–618
T'ang	618–906
Five Dynasties	906–959
Sung	960–1279
Yüan (Mongol)	1280–1368
Ming	1368–1644
Ch'ing (Manchu)	1644–1912

ITALIAN PRESIDENTS

Enrico de Nicola	1946–1948
Luigi Einaudi	1948–1955
Giovanni Gronchi	1955–1962
Antonio Segni	1962–1964
Giuseppe Saragat	1964–1971
Giovanni Leone	1971–1978
Alessandro Pertini	1978–1985
Francesco Cossiga	1985–

INDIAN PRIME MINISTERS

Jawaharlal Nehru	1950–1964
Lal Bahadur Shastri	1964–1966
Indira Gandhi	1966–1977
Morarji Desai	1977–1979
Indira Gandhi	1979–1984
Rajiv Gandhi	1984–

INDIAN PRESIDENTS

Rajendra Prasad	1950–1962
Sarvepalli Radhakrishnan	1962–1967
Zakir Husain	1967–1969
Varahagiri Venkata Giri	1969–1974
Sakhruddin Ali Ahmed	1974–1977
V. D. Jatti	1977
Meelam Sanjira Reddy	1977–1982
Giani Zail Singh	1982–

AUSTRALIAN PRIME MINISTERS

Edmund Barton	1901–1903
Alfred Deakin	1903–1904
John C. Watson	1904
George Houston Reid	1904–1905
Alfred Deakin	1905–1908
Andrew Fisher	1908–1909
Alfred Deakin	1909–1910
Andrew Fisher	1910–1913
Joseph Cook	1913–1914
Andrew Fisher	1914–1915
William M. Hughes	1915–1923
Stanley M. Bruce	1923–1929
James H. Scullin	1929–1931
Joseph A. Lyons	1932–1939
Robert Gordon Menzies	1939–1941
Arthur William Fadden	1941
John Curtin	1941–1945
Joseph Benedict Chifley	1945–1949
Robert Gordon Menzies	1949–1966
Harold Edward Holt	1966–1967
John Grey Gorton	1968–1971
William McMahon	1971–1972
Edward Gough Whitlam	1972–1975
John Malcolm Fraser	1975–1983
Robert James Hawke	1983–

CANADIAN PRIME MINISTERS

Sir John MacDonald	1867–1873
Alexander Mackenzie	1873–1878
Sir John MacDonald	1878–1891
Sir John Abbott	1891–1892
Sir John Thompson	1892–1894
Sir Mackenzie Bowell	1894–1896
Sir Charles Tupper	1896
Sir Wilfred Laurier	1896–1911
Sir Robert L. Borden	1911–1920
Arthur Meighen	1920–1921
W. L. Mackenzie King	1921–1930
R. B. Bennett	1930–1935
W. L. Mackenzie King	1935–1948
Louis St Laurent	1948–1957
John G. Diefenbaker	1957–1963
Lester B. Pearson	1963–1968
Pierre Elliott Trudeau	1968–1979
Joe Clark	1979–1980
Pierre Elliott Trudeau	1980–1984
John Turner	1984
Brian Mulroney	1984–

PRIME MINISTERS OF NEW ZEALAND

Henry Sewell	1856
William Fox	1856
Edward William Stafford	1856–1861
William Fox	1861–1862
Alfred Domett	1862–1863
Frederick Whittaker	1863–1864
Frederick Aloysius Weld	1864–1865
Edward William Stafford	1865–1869
William Fox	1869–1872
Edward William Stafford	1872
George Marsden Waterhouse	1872–1873
William Fox	1873
Julius Vogel	1873–1875
Daniel Pollen	1875–1876
Julius Vogel	1876
Harry Albert Atkinson	1876–1877
George Grey	1877–1879
John Hall	1879–1882
Frederick Whitaker	1882–1883
Harry Albert Atkinson	1883–1884
Robert Stout	1884
Harry Albert Atkinson	1884
Robert Stout	1884–1887
Harry Albert Atkinson	1887–1891
John Ballance	1891–1893
Richard John Seddon	1893–1906
William Hall-Jones	1906
Joseph George Ward	1906–1912
Thomas Mackenzie	1912
William Ferguson Massey	1912–1925
Francis Henry Dillon Bell	1925
Joseph Gordon Coates	1925–1928
Joseph George Ward	1928–1930
George William Forbes	1930–1935
Michael J. Savage	1935–1940
Peter Fraser	1940–1949
Sidney J. Holland	1949–1957
Keith J. Holyoake	1957
Walter Nash	1957–1960
Keith J. Holyoake	1960–1972
Sir John Marshall	1972
Norman Kirk	1972–1974
Wallace Rowling	1974–1975
Robert Muldoon	1975–1984
David Lange	1984–

GREAT ANCIENT CIVILIZATIONS

CIVILIZATION AND LOCATION	DATES	ACHIEVEMENTS	MAJOR CITIES
Sumerians Lived between the Tigris and Euphrates rivers in what is now Iraq.	3500 B.C. — 2000 B.C.	First people to develop word-writing, before 3000 B.C. Called *cuneiform* (wedge-shaped) writing, written on lumps of clay.	Kish, Lagash, Ur
Egyptians Lived along the Nile River.	3100 B.C. — 525 B.C.	Built huge temples and large tombs called pyramids out of stone. Invented another form of word-writing called *hieroglyphics*.	Memphis, Thebes, Akhetaton, Alexandria
Minoans Lived on the island of Crete near Greece.	3000 B.C. — 1100 B.C.	Made pottery and wall paintings full of bright patterns. Built large outdoor theaters and loved to watch outdoor sports.	Knossos, Phaestos
Babylonians Lived between the Tigris and Euphrates rivers in what is now Iraq.	1900 B.C. — 538 B.C.	Great lawmakers. The Code of Hammurabi is one of the oldest known sets of written law. There were many scientists and mathematicians. The first people to count seconds and minutes by 60s.	Babylon
Phoenicians Lived along eastern coast of the Mediterranean.	1100 B.C. — 842 B.C.	Invented an alphabet improved by the Greeks and used in the west today. Very skillful in making cloth and other goods. Traded all over the world. Good sailors.	Byblos, Tyre, Sidon, Ugarit
Hebrews Originally nomadic. Lived at various times in what is now Israel and Jordan.	1000 B.C. — 587 B.C.	Created a great literature. Most important was the Old Testament of the Bible, the books of which were probably written between about 900 B.C. and 150 B.C. King Solomon, a well-known king of Israel, built a great temple in Jerusalem.	Jerusalem, Hebron
Assyrians Lived along the Tigris River in what is now Iraq.	800 B.C. — 612 B.C.	Formed the first great army with iron weapons. This helped them to win many battles.	Assur, Nineveh
Greeks Lived in the southern part of what is now Greece.	800 B.C. — 197 B.C.	Built fine buildings and sculptures. Wrote great poetry and drama. Had many wise scientists and philosophers. Democracy began in Greece.	Athens, Sparta, Thebes, Corinth
Persians Lived in an area from the Indus River to the Aegean Sea at the height of the empire.	700 B.C. — 331 B.C.	Built huge palaces of mud, brick, and stone. Legendary beasts appeared in their wall paintings and sculptures. Mail was delivered by "Pony Express."	Persepolis
Romans Spread from the city of Rome west to England and east to Mesopotamia. At its height, included all lands around the Mediterranean Sea.	735 B.C. — 476 A.D.	Excellent administrators; first to control a vast area from a central place and still let cities govern themselves. Used their army to build bridges and roads to improve the lives of conquered peoples.	Rome, Pompeii, Byzantium

Science

Nature and Nature's Laws lay hid in Night:
God said, Let Newton be! and all was Light.

> Epitaph, intended for Sir Isaac Newton;
> written by Alexander Pope (1688–1744)

Unfortunately, science being what it is, even Sir Isaac Newton's laws are no longer quite true. They do not apply,

▲ **The circuitry of a silicon chip** photographed through a microscope.

for example, to bodies moving at extremely high speeds. But the vast body of science remains more or less constant, even though established scientific laws can never be regarded as the absolute truth. They are merely the best available explanation of observed events and may be changed as the need arises. For all practical purposes, Newton's laws of motion and gravitation are as sound today as when Alexander Pope penned his famous lines more than two hundred years ago.

BRANCHES OF SCIENCE

Science   **Study of**

EARTH SCIENCES

Geology	Rocks, earthquakes, volcanoes, and fossils
Meteorology	The atmosphere and weather
Mineralogy	Minerals, their location and mining
Oceanography	Waves, tides, currents, trenches, and ocean life
Palaeontology	Plant and animal fossils
Petrology	Formation and structure of rocks; their chemical content

LIFE SCIENCES

Agronomy	Land management of crops and cultivation
Anatomy	Structure, form, and arrangement of the body
Bacteriology	Bacteria, their growth and behavior
Biology	Animals and plants; origin, morphology, and environment
Botany	The plant world
Cytology	Structure, function, and life of cells
Ecology	Relationship between living things and environment
Medicine	Cause, prevention, and cure of disease
Nutrition	Supply of adequate and correct foods to satisfy the body's requirements
Pharmacology	Drugs; their preparation, use, and effects
Physiology	The function of living things
Psychology	Behavior of humans and animals; working of the brain
Zoology	Animals

MATHEMATICAL SCIENCES

Logic	Reasoning by mathematics; used by computers
Mathematics	The application of geometry, algebra, arithmetic, etc.; application of these to concrete data
Statistics	Numerical information which is to be analyzed

PHYSICAL SCIENCES

Aerodynamics	The properties and forces of flowing air on solid objects
Astronomy	Heavenly bodies and their motions
Chemistry	Properties and behavior of substances
Electronics	Behavior of electrons in a vacuum, in gases, and in semiconductors
Engineering	Application of scientific principles to industry
Mechanics	The invention and construction of machines, their operation, and the calculation of their efficiency

Physical Sciences continued	
Metallurgy	The working of metals; smelting and refining
Physics	Nature and behavior of matter and energy

SOCIAL SCIENCES

Anthropology	Origin, culture, development, and distribution of human beings
Archaeology	Remains, monuments left by prehistoric people
Economics	Use of natural resources to the best advantage
Geography	Location of Earth's features and our relation to them
Linguistics	Languages and their relationship to each other
Political Science	Function of states and governments
Sociology	Relationship between groups and individuals

Chronology of Medical Discovery

400 B.C. The ancient Greeks were very interested in the body and how it worked. One of their most famous doctors at this time was Hippocrates. He laid down certain rules called the Hippocratic Oath. Doctors still follow rules based on this oath today.

1543 Andreas Vesalius, a Flemish doctor, made the first accurate studies of the human body. He published a book on anatomy called *The Working of the Human Body.*

1600 The microscope was invented by Hans and Zacharias Janssen around this time. It became well known in 1665 through the work of Robert Hooke in England, and soon afterward Van Leeuwenhoek saw the first microorganisms in a sample of his own saliva.

In the early 1600s Sanctorius invented the first thermometer for taking human temperatures, and quinine was discovered as a treatment for malaria in South America.

▲ **Andreas Vesalius's** book contained many precise drawings. Dissecting bodies for research was not allowed at this time and so Vesalius had to use stolen corpses.

115

1628 William Harvey, a physician to James I, wrote a book called *Concerning the Motion of the Heart and Blood*. It was the first time that the circulation of the blood had been described.

1796 Edward Jenner discovered that injecting people with cowpox virus prevented them from catching smallpox. He had "invented" vaccination.

1816 René Laennec made one of the first stethoscopes from rolled paper. Later, a wooden one was made in England by John Elliotson.

1839 Theodore Schwann and Matthias Schleiden first suggested that living things were made up of cells.

1844 Horace Wells, an American dentist, used nitrous oxide or "laughing gas" to put his patients to sleep while he gave them treatment. Before this, patients were either made drunk before operations or were held down.

1847 Dr. James Simpson first used chloroform as an anesthetic.

1860 Joseph Lister began using weak carbolic acid as an antiseptic after he realized that many people were dying after operations because they developed infections.

1865 In the early 1860s, Louis Pasteur discovered that bacteria in the air cause perishable food to go bad very quickly. He invented "pasteurization" (treating food with heat) to kill the bacteria.

Between 1879 and 1885 Pasteur found ways of weakening harmful micro-organisms so that they could be made into vaccines. He developed vaccines against cholera, rabies, anthrax, and swine plague.

1883 Robert Koch, a German scientist, developed techniques for the study of bacteria. He is most famous for the discovery of the bacterium that causes tuberculosis (TB).

1895 Wilhelm Roentgen discovered X rays as a way of looking at bones.

1895 Sigmund Freud, an Austrian psychiatrist, founded psychoanalysis. He believed that childhood experiences helped to explain adult behavior and feelings. He also thought that dreams were a clue to the unconscious and published *The Interpretation of Dreams* in 1900.

▲ **Van Leeuwenhoek's microscope** (1600s) was very simple, but powerful enough to see bacteria.

1902 Marie and Pierre Curie discovered radium and polonium—two radioactive substances that can be used to treat cancer. Today, cobalt 60 is used instead.

1910 The four blood groups—A, AB, B, and O—were discovered by Dr. Karl Landsteiner.

1928 Sir Alexander Fleming discovered penicillin, a mold that could kill bacteria. This was the first antibiotic.

1944 The first kidney machine was developed by Dr. Wilhelm Kolff, in secret, during the German occupation of Holland. This was the first machine to take the place of a major organ of the human body.

1950 The first kidney transplant was performed by Dr. R. Lawler in Chicago.

1952 Jonas Salk, an American microbiologist, produced the first vaccine that prevented polio.

1957 Arthur Kornberg grew DNA—the molecule of life that controls heredity—in a test tube.

1958 The first internal heart pacemaker was fitted to Arne Larsson in Stockholm by Dr. A. Stenning.

1967 The first human heart transplant was performed on Louis Washkansky by Dr. Christiaan Barnard in South Africa.

1978 Louise Brown, the world's first "test-tube" baby, was born in Oldham, Lancashire, Great Britain. Doctors implanted a fertilized ovum into the

▲ **Mass vaccination against polio** began in the mid 1950s. By 1960, the occurrence of polio had been greatly reduced.

mother's womb, where it proceeded to develop normally. The ovum was fertilized in a laboratory run by the pioneers of this technique—Robert Edwards and Patrick Steptoe.

1982 The first artificial heart transplant was carried out in the U.S.A. The patient's name was Barney Clarke.

1986 The world's first triple transplant (heart, lung, and liver) was performed on a woman in December. It took place at Papworth Hospital, Cambridgeshire, Great Britain.

MAIN CAUSES OF DEATH IN THE U.S.A.

Cause	Number per 100,000 people (over 11 months, 1985)
Cardiovascular (heart) disease	408
Malignant neoplasms (cancer)	193
Cerebrovascular (brain) disease	64

(Deaths from motor accidents were 19.1 or 45,600)

● No one knows why we "age."

● The longest a person is known to have lived is 120 years. This was Shigechiyo Izumi from Asan, on Tokunoshima, an island southwest of Tokyo, Japan. He was born in Asan on June 29, 1865, and died of pneumonia in Asan on February 21, 1986.

● The death rate in the United States is about 9 per thousand inhabitants, about the same as other industrial nations. The birthrate is just over 15 per thousand inhabitants, higher than that of most of Western Europe.

HOW LONG DO WE LIVE?

Life expectancy at birth varies enormously from country to country and between the sexes. A baby girl born in Sweden today can expect on average to live until she is 80. A baby boy born in Guinea can expect to live only half that long—until he is 39. The chart below shows life expectancy in a sample country—England—through the ages.

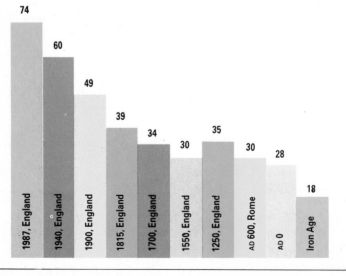

1987, England	1940, England	1900, England	1815, England	1700, England	1550, England	1250, England	AD 600, Rome	AD 0	Iron Age
74	60	49	39	34	30	35	30	28	18

PHYSICAL FIGURES

● The human body is made up of 50 million cells. It has a network of blood vessels that comprises 60,000 miles of tubing, and more than 500 chemical processes take place in the liver alone. The body regulates temperature, blood pressure, water concentration, digestion, and countless other aspects of our physical well-being. Its control center, the brain, records and stores a much greater range of information than any computer.

● Too much growth hormone—from the pituitary gland—can make a person a giant and too little can make him or her a dwarf. The tallest known person was 8 feet 10 inches tall and the shortest was 27.5 inches. Today, children with pituitary disorders can be treated so that they grow to normal size.

● Adults' lungs hold about 5 pints of air. In quiet breathing the diaphragm moves up and down about ½ inch and about 1 pint of air is breathed in and out, roughly 15 times every minute. During vigorous exercise, the breathing rate increases and breathing is much deeper, because the diaphragm can move as much as 2 inches.

● The area of your lungs is 753 square feet, about 40 times greater than the area covered by your skin. This is because of the enormous number of tiny alveoli and means that you can take in the amount of air that you need.

● Skin is about 0.04 inch thick on your eyelids, 0.1 inch thick on the palms of your hands and soles of your feet, and about 0.08 inch thick elsewhere.

● Muscles account for 40 percent of your total body weight.

● You use over 200 different muscles when you walk.

● Hair grows about ½ inch each month and most hairs can grow to a length of about 27.5 inches before they fall out.

● About 50 hairs fall from your head each day.

● Boys may continue to grow until the age of 23, whereas most girls are fully grown by about 20.

● There are 29 bones in your skull. This includes all the bones in your face and the 3 small bones inside your ear.

● An adult's body contains over 8 pints of blood.

● 1cc (a few drops) of blood contains about 5,000 million red blood cells and about 11 million white cells.

● At 9 years old, an average healthy, well-nourished boy will be three-fourths of his full adult height. A girl will be three-fourths of her adult height when she is 7½. By the time the girl and boy are 18 years old, the boy will be twice the height he was at 2 and the girl should be about twice the height she was when she was 18 months of age.

119

THE HUMAN SKELETON

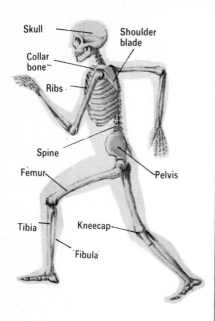

Skull
Shoulder blade
Collar bone
Ribs
Spine
Femur
Pelvis
Tibia
Kneecap
Fibula

BODY TEMPERATURE

°F	°C	
		Unconsciousness, possibly death
106	41	Heat stroke Pulse rate rises
100	37.7	Fever
99	37.2	Normal body
97	36	temperature
95	35	Shivering
93	34	Pulse rate falls
86	30	Unconsciousness
82	28	Respiration stops
77	25	Death

The average or "normal" temperature inside the human body is 98.4F° (37°C), though different people may have normal temperatures that are very slightly higher or lower than this. Maintaining a constant body temperature is vital, as people can be very ill if their temperature goes up or down by just a few degrees.

▼ **The four blood groups**—A, B, AB, and O. Antibodies in the plasma of one blood group can react against substances on the red blood cells of another group. This causes your body to reject a transfusion of blood unless it matches with your own blood type.

BLOOD GROUPS

BLOOD GROUP	CONTAINS ANTIBODIES WHICH REACT AGAINST	CAN GIVE BLOOD TO	CAN RECEIVE BLOOD FROM
A	B	A or AB	O, A
B	A	B or AB	O, B
AB	no antibodies against other blood groups	AB	A, B, AB, O
O	A&B	A, B, AB, O	O

CALORIES NEEDED PER DAY

Because foods, the body's fuel, vary in the amount of energy they liberate when "burned" or metabolized, it is convenient to express their value in units of heat or Calories. A Calorie is the amount of heat needed to warm a kilogram of water by 1°C (34°F). These Calories are kilocalories, which can also be expressed as kilojoules (1 Calorie = 4.2 kilojoules).

Age	Both sexes	Age	Male	Female
0–1	800	9–12	2,500	2,300
1–2	1,200	12–15	2,800	2,300
2–3	1,400	15–18	3,000	2,300
3–5	1,600			2,200 (normal life)
5–7	1,800	18–35	2,700 (normal life)	2,500 (very active)
7–9	2,100		3,600 (very active)	2,400 (pregnant)
				2,700 (breast feeding)
		35–65	2,600	2,200
		65–75	2,300	2,100
		75+	2,100	1,900

VITAMINS

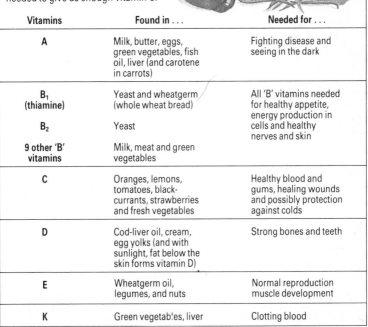

▶Plenty of fresh fruit and vegetables is needed to give us enough vitamin C.

Vitamins	Found in . . .	Needed for . . .
A	Milk, butter, eggs, green vegetables, fish oil, liver (and carotene in carrots)	Fighting disease and seeing in the dark
B₁ (thiamine) B₂ 9 other 'B' vitamins	Yeast and wheatgerm (whole wheat bread) Yeast Milk, meat and green vegetables	All 'B' vitamins needed for healthy appetite, energy production in cells and healthy nerves and skin
C	Oranges, lemons, tomatoes, black-currants, strawberries and fresh vegetables	Healthy blood and gums, healing wounds and possibly protection against colds
D	Cod-liver oil, cream, egg yolks (and with sunlight, fat below the skin forms vitamin D)	Strong bones and teeth
E	Wheatgerm oil, legumes, and nuts	Normal reproduction muscle development
K	Green vegetables, liver	Clotting blood

PHYSIOLOGY AND MEDICINE: NOBEL PRIZE WINNERS

This Nobel prize is awarded by the Caroline Institute of Stockholm.

1901	Emil von Behring (German)
1902	Sir Ronald Ross (British)
1903	Niels Finsen (Danish)
1904	Ivan Pavlov (Russian)
1905	Robert Koch (German)
1906	Camillo Golgi (Italian) & Santiago Ramón y Cajal (Spanish)
1907	Charles Laveran (French)
1908	Paul Ehrlich (German) & Elie Metchnikoff (Russian/French)
1909	Emil Theodor Kocher (Swiss)
1910	Albrecht Kossel (German)
1911	Allvar Gullstrand (Swedish)
1912	Alexis Carrel (French)
1913	Charles Richet (French)
1914	Robert Bárány (Austrian)
1915–18	*No award*
1919	Jules Bordet (Belgian)
1920	August Krogh (Danish)
1921	*No award*
1922	Archibald Hill (British) & Otto Meyerhof (German)
1923	Sir Frederick Banting (Canadian) & John Macleod (British)
1924	Willem Einthoven (Dutch)
1925	*No award*
1926	Johannes Fibiger (Danish)
1927	Julius Wagner-Jauregg (Austrian)
1928	Charles Nicolle (French)
1929	Christiaan Eijkman (Dutch) & Sir Frederick Hopkins (British)
1930	Karl Landsteiner (American)
1931	Otto Warburg (German)
1932	Edgar Adrian & Sir Charles Sherrington (British)
1933	Thomas H. Morgan (American)
1934	George Minot, William P. Murphy & George Whipple (American)
1935	Hans Spemann (German)
1936	Sir Henry Dale (British) & Otto Loewi (German/Austrian)
1937	Albert Szent-Györgyi (Hungarian)
1938	Corneille Heymans (Belgian)
1939	Gerhard Domagk (German) – declined
1940–42	*No award*
1943	Henrik Dam (Danish) & Edward Doisy (American)
1944	Joseph Erlanger & Herbert Gasser (American)
1945	Sir Alexander Fleming, Howard Florey & Ernst Chain (British)

1946	Hermann Muller (American)
1947	Carl and Gerty Cori (American) & Bernardo Houssay (Argentinian)
1948	Paul Müller (Swiss)
1949	Walter Hess (Swiss) & Antonio Moniz (Portuguese)
1950	Philip Hench & Edward Kendall (American), Tadeus Reichstein (Swiss)
1951	Max Theiler (S. African/American)
1952	Selman Waksman (American)
1953	Fritz Lipmann (German/American) & Hans Krebs (German/British)
1954	John Enders, Thomas Weller & Frederick Robbins (American)
1955	Hugo Theorell (Swedish)
1956	André Cournand & Dickinson Richards Jr (American) and Werner Forssmann (German)
1957	Daniel Bovet (Italian)
1958	George Beadle, Edward Tatum & Joshua Lederberg (American)
1959	Severo Ochoa & Arthur Kornberg (American)
1960	Sir Macfarlane Burnet (Australian) & Peter Medawar (British)
1961	Georg von Békésy (Hungarian American)
1962	Francis Crick & Maurice Wilkins (British) & James Watson (American)
1963	Alan Hodgkin & Andrew Huxley (British) & Sir John Eccles (Australian)
1964	Konrad Bloch (German/American) & Feodor Lynen (German)
1965	François Jacob, André Lwoff & Jacques Monod (French)
1966	Charles Huggins & Francis Peyton Rous (American)
1967	Ragnar Granit (Swedish) & Haldan Hartline & George Wald (American)
1968	Robert Holley, Har Gobind Khorana & Marshall Nirenberg (American)
1969	Max Delbrück, Alfred Hershey & Salvador Luria (American)
1970	Sir Bernard Katz (British), Ulf von Euler (Swedish) & Julius Axelrod (American)
1971	Earl Sutherland, Jr. (American)

1972	Rodney Porter (British) & Gerald Edelman (American)	**1980**	George Snell (American), Jean Dausset (French) & Barui Benacerraf (Venezuelan)
1973	Karl von Frisch & Konrad Lorenz (Austrian) & Nikolaas Tinbergen (Dutch)	**1981**	David Hubel, Roger Sperry (American) & Torsten Wiesel (Swedish)
1974	Albert Claude & Christian de Duve (Belgian) & George Palade (Romanian American)	**1982**	Sune Bergstrom & Bengt Samuelsson (Swedish)
1975	David Baltimore & Howard Temin (American), Renato Dulbecco (Italian)	**1983**	Barbara McClintock (American)
		1984	Cesar Milstein (British/ Argentinian), Georges F. Koehler (German) & Niels K. Jerne (British/ Danish)
1976	B. S. Blumberg & D. G. Gajdusek (American)		
1977	Rosalyn Yalow, R. Guillemin & A. Schally (American)	**1985**	Michael S. Brown & Joseph L. Goldstein (American)
1978	W. Arber (Swiss), D. Nathans & H. Smith (American)	**1986**	Stanley Cohen (British) & Rita Levi-Montalcini (Italian)
1979	Godfrey Newbold Hounsfield (British) & Allan McLeod Cormack (American)	**1987**	Susumu Tonegawa (Japanese)

Inventions

Inventions only succeed when people need them. The ancient peoples of Central America knew of the wheel, but since they had no domestic animals large enough to pull carts, they had no use for it. When Marconi first demonstrated the radio, the Italian government could see little purpose in it.

4000–3000 B.C. Bricks—in Egypt and Assyria
*c.*3000 B.C. Wheel—in Asia
*c.*3000 B.C. Plow—in Egypt and Mesopotamia
*c.*500 B.C. Abacus—the Chinese
*c.*300 B.C. Geometry—Euclid (Gk.)
200s B.C. Screw (for raising water)—Archimedes (Gk.)
A.D. 105 Paper (from pulp)—Ts'ai Lun (Chin.)
A.D. 250 Algebra—Diophantus (Gk.)
*c.*1000 Gunpowder—the Chinese
*c.*1100 Magnetic compass—the Chinese
*c.*1100 Rocket—the Chinese
*c.*1440 Printing press (movable type)—Johannes Gutenberg (Ger.)
1520 Rifle—Joseph Kotter (Ger.)
1589 Knitting machine—William Lee (Eng.)
*c.*1590 Compound microscope—Zacharias Janssen (Neth.)
1593 Thermometer—Galileo (It.)

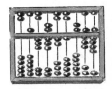

▲ **Until the invention of the electronic calculator,** the abacus was our most efficient number handler.

123

1608	Telescope—Hans Lippershey (Neth.)
1614	Logarithms—John Napier (Scot.)
1636	Micrometer—William Gascoigne (Eng.)
1637	Coordinate geometry—René Descartes (Fr.)
1640	Theory of numbers—Pierre de Fermat (Fr.)
1642	Calculating machine—Blaise Pascal (Fr.)
1643	Barometer—Evangelista Torricelli (It.)
1650	Air pump—Otto von Guericke (Ger.)
1656	Pendulum clock—Christian Huygens (Neth.)
1665–75	Calculus—Sir Isaac Newton (Eng.) & Gottfried Leibniz (Ger.) independently
1675	Pressure cooker—Denis Papin (Fr.)
1698	Steam pump—Thomas Savery (Eng.)
1712	Steam engine—Thomas Newcomen (Eng.)
1714	Mercury thermometer—Gabriel Fahrenheit (Ger.)
1725	Stereotyping—William Ged (Scot.)
1733	Flying shuttle for loom—John Kay (Eng.)
1735	Chronometer—John Harrison (Eng.)
1752	Lightning conductor—Benjamin Franklin (U.S.)
1764	Spinning jenny—James Hargreaves (Eng.)
1765	Condensing steam engine—James Watt (Scot.)
1768	Hydrometer—Antoine Baumé (Fr.)
1783	Parachute—Louis Lenormand (Fr.)
1785	Power loom—Edmund Cartwright (Eng.)
1793	Cotton gin—Eli Whitney (U.S.)
1796	Lithography—Aloys Senefelder (Ger.)
1800	Electric battery—Count Alessandro Volta (It.)
1800	Lathe—Henry Maudslay (Eng.)
1804	Steam locomotive—Richard Trevithick (Eng.)
1815	Miner's safety lamp—Sir Humphry Davy (Eng.)
1816	Metronome—Johann Mälzel (Ger.)
1816	Bicycle—Karl von Sauerbronn (Ger.)
1817	Kaleidoscope—David Brewster (Scot.)
1822	Camera—Joseph Niepce (Fr.)
1823	Digital calculating machine—Charles Babbage (Eng.)
1824	Portland cement—Joseph Aspdin (Eng.)
1825	Electromagnet—William Sturgeon (Eng.)
1826	Photograph (permanent)—Joseph Niepce (Fr.)
1827	Match—John Walker (Eng.)
1828	Blast furnace—James Nielson (Scot.)
1831	Dynamo—Michael Faraday (Eng.)
1834	Reaping machine—Cyrus McCormick (U.S.)
1836	Revolver—Samuel Colt (U.S.)

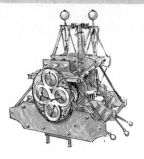

▲ **Harrison's marine chronometer** was accurate to within five seconds after many weeks at sea.

▼ **This photograph** was taken by Joseph Niepce in 1827.

◀ **The cowboy's favorite weapon**—the Colt revolver. It was first used by American troops against the Indians, and was the first completely mass-produced weapon.

1837	Telegraph—Samuel F. B. Morse (U.S.)
1839	Vulcanized rubber—Charles Goodyear (U.S.)
1844	Safety match—Gustave Pasch (Swed.)
1846	Sewing machine—Elias Howe (U.S.)
1849	Safety pin—Walter Hunt (U.S.)
1852	Gyroscope—Léon Foucault (Fr.)
1853	Passenger elevator—Elisha Otis (U.S.)
1855	Celluloid—Alexander Parkes (Eng.)
1855	Bessemer converter—Henry Bessemer (Eng.)
1855	Bunsen burner—Robert Bunsen (Ger.)
1858	Refrigerator—Ferdinand Carré (Fr.)
1858	Washing machine—Hamilton Smith (U.S.)
1859	Internal-combustion engine—Etienne Lenoir (Fr.)
1861	Linoleum—Frederick Walton (Eng.)
1862	Rapid-fire gun—Richard Gatling (U.S.)
1865	Cylinder lock—Linus Yale, Jr (U.S.)
1866	Dynamite—Alfred Nobel (Swed.)
1867	Typewriter—Christopher Sholes (U.S.)
1868	Lawnmower—Amariah Hills (U.S.)
1870	Margarine—Hippolyte Mège-Mouriés (Fr.)
1873	Barbed wire—Joseph Glidden (U.S.)
1876	Telephone—Alexander Graham Bell (U.S.)
1876	Carpet sweeper—Melville Bissell (U.S.)
1877	Phonograph—Thomas Edison (U.S.)
1878	Microphone—David Edward Hughes (Eng./U.S.)
1879	Incandescent lamp—Thomas Edison (U.S.)
1879	Cash register—James Ritty (U.S.)
1884	Fountain pen—Lewis Waterman (U.S.)
1884	Linotype—Ottmar Mergenthaler (U.S.)
1885	Motorcycle—Gottlieb Daimler (Ger.)
1885	Vacuum flask—James Dewar (Scot.)
1885	Electric transformer—William Stanley (U.S.)
1885	Automobile engine—Gottlieb Daimler & Karl Benz (Ger.), independently
1886	Electric fan—Schuyler Wheeler (U.S.)
1886	Halftone engraving—Frederick Ives (U.S.)
1887	Gramophone—Emile Berliner (Ger./U.S.)
1887	Monotype—Tolbert Lanston (U.S.)
1888	Pneumatic tire—John Boyd Dunlop (Scot.)
1888	Kodak camera—George Eastman (U.S.)
1890	Rotogravure printing—Karl Klic (Czech.)
1892	Zipper—Whitcomb Judson (U.S.)
1895	Radio—Guglielmo Marconi (It.)
1895	Photoelectric cell—Julius Elster & Hans Geitel (Ger.)
1895	Safety razor—King C. Gillette (U.S.)
1897	Diesel engine—Rudolf Diesel (Ger.)
1898	Submarine—John P. Holland (Ire./U.S.)

▲ **The skyscraper** had to wait for the invention of the passenger elevator.

▲ **Thomas Edison's** incandescent lamp (1879).

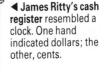

◀ **James Ritty's cash register** resembled a clock. One hand indicated dollars; the other, cents.

1899	Tape recorder—Valdemar Poulsen (Den.)
1901	Vacuum cleaner—Cecil Booth (Eng.)
1902	Radiotelephone—Reginald Fessenden (U.S.)
1903	Airplane—Wilbur & Orville Wright (U.S.)
1904	Diode—John Fleming (Eng.)
1906	Triode—Lee De Forest (U.S.)
1908	Bakelite—Leo Baekeland (Belg./U.S.)
1908	Cellophane—Jacques Brandenberger (Switz.)
1911	Combine harvester—Benjamin Holt (U.S.)
1913	Geiger counter—Hans Geiger (Eng.)
1914	Tank—Ernest Swinton (Eng.)
1915	Tungsten filament lamp—Irving Langmuir (U.S.)
1918	Automatic rifle—John Browning (U.S.)
1925	Television (working system)—John Logie Baird (Scot.) & others
1925	Frozen food process—Clarence Birdseye (U.S.)
1926	Rocket (liquid fuel)—Robert H. Goddard (U.S.)
1928	Electric shaver—Jacob Schick (U.S.)
1930	Jet engine—Frank Whittle (Eng.)
1931	Cyclotron—Ernest Lawrence (U.S.)
1935	Nylon—Wallace Carothers (U.S.)
1935	Parking meter—Carlton Magee (U.S.)
1939	Electron microscope—Vladimir Zworykin and others (U.S.)
1939	Betatron—Donald Kerst (U.S.)
1944	Automatic digital computer—Howard Aiken (U.S.)
1946	Electronic computer—J. Presper Eckert & John W. Mauchly (U.S.)
1947	Polaroid camera—Edwin Land (U.S.)
1948	Transistor—John Bardeen, Walter Brattain & William Shockley (U.S.)
1948	Xerography—Chester Carlson (U.S.)
1948	Long-playing record—Peter Goldmark (U.S.)
1954	Maser—Charles H. Townes (U.S.)
1960	Laser—Theodore Maiman (U.S.)
1965	Holography (an idea conceived in 1948 and subsequently developed using laser)—T. Gabor (Brit.)
1971	EMI-Scanner—Godfrey Hounsfield (Eng.) (developed from his invention of computed tomography in 1967)
1978	Compact disc—Philips (U.S.)

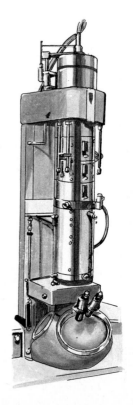

▶ **An early vacuum cleaner** used bellows to suck up the dust.

▶ **The electron microscope** allows a study of the internal structure of matter.

Discoveries

▶ **Isaac Newton**—the apple and gravity.

1543	Sun as center of solar system—Copernicus (Pol.)
1590	Law of falling bodies—Galileo (It.)
1609–19	Laws of planetary motion—Johannes Keplér (Ger.)
1662	Relation between gas pressure and volume—Robert Boyle (Eng./Ire.)
1669	Phosphorus—Hennig Brand (Ger.)
1675	Measurement of speed of light—Olaus Römer (Dan.)
1678	Wave theory of light—Christian Huygens (Dut.)
1687	Laws of gravitation and motion—Isaac Newton (Eng.)
1751	Nickel—Axel Cronstedt (Swe.)
1755	Magnesium—Sir Humphry Davy (Brit.)
1766	Hydrogen—Henry Cavendish (Brit.)
1772	Nitrogen—Daniel Rutherford (Brit.)
1774	Oxygen—Joseph Priestly (Brit.); Karl Scheele (Swe.)
1774	Chlorine—Karl Scheele (Swe.)
1781	Uranus (planet)—William Herschel (Brit.)
1783	Tungsten—Fausto & Juan José de Elhuyar (Sp.)
1789	True nature of combustion—Antoine Lavoisier (Fr.)
1797	Chromium—Louis Vauquelin (Fr.)
1803	Atomic structure of matter—John Dalton (Brit.)
1811	Molecular hypothesis—Amadeo Avogadro (It.)
1817	Cadmium—Friedrich Stromeyer (Ger.)
1820	Electromagnetism—Hans Christian Oersted (Dan.)
1824	Silicon—Jöns Berzelius (Swe.)
1826	Bromine—Antoine Balard (Fr.)
1826	Laws of electromagnetism—André Ampère (Fr.)
1827	Law of electric conduction—Georg Ohm (Ger.)
1827	Aluminum—Hans Christian Oersted (Dan.)
1831	Electromagnetic induction—Michael Faraday (Brit.); discovered previously, but not published, by Joseph Henry (U.S.)
1839	Ozone—Christian Schönbein (Ger.)
1841	Uranium—Martin Klaproth (Ger.)
1846	Neptune (planet)—Johann Galle (Ger.), from predictions of others

▲ **Atomic structure of water.** Two hydrogen atoms and one of oxygen give H_2O.

▼ **A primitive electricity producer**—Faraday's disk dynamo.

1864	Electromagnetic theory of light—James Clerk Maxwell (Brit.)
1868	Helium—Sir William Ramsay (Brit.)
1869	Periodic arrangement of elements—Dmitri Mendeleev (Russ.)
1886	Electromagnetic waves—Heinrich Hertz (Ger.)
1886	Fluorine—Henri Moissan (Fr.)
1894	Argon—Sir William Ramsay & Baron Rayleigh (Brit.)
1895	X rays—Wilhelm Roentgen (Ger.)
1896	Radioactivity—Antoine Becquerel (Fr.)
1897	Electron—Sir Joseph Thomson (Brit.)
1898	Radium—Pierre & Marie Curie (Fr.)
1900	Quantum theory—Max Planck (Ger.)
1905	Special theory of relativity—Albert Einstein (Ger.)
1910	Russell-Hertzsprung diagram (star pattern)—Henry Russell & Eijnar Hertzsprung (U.S.)
1913	Atomic number—Henry Moseley (Brit.)
1915	General theory of relativity—Albert Einstein (Ger.)
1919	Proton—Ernest Rutherford (Brit.)
1924	Wave nature of electron—Louis de Broglie (Fr.)
1926	Wave mechanics—Erwin Schrödinger (Aus.)
1927	Uncertainty principle—Werner Heisenberg (Ger.)
1930	Pluto (planet)—Clyde Tombaugh (U.S.) from prediction by Percival Lowell (U.S.) in 1905
1931	Existence of neutrino (atomic particle)—Wolfgang Pauli (Ger.)
1931	Deuterium (heavy hydrogen)—Harold Urey (U.S.)
1932	Neutron—James Chadwick (Brit.)
1932	Positron—Carl Anderson (U.S.)
1935	Existence of meson (atomic particle)—Hideki Yukawa (Jap.)
1940	Plutonium—G. T. Seaborg *et al.* (U.S.)
1950	Unified field theory—Albert Einstein (Ger./U.S.)
1950	Theory of continuous creation of matter—Fred Hoyle (Brit.)
1955	Antiproton—Emilio Segré & Owen Chamberlain (U.S.)
1958	Radiation belts surrounding Earth—James Van Allen (U.S.)
1963	Quasars—Thomas Matthews & Allan Sandage (U.S.)

▼ **Marie and Pierre Curie** in 1903, the year of their joint Nobel Prize.

▼ **Albert Einstein,** father of relativity.

▶ **Wilhelm Conrad Roentgen**'s X-ray machine.

1964	Omega particle—Brookhaven Laboratory, New York (U.S.)
1967	Pulsars—Radio Astronomy Group, University of Cambridge (Brit.)
1974	Psi particle—discovered independently by two U.S. laboratories
1977	Chiron, distant asteroid orbiting between Saturn and Uranus—Charles Kowal (U.S.)
1984	Three more subatomic particles: W & Z and the sixth quark particle ("top")—CERN Laboratory team, Geneva (Swi.)

PHYSICS: NOBEL PRIZE WINNERS

This Nobel prize is awarded by the Royal Academy of Science in Stockholm.

1901 Wilhelm Roentgen (German)
1902 Hendrik Lorentz & Pieter Zeeman (Dutch)
1903 Pierre and Marie Curie & Henri Becquerel (French)
1904 Lord Rayleigh (British)
1905 Philipp Lenard (German)
1906 Sir Joseph Thomson (British)
1907 Albert Michelson (American)
1908 Gabriel Lippmann (French)
1909 Guglielmo Marconi (Italian) & Ferdinand Braun (German)
1910 Johannes van der Waals (Dutch)
1911 Wilhelm Wien (German)
1912 Nils Gustav Dalén (Swedish)
1913 Heike Kamerlingh-Onnes (Dutch)
1914 Max von Laue (German)
1915 Sir William H. Bragg & William L. Bragg (British)
1916 *No award*
1917 Charles Barkla (British)
1918 Max Planck (German)
1919 Johannes Stark (German)
1920 Charles Guillaume (Swiss)
1921 Albert Einstein (German)
1922 Niels Bohr (Danish)
1923 Robert Millikan (American)
1924 Karl Siegbahn (Swedish)
1925 James Franck & Gustav Hertz (German)
1926 Jean Perrin (French)
1927 Arthur Compton (American) & Charles T. R. Wilson (British)
1928 Owen Richardson (British)
1929 Prince Louis Victor de Broglie (French)
1930 Sir Chandrasekhara Raman (Indian)
1931 *No award*
1932 Werner Heisenberg (German)
1933 Erwin Schrödinger (Austrian) & Paul Dirac (British)
1934 *No award*
1935 James Chadwick (British)

1936 Victor Hess (Austrian) & Carl Anderson (American)
1937 Clinton Davisson (American) & George Thomson (British)
1938 Enrico Fermi (Italian)
1939 Ernest O. Lawrence (American)
1940–1942 *No award*
1943 Otto Stern (American)
1944 Isidor Isaac Rabi (American)
1945 Wolfgang Pauli (Austrian)
1946 Percy Bridgman (American)
1947 Sir Edward Appleton (British)
1948 Patrick M. S. Blackett (British)
1949 Hideki Yukawa (Japanese)
1950 Cecil Frank Powell (British)
1951 Sir John Cockcroft (British) & Ernest Walton (Irish)
1952 Edward Purcell & Felix Bloch (American)
1953 Frits Zernike (Dutch)
1954 Max Born (German/British) & Walther Bothe (German)
1955 Polykarp Kusch & Willis Lamb Jr (American)
1956 William Shockley, Walter Brattain & John Bardeen (American)
1957 Tsung Dao Lee & Chen Ning Yang (Chinese/American)
1958 Pavel Cherenkov, Ilya Frank & Igor Tamm (Russian)
1959 Emilio Segrè & Owen Chamberlain (American)
1960 Donald Glaser (American)
1961 Robert Hofstadter (American) & Rudolf Mössbauer (German)
1962 Lev Landau (Russian)
1963 Eugene Wigner (American), Maria Goeppert-Mayer (German/American) & Hans Jensen (German)
1964 Charles Townes (American) & Nikolai Basov & Alexandr Prokhorov (Russian)

1965	Richard Feynman & Julian Schwinger (American) & Shinichiro Tomonaga (Japanese)	1978	P. J. Kapitsa (Russian), A. A. Penzias & R. W. Wilson (American)
1966	Alfred Kastler (French)	1979	Sheldon Glashow (American), Abdus Salam (Pakistan) & Stephen Weinberg (American)
1967	Hans Bethe (American)		
1968	Luis Alvarez (American)		
1969	Murray Gell-Mann (American)	1980	James Cronin & Val Fitch (American)
1970	Hannes Alfvén (Swedish) & Louis Néel (French)		
		1981	Kai Siegbahn (Swedish), Nicolaas Bloembergen & Arthur Schawlaw (American)
1971	Dennis Gabor (British)		
1972	John Bardeen, Leon Cooper & John Schrieffer (American)		
		1982	Kenneth G. Wilson (American)
1973	Ivar Giaever (American), Leo Esaki (Japanese) & Brian Josephson (British)	1983	Subrahmanyan Chandrasekhar & William A. Fowler (American)
1974	Sir Martin Ryle & Antony Hewish (British)	1984	Carlo Rubbia (Italian) & Simon van der Meere (Dutch)
1975	James Rainwater (American), Aage Bohr & Benjamin Mottelson (Danish)	1985	Klaus von Klitzing (German)
		1986	Ernest Ruska (German), Gerd Binnig (German) & Heinrich Rohrer (Swiss)
1976	B. Richter & G. Ting (American)		
1977	Sir Nevill Mott (British), J. Van Vleck and P. Anderson (American)	1987	Alex Müller (German) & Georg Bednorz (Swiss)

CHEMISTRY: NOBEL PRIZE WINNERS

This Nobel prize is awarded by the Royal Academy of Science in Stockholm.

1901	Jacobus van't Hoff (Dutch)	1926	Theodor Svedberg (Swedish)
1902	Emil Fischer (German)	1927	Heinrich Wieland (German)
1903	Svante Arrhenius (Swedish)	1928	Adolf Windaus (German)
1904	Sir William Ramsay (British)	1929	Arthur Harden (British) & Hans von Euler-Chelpin (German/ Swedish)
1905	Adolf von Baeyer (German)		
1906	Henri Moissan (French)		
1907	Eduard Buchner (German)		
1908	Ernest Rutherford (New Zealand/ British)	1930	Hans Fischer (German)
		1931	Carl Bosch & Friedrich Bergius (German)
1909	Wilhelm Ostwald (German)		
1910	Otto Wallach (German)	1932	Irving Langmuir (American)
1911	Marie Curie (French)	1933	No award
1912	Victor Grignard & Paul Sabatier (French)	1934	Harold Urey (American)
		1935	Frédéric and Irène Joliot-Curie (French)
1913	Alfred Werner (Swiss)		
1914	Theodore Richards (American)	1936	Peter Debye (Dutch)
1915	Richard Willstätter (German)	1937	Walter Haworth (British) & Paul Karrer (Swiss)
1916–1917	No award		
1918	Fritz Haber (German)	1938	Richard Kuhn (German)
1919	No award	1939	Adolf Butenandt (German) & Leopold Ružička (Swiss)
1920	Walther Nernst (German)		
1921	Frederick Soddy (British)	1940–1942	No award
1922	Francis Aston (British)	1943	Georg von Hevesy (Hungarian/ Swedish)
1923	Fritz Pregl (Austrian)		
1924	No award	1944	Otto Hahn (German)
1925	Richard Zsigmondy (German)	1945	Artturi Virtanen (Finnish)

1946	James Sumner, John Northrop & Wendell Stanley (American)
1947	Sir Robert Robinson (British)
1948	Arne Tiselius (Swedish)
1949	William Giauque (American)
1950	Otto Diels & Kurt Alder (German)
1951	Glenn Seaborg & Edwin McMillan (American)
1952	Archer Martin & Richard Synge (British)
1953	Hermann Staudinger (German)
1954	Linus Pauling (American)
1955	Vincent du Vigneaud (American)
1956	Sir Cyril Hinshelwood (British) & Nikolai Semenov (Russian)
1957	Sir Alexander Todd (British)
1958	Frederick Sanger (British)
1959	Jaroslav Heyrovsky (Czechoslovakian)
1960	Willard Libby (American)
1961	Melvin Calvin (American)
1962	Max Perutz & John Kendrew (British)
1963	Karl Ziegler (German) & Giulio Natta (Italian)
1964	Dorothy Crowfoot Hodgkin (British)
1965	Robert Woodward (American)
1966	Robert Mulliken (American)
1967	Ronald Norrish & George Porter (British) & Manfred Eigen (German)
1968	Lars Onsager (American)
1969	Derek Barton (British) & Odd Hassel (Norwegian)
1970	Luis Leloir (Argentinian)
1971	Gerhard Herzberg (Canadian)
1972	Christian Anfinsén, Stanford Moore & William Stein (American)
1973	Ernst Otto Fischer (German) & Geoffrey Wilkinson (British)
1974	Paul Flory (American)
1975	John Cornforth (Australian) & Vladmir Prelog (Swiss)
1976	W. N. Lipscomb (American)
1977	L. Prigogine (Belgian)
1978	Peter Mitchell (British)
1979	Herbert C. Brown (American) & George Witting (German)
1980	Paul Berg, Walter Gilbert (American) & Frederick Sanger (British)
1981	Kenichi Fukui (Japanese) & Roald Hoffman (American)
1982	Aaron Klug (S. African)
1983	Henry Taube (Canadian)
1984	Bruce Merrifield (American)
1985	Herbert A. Hauptman & Jerome Karle (American)
1986	Dudley Herschbach, Yuan Tseh Lee (American) & John Polanyi (Canadian)
1987	Charles Pedersen, Donald Cram (American) & Jean Marie Lehn (French)

▼ **Alfred Nobel** (1833–96), the Swedish inventor of dynamite (1866) who donated $9,000,000 so that the interest on that sum could be awarded annually as prizes for outstanding achievement in certain fields.

DECIMAL MULTIPLES

Factor	Name of prefix	Symbol
10	deca-	da
10^2	hecto-	h
10^3	kilo-	k
10^6	mega-	M
10^9	giga-	G
10^{12}	tera-	T
10^{-1}	deci-	d
10^{-2}	centi-	c
10^{-3}	milli-	m
10^{-6}	micro-	μ
10^{-9}	nano-	n
10^{-12}	pico-	p
10^{-15}	femto-	f
10^{-18}	atto-	a

CHEMICAL ELEMENTS

An element is a substance consisting entirely of atoms of the same atomic number. Less than a hundred elements are found in nature; the others can only be made artificially.

Name	Symbol	Atomic number	Atomic weight	Valence number
Actinium	Ac	89	(227)	
Aluminum	Al	13	26.98154	3
Americium	Am	95	(243)	3,4,5,6
Antimony	Sb	51	121.75	3,5
Argon	Ar	18	39.948	0
Arsenic	As	33	74.9216	3,5
Astatine	At	85	(210)	1,3,5,7
Barium	Ba	56	137.34	2
Berkelium	Bk	97	(247)	3,4
Beryllium	Be	4	9.01218	2
Bismuth	Bi	83	208.9804	3,5
Boron	B	5	10.81	3
Bromine	Br	35	79.904	1,3,5,7
Cadmium	Cd	48	112.40	2
Caesium	Cs	55	132.9054	1
Calcium	Ca	20	40.08	2
Californium	Cf	98	(251)	
Carbon	C	6	12.011	2,4
Cerium	Ce	58	140.12	3,4
Chlorine	Cl	17	35.453	1,3,5,7
Chromium	Cr	24	51.996	2,3,6
Cobalt	Co	27	58.9332	2,3
Copper	Cu	29	63.546	1,2
Curium	Cm	96	(247)	3
Dysprosium	Dy	66	162.50	3
Einsteinium	Es	99	(254)	
Erbium	Er	68	167.26	3
Europium	Eu	63	151.96	2,3
Fermium	Fm	100	(257)	
Fluorine	F	9	18.99840	1
Francium	Fr	87	(223)	1
Gadolinium	Gd	64	157.25	3
Gallium	Ga	31	69.72	2,3
Germanium	Ge	32	72.59	4
Gold	Au	79	196.9665	1,3
Hafnium	Hf	72	178.49	4
Hahnium	Ha	105		
Helium	He	2	4.00260	0
Holmium	Ho	67	164.9304	3
Hydrogen	H	1	1.0079	1
Indium	In	49	114.82	3
Iodine	I	53	126.9045	1,3,5,7
Iridium	Ir	77	192.22	3,4
Iron	Fe	26	55.847	2,3
Krypton	Kr	36	83.80	0
Lanthanum	La	57	138.9055	3
Lawrencium	Lr	103	(260)	
Lead	Pb	82	207.2	2,4
Lithium	Li	3	6.941	1
Lutetium	Lu	71	174.97	3
Magnesium	Mg	12	24.305	2
Manganese	Mn	25	54.9380	2,3,4,6,7
Mendelevium	Md	101	(258)	
Mercury	Hg	80	200.59	1,2

Name	Symbol	Atomic number	Atomic weight	Valence number
Molybdenum	Mo	42	95.94	3,4,6
Neodymium	Nd	60	144.24	3
Neon	Ne	10	20.179	0
Neptunium	Np	93	237.0482	4,5,6
Nickel	Ni	28	58.70	2,3
Niobium	Nb	41	92.9064	3,5
Nitrogen	N	7	14.0067	3,5
Nobelium	No	102	(255)	
Osmium	Os	76	190.2	2,3,4,8
Oxygen	O	8	15.9994	2
Palladium	Pd	46	106.4	2,4,6
Phosphorus	P	15	30.97376	3,5
Platinum	Pt	78	195.09	2,4
Plutonium	Pu	94	(244)	3,4,5,6
Polonium	Po	84	(209)	
Potassium	K	19	39.098	1
Praseodymium	Pr	59	140.9077	3
Promethium	Pm	61	(145)	3
Protactinium	Pa	91	231.0359	
Radium	Ra	88	226.0254	2
Radon	Rn	86	(222)	0
Rhenium	Re	75	186.207	
Rhodium	Rh	45	102.9055	3
Rubidium	Rb	37	85.4678	1
Ruthenium	Ru	44	101.07	3,4,6,8
Rutherfordium	Ru	104		
Samarium	Sm	62	105.4	2,3
Scandium	Sc	21	44.9559	3
Selenium	Se	34	78.96	2,4,6
Silicon	Si	14	28.086	4
Silver	Ag	47	107.868	1
Sodium	Na	11	22.98977	1
Strontium	Sr	38	87.62	2
Sulfur	S	16	32.06	2,4,6
Tantalum	Ta	73	180.9479	5
Technetium	Tc	43	(97)	6,7
Tellurium	Te	52	127.60	2,4,6
Terbium	Tb	65	158.9254	3
Thallium	Tl	81	204.37	1,3
Thorium	Th	90	232.0381	4
Thulium	Tm	69	168.9342	3
Tin	Sn	50	118.69	2,4
Titanium	Ti	22	47.90	3,4
Tungsten (Wolfram)	W	74	183.85	6
Uranium	U	92	238.029	4,6
Vanadium	V	23	50.9414	3,5
Xenon	Xe	54	131.30	0
Ytterbium	Yb	70	173.04	2,3
Yttrium	Y	39	88.9059	3
Zinc	Zn	30	65.38	2
Zirconium	Zr	40	91.22	4

Notes: The atomic weights are based on the exact number 12 as assigned to the atomic mass of the principal isotope of carbon, carbon-12. Valence number is the combining power of an atom, the number of hydrogen atoms which an atom will combine with or replace. For example, the valence number of oxygen in water, H_2O, is 2.

Values in parentheses are for certain radioactive elements whose atomic weights cannot be quoted precisely without knowledge of origin; the value given in each case is the atomic mass no. of the isotope of longest known half-life.

NB: Gold and platinum occur in the earth as elements. Cadmium compounds are found in zinc ores.

SELECTED SPECIFIC GRAVITIES

Specific gravity is the ratio of a substance to the density of water at 39°F (4°C). It is numerically equal to the *density* in grams per cubic centimeter.

Substance	S.G.	Substance	S.G.
Alcohol	0.8	Pitch	1.1
Aluminum	2.7	Plaster of Paris	1.8
Asbestos	2.4	Platinum	21.9
Benzene	0.7	Polystyrene	1.06
Borax	1.7	Polythene	0.93
Butter	0.9	PVC	1.4
Charcoal	0.4	Sand	1.6
Copper	8.9	Silver	10.5
Cork	0.25	Steel (stainless)	7.8
Corundum	4.0	Talc	2.8
Diamond	3.5	Tar	1.0
Gold	19.3	Tin	7.3
Granite	2.7	Tungsten	19.3
Ice (at 32°F, 0°C)	0.92	Turpentine	0.85
Iridium	22.42	Uranium	19.0
Lead	11.3	Water	1.0
Limestone	2.6	sea water	1.03
Marble	2.7	Wood:	
Milk	1.03	balsa	0.2
Nylon	1.14	bamboo	0.4
Olive oil	0.9	beech	0.75
Osmium*	22.57	boxwood	1.0
Paraffin oil	0.8	cedar	0.55
Perspex	1.2	mahogany	0.8
Petroleum	0.8	teak	0.9

*Densest of all measurable elements

SIGNS USED IN ELECTRICAL DC CIRCUITS

Some signs used in drawing up electrical circuits.

Cell

Conventional current flow

Switch

Resistance

Variable resistance

Lamp

Capacitor

Galvanometer

CHEMICAL NAMES OF EVERYDAY SUBSTANCES

Substance	Chemical name
Baking powder	Sodium bicarbonate
Boracic acid	Boric acid
Borax	Sodium borate
Chalk	Calcium carbonate
Common salt	Sodium chloride
Epsom salts	Magnesium sulfate
Lime	Calcium oxide
Magnesia	Magnesium oxide
Plaster of Paris	Calcium sulfate
Red lead	Triplumbic tetroxide
Saltpeter	Potassium nitrate
Sal volatile	Ammonium carbonate
Vinegar	Dilute acetic acid
Washing soda	Crystalline sodium carbonate

Chalk

SI UNITS*

Basic units	Symbol	Measurement
meter	m	length
kilogram	kg	mass
second	s	time
ampere	A	electric current
kelvin	K	thermodynamic temperature
mole	mol	amount of substance
candela	cd	luminous intensity

Derived units

hertz	Hz	frequency
newton	N	force
pascal	Pa	pressure, stress
joule	J	energy, work, quantity of heat
watt	W	power, radiant flux
coulomb	C	electric charge, quantity of electricity
volt	V	electric potential, potential difference, emf
farad	F	capacitance
ohm	Ω	electric resistance
siemens	S	conductance
weber	Wb	magnetic flux
tesla	T	magnetic flux density
henry	H	inductance
lumen	lm	luminous flux
lux	lx	illuminance

Supplementary units

radian	rad	plane angle
steradian	sr	solid angle

* SI means *systéme internationale*

CHEMICAL INDICATORS

Indicators show whether a substance is alkaline or acid. The following list gives the effect of adding an indicator.

alkaline indicator:

litmus: turns blue

methyl orange: turns yellow

acid indicator:

litmus: turns red

methyl orange: turns pink

▼ **Quartz, shown below, is so hard** that it can cut glass. It often remains in the ground when other, softer minerals have worn away.

MOHS HARDNESS SCALE

Mineral	Simple hardness test	Mohs hardness
Talc	Crushed by fingernail	1.0
Gypsum	Scratched by fingernail	2.0
Calcite	Scratched by copper coin	3.0
Fluorspar	Scratched by glass	4.0
Apatite	Scratched by a penknife	5.0
Feldspar	Scratched by quartz	6.0
Quartz	Scratched by a steel file	7.0
Topaz	Scratched by corundum	8.0
Corundum	Scratched by diamond	9.0
Diamond		10.0

METALS AND THEIR ORES

More than 80 of the known chemical elements are metals. Ores are minerals from which metals can be produced commercially.

Metal	Ores	Important Uses
Aluminum	Bauxite	Cooking utensils, aircraft, foil, power lines
Antimony	Stibnite	Bearings, metal type (printing)
Beryllium	Beryl; chrysoberyl	In alloys to give strength and elasticity
Bismuth	Bismuth glance; bismite	Low-melting alloys
Calcium	Limestone; chalk; gypsum; apatite	Quicklime, bleaching powder
Chromium	Chromite	Stainless steel, toasters, heaters, resistance wire
Cobalt	Smaltite; cobaltite	Magnetic alloys, turbines, jet aircraft, cutting steel
Copper	Chalcopyrite; chalcocite; bornite	Electrical conductors, brass, bronze
Iron	Hematite; magnetite; siderite	Steel making
Lead	Galena	Car batteries, ammunition
Lithium	Spodumene	Lightweight alloys
Magnesium	Magnesite; dolomite; kieserite; carnallite	Lightweight alloys, tools
Manganese	Pyrolusite; hausmannite	Steel making
Mercury	Cinnabar	Thermometers, electric switches
Molybdenum	Molybdenite; powellite	Steel, X-ray tubes
Nickel	Pentlandite; millerite	Stainless steel, coins, plating
Potassium	Carnallite; saltpeter	Fertilizers, medicine, photography
Silver	Argentite; horn silver	Coins, tableware, jewelry
Sodium	Rock salt; chile saltpeter	Metallurgy, anti-knock gasoline, detergents, dyestuffs
Strontium	Strontianite; celestine	Fireworks, sugar refining
Tin	Cassiterite	Coating cans, solder, bronze
Titanium	Rutile; ilmenite	Aerospace, surgical aids
Uranium	Pitchblende	Nuclear fuel
Zinc	Sphalerite; calamine	Galvanizing, brass, dry batteries

▼ **Precious and semiprecious stones** belonging to the group of minerals called beryl, including emerald, aquamarine, golden beryl, and morganite.

ALLOYS

An alloy is a substance composed of two or more metals or of a metal and a nonmetal. Most alloys are made by melting the metals and mixing them together.

Name	Composition
Aluminum bronze	90% Cu, 10% Al
Manganese bronze	95% Cu, 5% Mn
Gun-metal bronze	90% Cu, 10% Sn
Red brass	90% Cu, 10% Zn
Naval brass	70% Cu, 29% Zn, 1% Sn
Yellow brass	67% Cu, 33% Zn
Nickel silver	55% Cu, 18% Ni, 27% Zn
Steel	99% Fe, 1% C
Stainless steel	Fe with 0.1–2.0% C, up to 27% Cr or 20% W or 15% Ni and lesser amounts of other elements
18-carat gold	75% Au, 25% Ag & Cu
Palladium, or white gold	90% Au, 10% Pd
Sterling silver	92.5% Ag, 7.5% Cu
U.S. silver	90% Ag, 10% Cu
Britannia metal	90% Sn, 10% Sb
Dentist's amalgam	70% Hg, 30% Cu
Type metal	82% Pb, 15% Sb, 3% Sn
Pewter	91% Pb, 7% Sb, 2% Cu

GEMSTONES

Nearly all gemstones are minerals, as are those in this table. The four nonmineral gems are amber, coral, jet, and pearl.

Mineral	Color	Mohs hardness
Agate	brown, red, blue, green, yellow	7.0
Amethyst	violet	7.0
Aquamarine	sky blue, greenish blue	7.5
Beryl	green, blue, pink	7.5
Bloodstone	green with red spots	7.0
Chalcedony	all colors	7.0
Citrine	yellow	7.0
Diamond	colorless, tints of various colors	10.0
Emerald	green	7.5
Garnet	red and other colors	6.5–7.25
Jade	green, whitish, mauve, brown	7.0
Lapis lazuli	deep blue	5.5
Malachite	dark green banded	3.5
Moonstone	whitish with blue shimmer	6.0
Onyx	various colors with straight colored bands	7.0
Opal	black, white, orange-red, rainbow colored	6.0
Ruby	red	9.0
Sapphire	blue, and other colors	9.0
Serpentine	red and green	3.0
Soapstone	white, may be stained with impurities	2.0
Sunstone	whitish red-brown flecked with golden particles	6.0
Topaz	blue, green, pink, yellow, colorless	8.0
Tourmaline	brown-black, blue, pink, red, violet-red, yellow, green	7.5
Turquoise	greenish gray, sky blue	6.0
Zircon	all colors	7.5

Engineering Records

LONGEST BRIDGE SPANS			
	Location	Longest span (ft.) (m)	Opened
Suspension			
Akashi-Kaikyo	Japan	5,840 1,780	*
Humber Estuary	England	4,626 1,410	1980
Verrazano-Narrows	New York City	4,260 1,298	1964
Golden Gate	San Francisco	4,200 1,280	1937
Cantilever			
Quebec Railway	Canada	1,800 549	1917
Forth Rail	Scotland	1,710 518	1890
Steel Arch			
New River Gorge	W. Virginia	1,700 518	1977
Bayonne	New Jersey	1,652 504	1931
Sydney Harbor	Australia	1,650 503	1932
Cable-Stayed			
Second Hooghly	Calcutta, India	1,500 457	**
St. Nazaire	Loire, France	1,325 404	1975
Duisburg-Neuenkamp	W. Germany	1,148 350	1970
Continuous Truss			
Astoria	Oregon	1,232 376	1966
Concrete Arch			
Gladesville	Australia	1,000 305	1964
Longest bridge (total length)			
Pontchartrain Causeway	Louisiana	23.9 mi 38.4 km	1969

* Under construction, completion planned for 1988
** Under construction

LONGEST TUNNELS			
	miles:yards	km	Opened
Railway[1]			
Seikan (Japan)	33:860	53.9	1985
Oshimizu (Japan)	13:1,400	22.2	1982
Simplon I & II (Switz./Italy)	12:560	19.8	1906, 1922
Road			
Arlberg (Austria)	8:1,200	14.0	1978
Mont Blanc (France/Italy)	7:350	11.6	1965
Underwater			
Seikan (Japan)[2]	14:880	23.3	1985
Shin Kanmon	11:1,070	18.7	1974

[1] Longest continuous vehicular tunnel is the Belyaevo–Medvedkovo stretch of the Moscow Metro underground railway (completed 1978/9): 19 miles 135 yd (30.7 km).
[2] Length of the underwater section of the Seikan Railway Tunnel.

▲ **Golden Gate suspension bridge** spans the entrance to San Francisco Bay. The main span is 4,200 feet (1,280 meters) long and the supporting towers are 745 feet (227 meters) above high water. The main steel cables are 3 feet (93 cm) in diameter.

The oldest bridge in the world (that can be dated) spans the river Meles, Izmir, Turkey. This single-arch, slab-stone bridge dates back to c.850 B.C.

TALLEST STRUCTURES

The world's tallest building is the 110-story, 1,454-foot (443-meter) Sears Tower in Chicago, Illinois. With TV antennae, it reaches 1,559 feet (475.2 meters). The world's tallest structure is the 2,120-foot (646-meter) mast of Warszawa Radio at Konstantynow, near Plock, in Poland. Made of galvanized steel, it was completed in July 1974.

The highest structures of ancient times were the pyramids of Egypt. The Great Pyramid of Cheops, at el-Gizeh, built in about 2580 B.C., reached a height of 481 feet (146.5 meters). It was another 4,000 years before this was surpassed—by the central tower of Lincoln Cathedral, England, which was completed in 1548 and stood 525 feet (160 meters) before it toppled.

HIGHEST & LARGEST DAMS

Highest	Location	Type	(ft.)	(m)	Completed
Nurek	U.S.S.R.	earthfill	1040	317	1980
Grande Dixence	Switzerland	gravity	932	284	1962
Inguri	U.S.S.R.	arch	892	272	1980
Vajont	Italy	multi-arch	858	262	1961
Mica	Canada	rockfill	794	242	1973
Mauvoisin	Switzerland	arch	777	237	1958

Largest[1]	Location	(cub. yd)	(cub. m)	Completed
New Cornelia	Arizona	274,026,000	209,506,000	1973
Tarbela	Pakistan	186,000,000	148,000,000	1979
Fort Peck	Montana	125,600,000	96,000,000	1940
Oahe	S. Dakota	92,000,000	70,000,000	1963
Mangla	Pakistan	85,870,000	65,650,000	1967
Gardiner	Canada	85,740,000	65,550,000	1968
Oroville	California	78,000,000	60,000,000	1968

[1] All earthfill except Tarbela (earth and rockfill).

The Arts

Art is long, but life is short.
   Hippocrates, ancient Greek physician.

From cave paintings and primitive musical instruments made of sticks to electronic music and computer graphics, the arts have always been a part of our lives. The arts—writing, painting and sculpture, music, theater and dance—are tools of communication. Through the arts we can express our emotions and convey ideas to other people. The arts also mean entertainment. We can sit back and forget our everyday lives as we watch a comedy show or listen to an

▲ **Dutch artist Vincent Van Gogh** (1853–90) painted this country view—the Plain of the Crau, east of Arles in the south of France—in 1888. The scene is rural but full of human activity—farm workers, haystacks, carts, and cottages.

opera. Various art forms have a vital role in education. Colorful images and catchy tunes put ideas across in a way that is enjoyable and so easier to remember. This is very useful when working with people who have one sense that is not working properly. A child who cannot speak can communicate and learn through color and pictures. There is art in everyone's life—it is often just a question of learning to look for it.

Music

SYMBOLS AND NOTATION

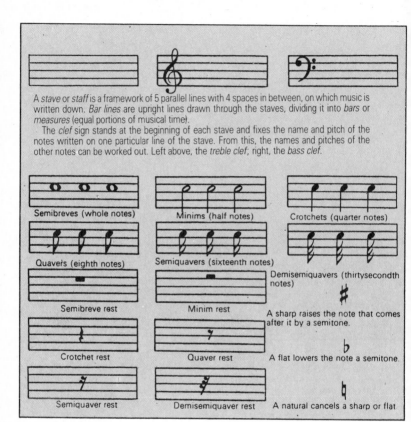

A *stave* or *staff* is a framework of 5 parallel lines with 4 spaces in between, on which music is written down. *Bar lines* are upright lines drawn through the staves, dividing it into *bars* or *measures* (equal portions of musical time).

The *clef* sign stands at the beginning of each stave and fixes the name and pitch of the notes written on one particular line of the stave. From this, the names and pitches of the other notes can be worked out. Left above, the *treble clef*; right, the *bass clef*.

Semibreves (whole notes)

Minims (half notes)

Crotchets (quarter notes)

Quavers (eighth notes)

Semiquavers (sixteenth notes)

Demisemiquavers (thirtysecondth notes)

Semibreve rest

Minim rest

A sharp raises the note that comes after it by a semitone.

Crotchet rest

Quaver rest

A flat lowers the note a semitone.

Semiquaver rest

Demisemiquaver rest

A natural cancels a sharp or flat

THE TONIC SOL-FA

The tonic sol-fa is a method of musical notation using letters and syllables instead of notes on a stave. It was devised by the English musician John Curwen (1816–80), who based it on the system known as solmization used in the Middle Ages.

The eight notes of a major scale are denoted by the syllables do, re, mi, fa, so (or sol), la, ti, do. It works for any scale by just changing the note which represents do. Sharpened and flattened notes are indicated by changing the vowel sounds (for example, sol sharp is se, and ti flat is taw).

INSTRUMENTS OF THE ORCHESTRA

Below you can see the major instruments in a classical orchestra and how they are arranged in relation to the conductor. The orchestra really developed in the 1700s. Today there can be more than 100 players in a symphony orchestra. Some types of music require more of one type of instrument. For example, the music of Bach, Mozart, and Beethoven needs a large string section, but small percussion, brass, and woodwind sections.

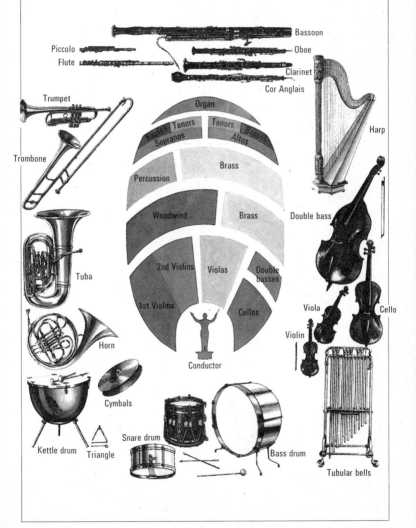

143

Musical Terms

allegro Fast and lively.

alto Higher in pitch than tenor, but lower than soprano.

andante At a moderate speed.

bar A division of music, marked by two bar-lines, containing a set number of beats.

baritone Low in pitch, but not as low as bass.

bass Generally low in pitch; also lower than baritone.

beat The basic pulse of a piece of music.

chord A group of notes played at the same time.

concerto A piece of music that features a solo instrument, such as a piano, with an orchestra.

flat (♭) A note one semitone below another note; B flat is a semitone below B. Also, slightly too low in pitch.

forte (f) Loud.

fortissimo (ff) Very loud.

key The basic note of the main scale used in a piece of music. Music in the key of G, for example, has the sound of being based on the note G and often returns to G as a home note.

largo Very slow.

major Music in a major key uses a major scale, in which the first three notes are the key note followed by intervals of a tone and then another tone (for example, C, D, E). It often has a cheerful, strong sound.

minor Music in a minor key uses a minor scale, in which the first three notes are the key note followed by intervals of a tone and then a semitone (for example, A, B, C). It often has a sad, melancholy sound.

movements The separate sections into which a long piece of music is divided.

natural A note that is neither flattened nor sharpened.

octave A note that sounds twice as high in pitch as another is an octave above the other note, and has the same letter naming it.

opus A single work or set of works by a composer.

pianissimo (pp) Very soft.

piano (p) Soft.

presto Very fast.

rallentando (rall) Getting slower.

scale A series of notes arranged in ascending or descending order of pitch.

semitone The smallest interval of pitch normally used in Western music. It is the interval between any two notes next to each other on a keyboard.

sharp (♯) Any note a semitone higher than another note; C sharp is a semitone higher than C. Also, slightly too high in pitch.

sonata A long work for one or two players, usually in three or four movements.

soprano The highest class of voice in pitch, or the highest-pitched members of a family of instruments.

symphony A large work for orchestra, usually in three or four movements.

tenor Lower in pitch than alto, but higher than baritone.

tone An interval equal to two semitones. Also, the sound quality of an instrument or voice.

treble Generally high in pitch.

THE ELEMENTS OF MUSIC

Pitch and Melody The pitch of a note depends on how high (*treble*) or low (*bass*) it sounds. A group of notes of different pitches gives a melody or *tune*.

Tempo and Rhythm The tempo of a piece of music is the speed at which it goes—fast, medium, or slow. Rhythm is the pattern made by the different lengths of the notes.

Harmony When two or more notes sound together, the combined sound is a harmony or *chord*.

Counterpoint When two different melodies are played together, counterpoint is produced.

Tone Tone is the quality of sound, either of a voice or of an instrument. (Also, *see entry above*.)

▶ *Above:* **The young Mozart** wearing splendid clothes given to him by the Empress Maria Theresa in Vienna in 1762. *Below:* Unlike Mozart, Joseph Haydn never fell on hard times because of his generous patrons, the Esterházy family. Today you can still see this family's magnificent palace at Eisenstadt, Austria.

FAMOUS CLASSICAL COMPOSERS

Antonio Vivaldi, Italian (*c.* 1678–1741)
George Frideric Handel, German (1685–1759)
Johann Sebastian Bach, German (1685–1750)
Joseph Haydn, Austrian (1732–1809)
Wolfgang Amadeus Mozart, Austrian (1756–91)
Ludwig van Beethoven, German (1770–1827)
Franz Schubert, Austrian (1797–1828)
Hector Berlioz, French (1803–69)
Felix Mendelssohn, German (1809–47)
Fréderic Chopin, Polish (1810–49)
Robert Schumann, German (1810–56)
Franz Liszt, Hungarian (1811–86)
Giuseppe Verdi, Italian (1813–1901)
Richard Wagner, German (1813–83)
Johannes Brahms, German (1833–97)
Georges Bizet, French (1838–75)
Peter Ilyich Tchaikovsky, Russian (1840–93)
Anton Dvořák, Czech (1841–1904)
Edvard Grieg, Norwegian (1843–1907)
Edward Elgar, British (1857–1934)
Giacomo Puccini, Italian (1858–1924)
Gustav Mahler, Austrian (1860–1911)
Claude Debussy, French (1862–1918)
Jean Sibelius, Finnish (1865–1957)
Sergei Rachmaninov, Russian (1873–1943)
Maurice Ravel, French (1875–1937)
Charles Ives, American (1874–1954)
Arnold Schoenberg, Austrian (1874–1951)
Béla Bartók, Hungarian (1881–1945)
Igor Stravinsky, Russian (1882–1971)
Sergei Prokofiev, Russian (1891–1953)
George Gershwin, American (1898–1937)
Dmitri Shostakovich, Russian (1906–75)
Benjámin Britten, British (1913–76)
Karlheinz Stockhausen, German (1928–)

Jazz

▲ **The Original Dixieland Jazz Band.**
Inset: Scott Joplin (1868–1917), father of ragtime music. Ragtime is a style of piano playing with an up-and-down rhythm or "ragged time." It became popular around 1900 and the craze spread to Europe. In the 1920s ragtime's popularity was overtaken by jazz.

The first jazz record was made in 1917. It featured "The Dark Town Strutters Ball" and "Indiana." The performers were the Original Dixieland Jazz Band.

Jazz owes a great debt to the Civil War. The music began in New Orleans when black people got together and played in the streets. Their instruments were cornets, clarinets, and trombones that had belonged to the army during the Civil War.

JAZZ GIANTS

Count Basie (1904–84) Pianist and band leader of the big-band swing sound.
Dave Brubeck (1920–) Jazz pianist and leader of famous quintet.
John Coltrane (1926–67) Influential improviser on tenor and alto saxophones.
Miles Davis (1926–) Important 1950s jazz trumpeter; advanced jazz/rock fusion in 1960s.
Duke Ellington (1899–1974) Major jazz composer, pianist, and band leader.
Dizzy Gillespie (1917–) Jazz trumpeter and pioneer of bebop style.
Benny Goodman (1909–86) Clarinettist and swing band leader.
Billie Holiday (1915–59) Great jazz singer at her best in 1930s and 1940s.
Jelly Roll Morton (1885–1941) Jazz pianist and composer; vital link between ragtime and jazz in 1920s.
Charlie "Bird" Parker (1920–55) Bebop alto saxophonist.
Oscar Peterson (1925–) Canadian jazz piano improviser.
Django Reinhardt (1910–53) First major European jazz musician. Belgian Gypsy guitarist with only seven fingers.
Bessie Smith (1894–1937) Blues singer; great influence on jazz and pop.
Grover Washington, Jr. (1943–) Saxophonist who successfully fused jazz with soul music.

◀ **Louis "Satchmo" Armstrong** (1900–71). Famous for his distinctive, gravelly singing style and for pioneering jazz improvisation in the 1920s with his trumpet solos.

▲ **Bob Geldof** (at microphone) organized a huge Live Aid pop concert in July 1985. Top artists performed in concerts—one in England and one in the United States—that took place simultaneously. More than $70 million was raised for the starving in Ethiopia.

Pop Music

The term "pop" is generally not used today to describe all "popular" (non-classical) music. Jazz and folk are popular forms that are usually considered separately. Today's mass-market, mainstream pop really started as rock and roll in the 1950s, which in turn grew out of the fusion of black rhythm and blues and white country-and-western music.

SOME GREATS OF POP

David Bowie (born 1947) British singer-songwriter with powerfully imaginative style and presentation.
Bob Dylan (born 1941) Influential American singer-songwriter who fused early 1960s folk style with rock.
Jimi Hendrix (1942–70) American, often said to be rock's all-time greatest guitarist.
Buddy Holly (1936–59) American singer-songwriter with simple, direct style. Very short career.
Bob Marley (1945–81) Jamaican who, with his group the Wailers, popularized reggae music.
Elvis Presley (1935–77) American singer who burst onto the scene in the 1950s with "new" music—rock 'n' roll. Rock's first superstar.
Stevie Wonder (born 1950) American singer-songwriter and musician, born blind; major figure for 20 years.

TOP RECORDS

● Greatest selling record to date is Irving Berlin's *White Christmas*. Bing Crosby's famous 1942 recording has sold 30 million, and more than 100 million copies of other versions have been sold.

● The greatest-selling pop record to date is *Rock Around the Clock*. Recorded in 1954 by Bill Haley and the Comets, it has sold around 25 million copies.

● Michael Jackson's *Thriller* is the biggest-selling album ever. By the end of 1985, 39 million copies had been sold.

● The most successful group in terms of record sales was the Beatles, from Liverpool, England. The Beatles split up in 1970. By summer 1985 estimates show that more than one billion Beatles records and tapes had been sold.
   The next most successful group is thought to be ABBA. These four Swedes had sold 215 million records and tapes by 1985.

● Paul McCartney, one-time member of the Beatles, and subsequently of Wings, is the biggest-selling songwriter ever. Either jointly or alone, he notched up 43 million-selling songs between 1962 and 1978.

Dance

THE BALLET

arabesque Position in which dancer stands on one leg with arms extended, body bent forward from hips, while other leg is stretched out backward.

ballerina Female ballet dancer.

barre Exercise bar fixed to classroom wall at hip level; dancers grasp it while exercising.

battement Beating movement made by raising and lowering leg, sideways, backward, or forward.

corps de ballet Main group of ballet dancers, as distinct from soloists.

entrechat Leap in which dancer rapidly strikes heels together in air.

fouetté Turn in which dancer whips free leg around.

glissade Gliding movement.

jeté Leap from one foot to another.

pas Any dance step.

pas de deux Dance for two.

pas seule Solo dance.

pirouette Movement in which dancer spins completely around on one foot.

plié Bending knees while keeping back straight.

positions Five positions of feet on which ballet is based (*see illustrations*). These were devised by Louis XIV's dance master—Pierre Beauchamp.

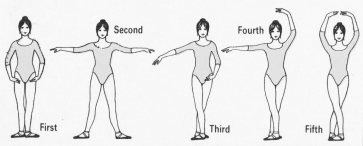

First   Second   Third   Fourth   Fifth

▶ **Traditional ballet**—principal dancers and the corps in a London Festival Ballet production of *Swan Lake*.

◀ **The more experimental style** of American choreographer, designer, and composer Alwin Nikolais.

Famous Dance Names

Ashton, Sir Frederick (William Mallandaine) (born 1906), a choreographer of classical lyrical style; born in Ecuador. He was a dancer and a choreographer with Ballet Club (later Ballet Rambert) and the Vic-Wells company (later the Royal Ballet), and later a director of the Royal Ballet.

Astaire, Fred (Frederick Austerlitz) (born 1899), American dancer and actor, began in vaudeville and musicals, moving on to success in films, often partnering Ginger Rogers.

De Valois, Dame Ninette (Edris Stannus) (born 1898), born in Ireland; a dancer in Diaghilev's Ballets Russes. In 1931, she created the Vic-Wells company (later the Royal Ballet) and directed it until 1963.

Diaghilev, Sergei (1872–1929), Russian, whose exciting Ballets Russes company toured Europe and America from 1909 to 1929.

Duncan, Isadora (1878–1927), American dancer, created a style of dancing based on simple, natural, and graceful movement, such as walking and running. Danced barefoot, dressed in simple tunics and long, flowing scarves, on a stage without any scenery.

Fokine, Michel (1880–1942), Russian-born dancer and choreographer, helped to create a more natural style of ballet. He choreographed over 60 ballets, most of them for Diaghilev's company.

Fonteyn, Dame Margot (Margaret Hookham) (born 1919), English ballerina, joined the Vic-Wells Ballet (now the Royal Ballet) in 1934 and became its leading ballerina. Danced as a guest artist all around the world.

Graham, Martha (born 1894). An American who pioneered new dance system of angular movements and floor work in the 1930s and 1940s.

Helpmann, Sir Robert (1909–86), Australian choreographer and film and theater actor; became a dancer in the Vic-Wells Ballet (now the Royal Ballet) in 1933. Also a director of the Australian Ballet.

Kelly, Gene (born 1912), American dancer, choreographer, actor, and director of stage and film musicals.

Markova, Dame Alicia (born 1910). One of the English dancers in Diaghilev's Ballet Russes. Later formed her own company.

Nijinsky, Vaslav (1890–1950), Russian, regarded by many as world's greatest ever ballet dancer. Noted for high leaps and brilliant entrechats. Joined Diaghilev's Ballets Russes in 1909, and also created several ballets.

Nureyev, Rudolf (born 1938), a Russian ballet dancer, choreographer, and producer, began his career in the Kirov Ballet in 1958. When on tour with the company in Paris in 1961, he ran away. He then danced with various companies in the West, and formed a long partnership with Margot Fonteyn in the Royal Ballet.

Pavlova, Anna (1881–1931), a Russian ballerina who settled in England, was prima ballerina in the Imperial Russian Ballet from 1906 to 1913. She also danced abroad and appeared with Diaghilev's company. In 1914, she formed her own company and toured the world presenting the classics.

Ulanova, Galina (born 1910), great Russian ballerina; with Kirov Ballet 1928–44 and Bolshoi Ballet until 1962.

Theater—Some Famous People

Beckett, Samuel (born 1906), Irish playwright and novelist, famous for plays that forcefully express the absurdity of humankind's existence, such as *Waiting for Godot* and *Endgame*.

Bernhardt, Sarah (1844–1923), the leading French actress of her day, notable for powerful acting in tragedies and beautiful voice. Roles included Cordelia in *King Lear*, Hamlet in *Hamlet*, and the Queen in *Ruy Blas*.

Brecht, Berthold (1898–1956), German writer and theater producer, in U.S.A. during Nazi era. Plays include *The Caucasian Chalk Circle* and *Threepenny Opera*.

Chekhov, Anton (1860–1904), Russian playwright. Plays include *Uncle Vanya*, *The Three Sisters*, and *The Cherry Orchard*. His plays are mainly about the behavior of passive, tragic characters.

Coward, Sir Noël (1899–1973), English playwright, musical composer, and actor, became famous as a playwright in the 1920s. Best plays include *Hay Fever, Private Lives, Blithe Spirit*, and *Present Laughter*. Also wrote successful revues and musicals.

Goethe, Johann Wolfgang von (1749–1832), German poet, playwright, and novelist. His most famous work, *Faust*, a long poetic drama in two parts, tells the legendary story of the man who sells his soul to the Devil.

Ibsen, Henrik (1828–1906), Norwegian dramatist, became internationally known for his realistic, but also increasingly symbolic, plays about problems of modern life. Plays include *Ghosts, A Doll's House, The Wild Duck*, and *Hedda Gabler*.

Jonson, Ben (c. 1573–1637), English poet and playwright; plays include *The Alchemist* and *Volpone*.

Molière (Jean Baptiste Poquelin) (1622–73), French writer of comedies and actor. Ran a theater company for which he wrote many plays. In them, he pokes fun at character faults such as miserliness, hypocrisy, and affectation. Plays include *The Miser, Tartuffe*, and *The Misanthrope*.

Olivier, Lord (Laurence Olivier) (born 1907), distinguished English actor, became famous as leading player of Shakespearean roles, but also acted in a wide range of plays and in many films. He also directed the National Theatre.

O'Neill, Eugene (1888–1953), American playwright; wrote series of successful plays between 1920 and 1934, of which *Mourning Becomes Electra* is best known. Later plays included *The Iceman Cometh*.

Osborne, John (born 1929), English playwright, became known for his play *Look Back in Anger* (1956), an attack

▼ **Henrik Ibsen** was one of the pioneers of "naturalistic" theater.

150

on contemporary Britain which was hailed as a turning point in modern drama. Other successes included *The Entertainer*, *Luther*, and *Inadmissible Evidence*.

Pinter, Harold (born 1930), English playwright and actor. The sparse, seemingly absurd dialogue in plays such as *The Birthday Party* and *The Caretaker* caused initial shock.

Shakespeare, William (1564–1616), Britain's greatest dramatist; also an actor and writer of beautiful sonnets. His 36 plays include historical dramas, such as *Henry V* and *Julius Caesar*; comedies— *A Midsummer Night's Dream* and *The Taming of the Shrew*; tragedies— *Hamlet*, *King Lear*, and *Romeo and Juliet*; and fantasy romances—*The Tempest*.

Shaw, George Bernard (1856–1950), Irish-born dramatist, wrote popular plays that expressed his own bold ideas in brilliant, witty dialogue. Best-known plays include *Arms and the Man*, *Man and Superman*, *Pygmalion*, *Heartbreak House*, and *Saint Joan*.

Sheridan, Richard Brinsley (1751–1816), Irish-born playwright, theater manager, and politician. His three great "comedy of manners" plays are *The Rivals*, *School for Scandal*, and *The Critic*.

Sophocles (c.496–c.406 B.C.), ancient Greek tragic playwright; seven surviving plays include *Antigone*, *Oedipus Rex*, and *Electra*.

Wilde, Oscar (1854–1900), Irish dramatist and novelist, best remembered for witty, social plays about the upper classes. These include *Lady Windermere's Fan*, *An Ideal Husband*, and *The Importance of Being Earnest*.

THEATER RECORDS

● The longest continuous run of any play at one theater ended on March 23, 1974, after 8,860 performances of *The Mousetrap*, by Agatha Christie. Having spent 22 years at the Ambassador's Theatre, London, it moved to the St. Martin's next door.

● The oldest indoor theater still in use is the Teatro Olimpico, in Vicenza, Italy. Completed in 1583, it was designed according to the principles of the Roman writer Vitruvius by Andrea di Pietro (also called Palladio).

● The first theater in Britain was built by James Burbage in 1576, and called simply "The Theatre." Later, it was dismantled and its timbers used to build Shakespeare's Globe Theatre.

● The oldest national theater in the world is the Comédie Française, established in 1680 by order of Louis XIV. It was formed by combining the three most important companies then playing in Paris.

LONG RUNS ON THE NEW YORK STAGE

*Chorus Line	6,371
*Oh! Calcutta! (revival)	5,358
*42nd Street	3,256
Grease	3,388
Fiddler on the Roof	3,242
Life With Father	3,224
Tobacco Road	3,182
Hello Dolly	2,844
My Fair Lady	2,717
Annie	2,377

* Still running in 1988

LONG RUNS ON THE LONDON STAGE

*The Mousetrap	14,280
No Sex Please, We're British	6,761
The Black and White Minstrel Show	4,354
Oh! Calcutta!	3,918
Jesus Christ Superstar	3,357
Evita	2,900
Oliver!	2,618
The Rocky Horror Show	2,599
There's a Girl in My Soup	2,547
Pyjama Tops	2,498

* Still running at time of going to press.

Motion Pictures

Today there are many different awards given around the world for outstanding achievement in the film industry. The most publicized and best-known award is the Oscar. Oscars are awarded by the United States Academy of Motion Picture Arts and Sciences.

ACADEMY AWARDS (OSCARS)

Best Film

1927–28	Wings
1928–29	The Broadway Melody
1929–30	All Quiet on the Western Front
1930–31	Cimarron
1931–32	Grand Hotel
1932–33	Cavalcade
1934	It Happened One Night
1935	Mutiny on the Bounty
1936	The Great Ziegfeld
1937	The Life of Emile Zola
1938	You Can't Take It With You
1939	Gone With the Wind
1940	Rebecca
1941	How Green Was My Valley
1942	Mrs. Miniver
1943	Casablanca
1944	Going My Way
1945	The Lost Weekend
1946	The Best Years of Our Lives
1947	Gentleman's Agreement
1948	Hamlet
1949	All the King's Men
1950	All About Eve
1951	An American in Paris
1952	The Greatest Show on Earth
1953	From Here to Eternity
1954	On the Waterfront
1955	Marty
1956	Around the World in 80 Days
1957	The Bridge on the River Kwai
1958	Gigi
1959	Ben Hur
1960	The Apartment
1961	West Side Story
1962	Lawrence of Arabia
1963	Tom Jones
1964	My Fair Lady
1965	The Sound of Music
1966	A Man for All Seasons
1967	In the Heat of the Night
1968	Oliver!
1969	Midnight Cowboy
1970	Patton
1971	The French Connection
1972	The Godfather
1973	The Sting
1974	The Godfather, Part II
1975	One Flew Over the Cuckoo's Nest
1976	Rocky
1977	Annie Hall
1978	The Deer Hunter
1979	Kramer vs. Kramer
1980	Ordinary People
1981	Chariots of Fire
1982	Gandhi
1983	Terms of Endearment
1984	Amadeus
1985	Out of Africa
1986	Platoon
1987	The Last Emperor

Best Actor

1927–28	Emil Jannings (The Way of All Flesh and The Last Command)
1928–29	Warner Baxter (In Old Arizona)
1929–30	George Arliss (Disraeli)
1930–31	Lionel Barrymore (A Free Soul)
1931–32	Frederick March (Dr. Jekyll and Mr. Hyde) Wallace Beery (The Champ)
1932–33	Charles Laughton (The Private Life of Henry VIII)
1934	Clark Gable (It Happened One Night)
1935	Victor McLaglen (The Informer)
1936	Paul Muni (The Story of Louis Pasteur)
1937	Spencer Tracy (Captains Courageous)
1938	Spencer Tracey (Boy's Town)
1939	Robert Donat (Goodbye Mr. Chips)
1940	James Stewart (The Philadelphia Story)
1941	Gary Cooper (Sergeant York)
1942	James Cagney (Yankee Doodle Dandy)
1943	Paul Lukas (Watch on the Rhine)
1944	Bing Crosby (Going My Way)
1945	Ray Milland (The Lost Weekend)
1946	Frederic March (The Best Years of Our Lives)

1947	Ronald Colman (*A Double Life*)
1948	Laurence Olivier (*Hamlet*)
1949	Broderick Crawford (*All the King's Men*)
1950	Jose Ferrer (*Cyrano de Bergerac*)
1951	Humphrey Bogart (*The African Queen*)
1952	Gary Cooper (*High Noon*)
1953	William Holden (*Stalag 17*)
1954	Marlon Brando (*On the Waterfront*)
1955	Ernest Borgnine (*Marty*)
1956	Yul Brynner (*The King and I*)
1957	Alec Guinness (*The Bridge on the River Kwai*)
1958	David Niven (*Separate Tables*)
1959	Charlton Heston (*Ben-Hur*)
1960	Burt Lancaster (*Elmer Gantry*)
1961	Maximilian Schell (*Judgment at Nuremberg*)
1962	Gregory Peck (*To Kill a Mockingbird*)
1963	Sidney Poitier (*Lilies of the Field*)
1964	Rex Harrison (*My Fair Lady*)
1965	Lee Marvin (*Cat Ballou*)
1966	Paul Scofield (*A Man for All Seasons*)
1967	Rod Steiger (*In the Heat of the Night*)
1968	Cliff Robertson (*Charly*)
1969	John Wayne (*True Grit*)
1970	George C. Scott (*Patton*)
1971	Gene Hackman (*The French Connection*)
1972	Marlon Brando (*The Godfather*)
1973	Jack Lemmon (*Save the Tiger*)
1974	Art Carney (*Harry and Tonto*)
1975	Jack Nicholson (*One Flew Over the Cuckoo's Nest*)
1976	Peter Finch (*Network*)
1977	Richard Dreyfus (*Goodbye Girl*)
1978	Jon Voight (*Coming Home*)
1979	Dustin Hoffman (*Kramer vs. Kramer*)
1980	Robert De Niro (*Raging Bull*)
1981	Henry Fonda (*On Golden Pond*)

▲ **In the 1977 film *Star Wars*,** Princess Leia sends a hologram of herself to ask for help. This film still stands at number two in the American all-time top 50 of films. *Star Wars* started a whole string of action-packed fantasy films with spectacular special effects. Alec Guinness, on the left, appears in a very different role from that which won him an Oscar twenty years before.

FILM FEATS

● Walt Disney (1901–66) holds the record number of Oscar awards—32 including certificates, plaques, etc.

● Katharine Hepburn is the only person to win four Oscar awards in major roles.

● All-time record for the highest value box office receipts in one day—$33 million—is held by the 1987 film *Beverly Hills Cop II*, starring Eddie Murphy.

1982	Ben Kingsley (*Gandhi*)
1983	Robert Duvall (*Tender Mercies*)
1984	F. Murray Abraham (*Amadeus*)
1985	William Hurt (*Kiss of the Spider Woman*)
1986	Paul Newman (*The Color of Money*)
1987	Michael Douglas (*Wall Street*)

Best Actress

1927–28	Janet Gaynor (*Seventh Heaven, Street Angel*, and *Sunrise*)
1928–29	Mary Pickford (*Coquette*)
1929–30	Norma Shearer (*The Divorcee*)
1930–31	Marie Dressler (*Min and Bill*)
1931–32	Helen Hayes (*The Sin of Madelon Claudet*)
1932–33	Katharine Hepburn (*Morning Glory*)
1934	Claudette Colbert (*It Happened One Night*)
1935	Bette Davis (*Dangerous*)
1936	Luise Rainer (*The Great Ziegfeld*)
1937	Luise Rainer (*The Good Earth*)
1938	Bette Davis (*Jezebel*)
1939	Vivien Leigh (*Gone With the Wind*)
1940	Ginger Rogers (*Kitty Foyle*)
1941	Joan Fontaine (*Suspicion*)
1942	Greer Garson (*Mrs. Miniver*)
1943	Jennifer Jones (*The Song of Bernadette*)
1944	Ingrid Bergman (*Gaslight*)
1945	Joan Crawford (*Mildred Pierce*)
1946	Olivia de Havilland (*To Each His Own*)
1947	Loretta Young (*The Farmer's Daughter*)
1948	Jane Wyman (*Johnny Belinda*)
1949	Olivia de Havilland (*The Heiress*)
1950	Judy Holliday (*Born Yesterday*)
1951	Vivien Leigh (*A Streetcar Named Desire*)
1952	Shirley Booth (*Come Back, Little Sheba*)
1953	Audrey Hepburn (*Roman Holiday*)
1954	Grace Kelly (*The Country Girl*)
1955	Anna Magnani (*The Rose Tattoo*)
1956	Ingrid Bergman (*Anastasia*)
1957	Joanne Woodward (*The Three Faces of Eve*)
1958	Susan Hayward (*I Want to Live*)
1959	Simone Signoret (*Room at the Top*)
1960	Elizabeth Taylor (*Butterfield 8*)
1961	Sophia Loren (*Two Women*)
1962	Anne Bancroft (*The Miracle Worker*)
1963	Patricia Neal (*Hud*)
1964	Julie Andrews (*Mary Poppins*)
1965	Julie Christie (*Darling*)
1966	Elizabeth Taylor (*Who's Afraid of Virginia Woolf?*)
1967	Katharine Hepburn (*Guess Who's Coming to Dinner*)
1968	Katharine Hepburn (*A Lion in Winter*) Barbra Streisand (*Funny Girl*)
1969	Maggie Smith (*The Prime of Miss Jean Brodie*)
1970	Glenda Jackson (*Women in Love*)
1971	Jane Fonda (*Klute*)
1972	Liza Minnelli (*Cabaret*)
1973	Glenda Jackson (*A Touch of Class*)
1974	Ellen Burstyn (*Alice Doesn't Live Here Any More*)
1975	Louise Fletcher (*One Flew Over the Cuckoo's Nest*)
1976	Faye Dunaway (*Network*)
1977	Diane Keaton (*Annie Hall*)
1978	Jane Fonda (*Coming Home*)
1979	Sally Field (*Norma Rae*)
1980	Sissy Spacek (*Coal Miner's Daughter*)
1981	Katharine Hepburn (*On Golden Pond*)
1982	Meryl Streep (*Sophie's Choice*)
1983	Shirley MacLaine (*Terms of Endearment*)
1984	Sally Field (*Places in the Heart*)
1985	Geraldine Page (*The Trip to Bountiful*)
1986	Marlee Matlin (*Children of a Lesser God*)
1987	Cher (*Moonstruck*)

FILMMAKING TERMS

dolly Mobile carriage to carry a camera.

dubbing Adding sound to a film.

intercut shots Two related series of shots shown alternately, such as the heroine tied to the railway lines and the train approaching.

library shot Film taken from material already made and in stock.

pan Short for panoramic shot—a sideways sweep by the camera.

prop Short for property—an object used by an actor, such as a gun or a telephone.

rushes The day's shots, before editing.

set An area prepared for a film scene, either in a studio or outdoors.

shoot To photograph a scene.

take Part of a scene shot without interruption.

track in, track back To move a camera on its dolly toward or away from the subject.

zooming Using a variable lens to give the effect of tracking in or back.

Pottery

SOME HISTORIC POTTERY AND PORCELAIN FACTORIES

Belleek (Ireland)	1857–
Bennington (U.S.A.)	1793–1894
Bow (England)	1744–1776
Bristol (England)	1749–1781
Caughley (England)	1754–1814
Chantilly (France)	1725–1800
Chelsea (England)	1745–1784
Coalport (England)	1796–
Copenhagen (Denmark)	1774–
Derby (England)	1750–1848
Derby, Royal Crown	1876–
Frankenthal (Germany)	1755–1799
Greenpoint (U.S.A.)	1848–
Hoechst (Germany)	1750–1798
Limoges (France)	1771–
Liverpool (England)	1710–c. 1800
Ludwigsburg (Germany)	1758–1824
Meissen (Germany)	1710–
Mennecy (France)	1735–1785
Nymphenburg (Germany)	1753–
Sèvres (France)	1756–
Spode (England)	1770–
Tucker (U.S.A.)	1826–1838
Vincennes (France)	1738–1756
Wedgwood (England)	1759–
Worcester (England)	1751–

▼ A pot dating back to the days of the ancient Greeks. Some of their pots, like the ones you can see at Knossos, on the island of Crete, were as tall as a person, or even larger. They were used for storing grain and other foodstuffs.

CHINESE DYNASTIES

Chinese pottery and porcelain is dated by the dynasty (royal family) or individual emperor in whose time it was made. Some of the most important are:

Dynasty	Dates
Han	206 B.C.–A.D. 220
Three Kingdoms	220–265
Six Dynasties	265–588
Sui	589–618
T'ang	618–906
Five Dynasties	906–959
Sung	960–1279
Yüan (Mongol)	1280–1368
Ming	1368–1644
Ch'ing (Manchu)	1644–1912

(Emperor Chi'en Lung 1736–1795)

ANCIENT GREEK VESSELS

Many different sorts of vessels made by the ancient Greeks have been found. Below is a list of the main kinds.

amphora	storage jar
crater	large, open bowl
cylix	drinking cup
hydria	water pot
lecythos	oil flask
oinochoë	wine pitcher
rhyton	head-shaped cup

155

Sculpture

Brancusi, Constantin (1876–1957), Romanian

Calder, Alexander (1898–1973), American (developer of the mobile)

Donatello, Donato Di Niccolo (c. 1386–1466), Florentine

Michelangelo, Buonarroti (1475–1564), Italian

Moore, Henry (1898–1986), English

Rodin, François Auguste René (1840–1917), French

▼ Spanish-born painter and sculptor **Pablo Picasso** (1881–1973) sculpted this bronze figure of a cock.

SCULPTURE MATERIALS AND METHODS

The main materials used to make sculptures are clay, stone, wood, bronze and other metals, plastics, and bone, including ivory. The four commonest methods used for making a sculpture are modeling, carving, casting, and construction.

Modeling. The materials for modeling are wet clay, plaster, and plasticine, which can be shaped in the hands. The wet model is usually baked in a special oven to harden it. Clay models are often covered by a thin film of *glaze* for protection.

Carving. Materials used for carving include stone (especially marble) and wood. Sharp knives and chisels are needed to carve wood. Stone sculpture requires a punch and mallet, a hammer with a pointed steel head for rough work, a chisel with several teeth for finer detail, and files for smoothing the finished sculpture.

Casting. Casting is the most complex method of sculpture. It is used to make sculptures from molten metal, usually bronze. First a clay model is made. Then one of several possible methods is followed. In the *cire perdue* (lost wax) method, a plaster mold is made outside the clay model. The mold is then lined with wax, which is then covered with plaster. The whole mold is then heated. The melted wax runs out and hot metal is poured into the space left between the plaster layers. The result is a thinly cast metal sculpture.

Construction. Sculptures can be made by fixing pieces of material together to build up an object. Large metal sculptures can be welded together using welding equipment. Small hanging *mobiles* can be made by linking pieces of metal, wood, or plastic together with wires.

Major Movements in the Visual Arts

Abstract art A form of art in which some features of a subject are selected, or *abstracted*, so that the result is not purely realistic.

Art Nouveau (new art) A European and North American art style of the 1890s and 1900s. It is characterized by flowing, swirling lines often suggested by plants. Examples: Aubrey Beardsley, Alphonse Mucha.

Baroque art A highly decorative style characterized by vigorous, swirling action and complex design. It was followed mainly by artists in southern Europe in the 1600s and early 1700s. Examples: Peter Paul Rubens (painting), Gianlorenzo Bernini (sculpture).

Byzantine art The splendid, sumptuously rich art of the Byzantine Empire from about A.D. 450 to 1450. Artists portrayed mainly religious subjects.

Cubism An art style of the early 1900s. Artists aimed to show three-dimensional objects, including people, on a flat canvas from various points of view all at the same time. Example: Pablo Picasso.

Dadaism A movement in literature as well as art. Centered on Zurich-based group from 1915 to 1922. Sought to overturn traditional artistic values and promote the irrational. Examples: Marcel Duchamp, Max Ernst.

Expressionism A style in which artists express feeling by exaggerating certain colors or shapes. Examples: Vincent Van Gogh, Edvard Munch.

Impressionism An art movement of the 1870s. Artists tried to paint subjects realistically by carefully reproducing the complex colors in the light that falls on them. Examples: Claude Monet, Camille Pissarro, Alfred Sisley.

Op art A technique used by artists since the 1960s to suggest optical illusions, often by means of pattern and color. Example: Victor Vasarely.

Pop art An art form of the 1950s and 1960s. Artists used unexpected, ordinary objects, such as photographs, bottles, and cartoon strips, as their subjects and painted them in gaudy colors. Examples: Robert Rauschenberg (painting), Eduardo Paolozzi (sculpture).

Pre-Raphaelites A group of British artists of the mid-1800s who aimed to paint in the style of Italian artists before Raphael (1483–1520). They painted medieval or religious subjects, using great detail and bright colors. Examples: Holman Hunt, Dante Gabriel Rossetti, John Millais.

Primitives Artists without formal training who come to show great artistic merit. Example: Henri Rousseau.

Rococo A highly decorative style in art and interior decoration in the 1700s. Graceful curves and daintiness are characteristic features. Example: Antoine Watteau (painting).

Romanticism A period in the arts in the mid-1800s in which artists sought freedom from restraint. Typical Romantic features are love of liberty, extreme emotion, medieval subjects, and exotic landscapes. Examples: Eugene Delacroix and William Blake (painting).

Surrealism An artistic movement that began in the 1920s. Artists created a dreamlike or fantasy world suggesting hidden meanings. Example: Salvador Dali (painting).

Some Famous Painters

Bosch, Hieronymus (*c.* 1450–1516; Dutch); busy fantasy paintings, often religious allegories.

Botticelli, Sandro (*c.* 1444–1510; Italian); spent most of his life in Florence. Most of his paintings were religious, with clear, delicate lines.

Braque, Georges (1882–1963; French); painter and sculptor; one of the founders of Cubism.

Brueghel, Pieter (The Elder; *c.* 1520–1569; Flemish); renowned for bustling pictures of village life, often with hundreds of people in them.

Cézanne, Paul (1839–1906; French); famous for bold, strongly colored landscapes and still lifes.

Constable, John (1776–1837; English); one of the greatest landscape painters, who caught the character of the English countryside.

Dali, Salvador (born 1904; Spanish); Surrealist painter whose very detailed work often borders on the nightmarish.

Degas, Edgar (1834–1917; French); Impressionist, noted for his pictures of ballet dancers.

Gainsborough, Thomas (1727–88; English); highly sought-after "society" portrait painter. Influenced by Rubens.

Gauguin, Paul (1848–1903; French); escaped to the Pacific island of Tahiti where he painted local subjects in flat, bright color.

Giotto (*c.* 1266–1337; Italian); greatly influenced Renaissance art. Developed more realistic style than most painters of his day.

Goya, Francisco (1746–1828; Spanish); painted court people truthfully rather than flatteringly.

Greco, El ("The Greek"; *c.*1548–1614; Greek-Spanish); born Domenikos Theotocopoulos in Crete, worked in Venice and Spain.

Holbein, Hans the Younger (*c.* 1497–1543; German); portrait artist whose very realistic paintings include that of King Henry VIII of England.

Kandinsky, Wassily (1866–1944; Russian); Expressionist who is credited with having produced the first truly abstract painting.

Klee, Paul (1879–1940; Swiss); described his painting as "taking a line for a walk."

Leonardo da Vinci (1452–1519; Italian); painter, architect, sculptor, musician, inventor, and scientist.

Magritte, René (1898–1967; Belgian); Surrealist painter who created poetic paintings from the unusual arrangement of familiar objects.

▼ **A detail** taken from Cézanne's painting *The Bathers* (1898–1905). Cézanne's later work has been seen as early Cubism. Certainly his style here is beginning to look like that of later abstract artists.

Manet, Edouard (1832–83; French); rebellious Impressionist whose early work shocked the official art world.

Matisse, Henri (1869–1954; French); used bright, complimentary colors to capture natural light effects.

Michelangelo, Buonarroti (1475–1564; Italian); painted ceiling of Sistine Chapel, in the Vatican. Turned to architecture and designed the dome of St. Peter's Basilica, Rome.

Monet, Claude (1840–1926; French); Impressionist who used broken color to show natural light outdoors.

Picasso, Pablo (1881–1973; Spanish); spent most of his life in France. Introduced Cubism in 1907, which was to change the course of art.

Pollock, Jackson (1912–56; American); Abstract Expressionist, famous for his huge canvases covered with paint spills and drips—"action painting."

Raphael (1483–1520; Italian); greatly influenced by Michelangelo and Leonardo. Paintings have a serenity and perfect composition.

▼ **One of Rembrandt's** many self-portraits. This one was painted around 1660. Rembrandt's genius lay in painting portraits that really penetrated the character of the sitter.

Rembrandt van Rijn (1606–69; Dutch); fine portrait painter, made dramatic use of *chiaroscuro*. This is the effects of light and shade.

Renoir, Pierre Auguste (1841–1919; French); rich colors, especially pinks and reds, dominated his work.

Reynolds, Sir Joshua (1723–92; English); very influential person in the history of art. Prominent society portrait painter and, as the first president of the Royal Academy, his theories about art had enormous impact.

Rousseau, Henri (1844–1910; French); Primitive painter; childlike directness much admired by other painters.

Rubens, Peter Paul (1577–1640; Flemish); after eight years in Italy, became court painter in Antwerp, where assistants helped him produce huge religious and mythological paintings.

Titian (full name Tiziano Vecelli; *c.* 1487–1576; Italian); greatest Venetian painter. Painted many religious works for churches.

Turner, Joseph Mallord William (1775–1851; English); especially noted for watercolors and magnificent sunsets that became increasingly abstract.

Van Eyck, Jan (*c.* 1370–1441; Flemish); one of the earliest painters to use oil colors. Richly colored, detailed work.

Van Gogh, Vincent (1853–1890; Dutch); early, somber pictures gave way to bright, swirling style. Cut off part of one ear in a fit of madness.

Velasquez, Diego (1599–1660; Spanish); court painter in Madrid in 1623. Famous for portraits of Philip IV and his courtiers.

Vermeer, Jan (1632–75; Dutch); surviving paintings are beautiful, serene compositions with gentle play of light.

Architecture

ARCHITECTS

Adam, Robert (1728–92), Scottish
Bramante, Donato (1444–1514), Italian
Brunelleschi, Filippo (1377–1446), Italian
Gaudi, Antoni (1852–1926), Spanish
Gropius, Walter (1883–1969), German
Jones, Inigo (1573–1652), English
Le Corbusier (1887–1965), French-Swiss
Michelangelo (1475–1564), Italian
Mies van der Rohe, Ludwig (1886–1969), Ger./Amer.
Nash, John (1752–1835), English
Nervi, Pier Luigi (1891–1979), Italian
Palladio, Andrea (1508–80), Italian
Vitruvius Pollio, Marcus (1st century, A.D.), Roman
Wren, Sir Christopher (1632–1723), English
Wright, Frank Lloyd (1869–1959), American

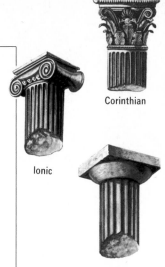

Corinthian

Ionic

Doric

PERIODS OF ARCHITECTURE

Greek	600s–100s B.C.
Roman	100s B.C.–A.D. 400s
Byzantine	A.D. 400s–1453
Romanesque	
(N. Europe)	mid-900s–late 1100s
Norman	
(England)	late 1000s–1100s
Gothic	mid-1100s–1400s
Renaissance	
(Italy)	1400s–1500s
French	
Renaissance	1500s
Baroque (Italy)	1600–1750
Georgian	
(England)	1725–1800
Rococo	mid-1700s
Regency	
(England)	1800–1825
Art Nouveau	
(Europe)	1890–1910
Expressionism	
(Germany)	1910–1930s
Functionalism	1920s–
International Style	1920s–
Brutalism	1950s–

▲ **The three** very different styles of Greek capital (column): Doric, Ionic, and Corinthian.

▼ **Sydney Opera House** in Sydney Harbor. Although it was not completed until 1973 it is a good example of 1960s architecture. Its complex design, based on the sails of boats, proved very difficult to build.

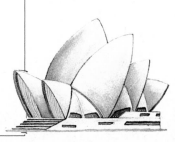

Literature – Some Important Writers

Andersen, Hans Christian (1805–75); Danish writer, famous for fairy tales such as *The Tinderbox*, *The Emperor's New Clothes*, and *The Snow Queen*.

Austen, Jane (1775–1817); English novelist, wrote about comfortably off country people, living by strict rules of behavior. Novels include *Sense and Sensibility*, *Pride and Prejudice*, and *Emma*.

Balzac, Honoré de (1799–1850); French novelist, wrote a series of 90 realistic stories about everyday life in France called the *Human Comedy*.

Brontë Family name of three English novelist sisters: **Charlotte** (1816–55), **Emily Jane** (1818–48), and **Anne** (1820–49). Charlotte's most famous novel is *Jane Eyre*. *Wuthering Heights*, a dramatic love story, is Emily's best work.

Byron, Lord George (1788–1824); English Romantic poet, wrote several long, narrative poems. The finest is *Don Juan*.

Carroll, Lewis (Charles Lutwidge Dodgson; 1832–98); best remembered for his stories *Alice's Adventures in Wonderland* and *Through the Looking Glass*.

Chaucer, Geoffrey (c. 1340–1400); English poet, famous for his *Canterbury Tales*, a collection of stories told by travelers on a journey.

Coleridge, Samuel Taylor (1772–1834); English Romantic poet, wrote the famous poem *The Rime of the Ancient Mariner*.

Dante, Alighieri (1265–1321); Italian poet, wrote *Divine Comedy*, a poem in three parts about a man's role on Earth.

Dickens, Charles (1812–70); English novelist, wrote stories about the harsh lives of ordinary people in industrial England such as *Great Expectations*, *David Copperfield*, and *Oliver Twist*.

Dostoevsky, Fyodor (1821–81); Russian novelist. Among his powerful stories are *Crime and Punishment*, *The Idiot*, and *The Brothers Karamazov*.

Eliot, George (Marian Evans) (1819–80); English novelist, whose novels include *The Mill on the Floss* and *Middlemarch*, a story about country people.

Eliot, T. S. (Thomas Stearns) (1888–1965); American-born British poet, dramatist, and critic; early poetry expressed frustration and despair.

Hemingway, Ernest (1898–1961); American novelist, wrote stories about adventurous, violent lives. Best known include *A Farewell to Arms* and *For Whom the Bell Tolls*.

Homer (700s B.C.); influential Greek poet, whose *Iliad* tells the story of the siege of Troy, while the *Odyssey* describes the travels of the hero Odysseus after the war.

Johnson, Dr. Samuel (1709–84); English poet and essayist, compiled a *Dictionary of the English Language*.

Joyce, James (1882–1941); Irish novelist, wrote stories about people in conflict with their surroundings.

Keats, John (1795–1821); English Romantic poet, composed narrative poems such as *Ode to Autumn* and *Ode to a Nightingale*.

Lawrence, D. H. (David Herbert) (1885–1930); English novelist whose best work is about working-class life, growing up, and natural love. *Sons and Lovers* and *Lady Chatterley's Lover*.

161

▲ **William Wordsworth.** Perhaps his most famous work is his long, autobiographical poem entitled *The Prelude*.

BRITISH POETS LAUREATE	
Ben Johnson	1619–1637
Sir William Davenant	1638–1668
John Dryden	1668–1688
Thomas Shadwell	1689–1692
Nahum Tate	1692–1715
Nicholas Rowe	1715–1718
Laurence Eusden	1718–1730
Colley Cibber	1730–1757
William Whitehead	1757–1785
Thomas Warton	1785–1790
Henry James Pye	1790–1813
Robert Southey	1813–1843
William Wordsworth	1843–1850
Lord Tennyson	1850–1892
Alfred Austin	1896–1913
Robert Bridges	1913–1930
John Masefield	1930–1967
Cecil Day Lewis	1968–1972
Sir John Betjeman	1972–1984
Ted Hughes	1984–

AMERICAN POETS LAUREATE	
Robert Penn Warren	1986
Richard Wilbur	1987
Howard Nemerov	1988

Milton, John (1608–74); English poet and religious and political writer. Most important works were long poems *Paradise Lost* and *Paradise Regained.*

Poe, Edgar Allan (1809–49); American short-story writer, poet, and critic; best known for his tales of mystery.

Rabelais, François (*c.* 1494–*c.* 1553); French priest and doctor, poked fun at life in his day in his books *Gargantua* and *Pantagruel.*

Scott, Sir Walter (1771–1832); Scottish novelist and poet. Wrote romantic adventures, often set in the Middle Ages, such as *Waverley* and *Ivanhoe.*

Shelley, Percy Bysshe (1792–1822); English Romantic poet, wrote idealistic poems including *Ode to a Skylark* and *The Cloud.*

Stevenson, Robert Louis (1850–94); Scottish novelist, wrote *Treasure Island* and *Kidnapped*, both adventure stories, and *Dr. Jekyll and Mr. Hyde*, a mystery.

Swift, Jonathan (1667–1745); Irish clergyman, wrote satirical pamphlets on religion and politics, but is best known for his story *Gulliver's Travels.*

Tennyson, Alfred Lord (1809–92); English poet, wrote *Break, Break, Break, The Charge of the Light Brigade*, and *Idylls of the King.*

Tolstoy, Count Leo (1828–1910); Russian novelist and playwright whose novel *War and Peace* traces the lives of several families during Napoleon's invasion of Russia.

Twain, Mark (Samuel Langhorne Clemens; 1835–1910); American novelist, wrote about American life, especially life along the Mississippi River, as in *The Adventures of Huckleberry Finn.*

Virgil (Publius Vergilius Maro) (70–19 B.C.); Roman poet, wrote the *Aeneid*, a famous long epic poem about the founding of Rome.

Wordsworth, William (1770–1850); an English poet, expressed his deep love of nature in beautiful, simple language.

Zola, Emile (1840–1902); French novelist and journalist.

LITERATURE: NOBEL PRIZE WINNERS

1901 René Sully Prudhomme (French)
1902 Theodor Mommsen (German)
1903 Björnstjerne Björnson (Norwegian)
1904 Frédéric Mistral (French) and José Echegaray (Spanish)
1905 Henryk Sienkiewicz (Polish)
1906 Giosuè Carducci (Italian)
1907 Rudyard Kipling (English)
1908 Rudolf Eucken (German)
1909 Selma Lagerlöf (Swedish)
1910 Paul von Heyse (German)
1911 Maurice Maeterlinck (Belgian)
1912 Gerhart Hauptmann (German)
1913 Sir Rabindranath Tagore (Indian)
1914 *No award*
1915 Romain Rolland (French)
1916 Verner von Heidenstam (Swedish)
1917 Karl Gjellerup and Henrik Pontoppidan (Danish)
1918 *No award*
1919 Carl Spitteler (Swiss)
1920 Knut Hamsun (Norwegian)
1921 Anatole France (French)
1922 Jacinto Benavente (Spanish)
1923 William Butler Yeats (Irish)
1924 Wladyslaw Reymont (Polish)
1925 George Bernard Shaw (Irish)
1926 Grazia Deledda (Italian)
1927 Henri Bergson (French)
1928 Sigrid Undset (Norwegian)
1929 Thomas Mann (German)
1930 Sinclair Lewis (American)
1931 Erik Karlfeldt (Swedish)
1932 John Galsworthy (English)
1933 Ivan Bunin (Russian)
1934 Luigi Pirandello (Italian)
1935 *No award*
1936 Eugene O'Neill (American)
1937 Roger Martin du Gard (French)
1938 Pearl S. Buck (American)
1939 Frans Eemil Sillanpää (Finnish)
1940–43 *No award*
1944 Johannes V. Jensen (Danish)
1945 Gabriela Mistral (Chilean)
1946 Hermann Hesse (Swiss)
1947 André Gide (French)

1948 Thomas Stearns Eliot (Anglo-American)
1949 William Faulkner (American)
1950 Bertrand Russell (English)
1951 Pär Lagerkvist (Swedish)
1952 François Mauriac (French)
1953 Sir Winston Churchill (English)
1954 Ernest Hemingway (American)
1955 Halldór Laxness (Icelandic)
1956 Juan Ramón Jiménez (Spanish)
1957 Albert Camus (French)
1958 Boris Pasternak (Russian) – declined
1959 Salvatore Quasimodo (Italian)
1960 Saint-John Perse (Alexis Saint-Léger) (French)
1961 Ivo Andric (Yugoslavian)
1962 John Steinbeck (American)
1963 George Seferis (Giorgios Seferiades) (Greek)
1964 Jean-Paul Sartre (French) – declined
1965 Mikhail Sholokhov (Russian)
1966 Shmuel Yosef Agnon (Israeli) and Nelly Sachs (Swedish)
1967 Miguel Angel Asturias (Guatemalan)
1968 Yasunari Kawabata (Japanese)
1969 Samuel Beckett (Irish)
1970 Alexander Solzhenitsyn (Russian)
1971 Pablo Neruda (Chilean)
1972 Heinrich Böll (W. German)
1973 Patrick White (Australian)
1974 Eyvind Johnson and Harry Edmund Martinson (Swedish)
1975 Eugenio Montale (Italian)
1976 Saul Bellow (American)
1977 V. Aleixandre (Spanish)
1978 Isaac Bashevis Singer (American)
1979 Odysseus Alepoudhelis (Greek) – known as Odysseus Elytis
1980 Czeslaw Milosz (Polish/American)
1981 Elias Canetti (Bulgarian)
1982 Gabriel Garcia Marquez (Colombian/Mexican)
1983 William Golding (British)
1984 Jaroslav Siefert (Czechoslovakian)
1985 Claude Simon (French)
1986 Wole Soyinka (Nigerian)
1987 Joseph Brodsky (Russian/American)

The Natural World

Life began on our planet more than three billion years ago.
Early life forms were very simple—they were probably all
single cells. Slowly, over many thousands of years, some of
these forms changed—evolved—into more complex forms.
By about two billion years ago, life had become clearly
separated into two groups: animals and plants. On pages 166
and 167, you can see how life developed through the various
ages of the Earth.

▲ **A bull's-eye moth** (from North America). It gets its name from its wing pattern. When it is threatened, the bull's-eye spreads its wings to frighten predators.

The 140,000 species of butterflies and moths form one of the largest insect orders. The Solomon Islands in the South Pacific are home to both the largest and rarest butterflies in the world. Females of the giant birdwing *Troides victoriae* can weigh over 0.18 oz (5 g), and have a wingspan exceeding 12 in (30 cm).

ERA	PERIOD	EPOCH	MILLIONS OF YEARS AGO
Cenozoic	Quaternary	Recent (Holocene)	
		Pleistocene	0.01
			2
	Tertiary	Pliocene	5
		Miocene	25
		Oligocene	35
		Eocene	60
		Paleocene	65
Mesozoic	Cretaceous		145
	Jurassic		210
	Triassic		245
Paleozoic	Permian		285
	Carboniferous		360
	Devonian		410
	Silurian		440
	Ordovician		505
	Cambrian		570

Precambrian time stretches back to the formation of the Earth, about 4.6 billion years ago.

HIGHLIGHTS OF PLANT AND ANIMAL LIFE

Modern human beings emerged and civilization began.

Ice Age in Northern Hemisphere, woolly mammals survived the cold.

"Ape-men" appeared. Many large mammals died out as the weather got colder.

Many apes in Africa. Herds of mammals grazed on the spreading grasslands.

Early apes appeared. Many modern mammals began to evolve. Flowering plants increased.

Strange mammals, including early horses and elephants. Plants mostly modern types.

Mammals evolved rapidly after most reptiles had died out.

Dinosaurs and many other reptiles died out at the end of the period. Ammonites disappeared. First flowering plants.

Dinosaurs ruled the land. Flying reptiles. First birds. Ammonites common. Some small mammals.

First dinosaurs and large sea reptiles. First mammals. Ammonites common. Cycads and Bennettitaleans evolved. Conifers spread. Luxuriant forests.

Reptiles increased. Amphibians less important. Trilobites died out. Primitive conifers and ginkgos.

Amphibians increased. First reptiles. Club mosses, ferns, and horsetails in coal-forming swamps.

The age of fishes (bony and cartilaginous). Amphibians evolved. Land plants more common.

Giant armored fishes. First land/marsh plants. Large sea scorpions—terrors of the seas.

First vertebrates (jawless fishes). Graptolites and trilobites abundant. Echinoderms and brachiopods spread.

Fossils abundant. Graptolites, trilobites, primitive shellfish, corals, crustaceans, etc.

Life began about 4 billion years ago? Oldest known fossils are Fig-Tree Cherts (3.1 billion yrs) and stromatolites (2.8 billion yrs). But fossils rare—probably because creatures were all soft-bodied (e.g. jellyfish, worms).

Classifying Animals

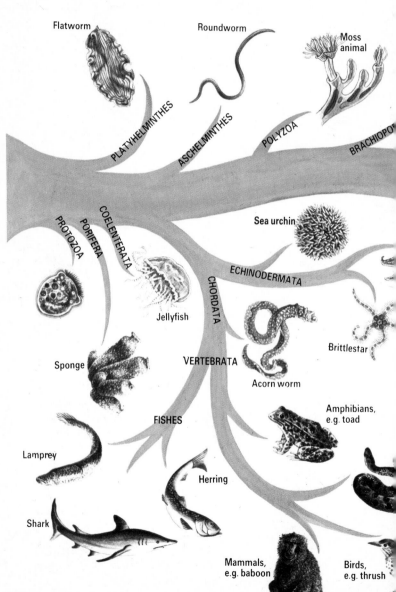

Flatworm

Roundworm

Moss animal

PLATYHELMINTHES

ASCHELMINTHES

POLYZOA

BRACHIOPO

PROTOZOA

PORIFERA

COELENTERATA

Sea urchin

ECHINODERMATA

CHORDATA

Jellyfish

Brittlestar

Sponge

VERTEBRATA

Acorn worm

Amphibians, e.g. toad

FISHES

Lamprey

Herring

Shark

Mammals, e.g. baboon

Birds, e.g. thrush

This "tree" shows the main groups into which the animal kingdom is divided. The smallest branches are classes. For example, a baboon is a mammal. Mammals form one class of the phylum Chordata. All members of this phylum have some kind of internal skeleton. On page 171 there is a detailed explanation of classification.

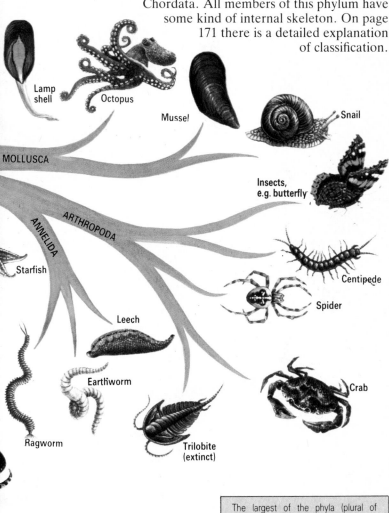

Lamp shell

Octopus

Mussel

Snail

MOLLUSCA

Insects, e.g. butterfly

ARTHROPODA

ANNELIDA

Starfish

Centipede

Spider

Leech

Earthworm

Crab

Ragworm

Trilobite (extinct)

The largest of the phyla (plural of phylum) is the *Arthropoda*. This phylum contains all the insects and spiders and their relatives—mostly small creatures with several pairs of legs. There are more than one million different kinds of arthropods.

169

Classifying Plants

On this page you can see that flowering plants are divided into two main groups—*Dicotyledons* and *Monocotyledons*.

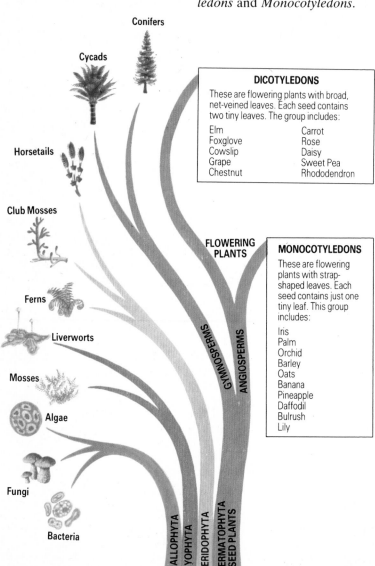

Conifers

Cycads

Horsetails

Club Mosses

Ferns

Liverworts

Mosses

Algae

Fungi

Bacteria

DICOTYLEDONS

These are flowering plants with broad, net-veined leaves. Each seed contains two tiny leaves. The group includes:

Elm
Foxglove
Cowslip
Grape
Chestnut

Carrot
Rose
Daisy
Sweet Pea
Rhododendron

FLOWERING PLANTS

MONOCOTYLEDONS

These are flowering plants with strap-shaped leaves. Each seed contains just one tiny leaf. This group includes:

Iris
Palm
Orchid
Barley
Oats
Banana
Pineapple
Daffodil
Bulrush
Lily

GYMNOSPERMS

ANGIOSPERMS

THALLOPHYTA

BRYOPHYTA

PTERIDOPHYTA

SPERMATOPHYTA or SEED PLANTS

Naming the Natural World

Classification enables us to compare plants and animals by grouping them according to similarities. The use of Latin or "scientific" names (as opposed to "common" names such as "cat") began in the 1700s. There have been many changes since then, and today experts still argue about classification.

In taxonomy—the science of classification—there are seven basic ranks, which are:

1. Kingdom: The highest rank. An organism can belong to either the Plantae or the Animalia kingdom. Some scientists make a claim for a third kingdom—the Protista—for organisms such as bacteria, which are on the borderline between the two kingdoms.

2. Phylum (plural phyla) or **Division** for plants: The largest subdivision. For example, all animals that have any kind of backbone belong to the phylum Chordata.

3. Class: Main subdivision of a phylum. The class Mammalia, for example, includes all animals that have mammary glands and suckle their young.

4. Order: Takes the subdivision a stage further. The Mammalia, for example, are divided into 18 orders—such as the Marsupialia, Primates, Rodentia, and Carnivora.

5. Family: Organisms that are recognizably similar. For example, among the order Carnivora (flesh-eating animals) the family Felidae includes all cat-like animals.

6. Genus (plural genera): A group of closely related organisms within a family. For example, the family Felidae includes the genera *Panthera*—big cats such as lions; *Felis*—cats that purr but do not roar; *Acinonyx*—the cheetah with its nonretractable claws, and *Lynx*—the lynx.

7. Species: The smallest division, defining organisms that are of the same kind and can breed together. Lions (*Panthera leo*) and tigers (*Panthera tigris*) are two different species in the genus *Panthera*. Sometimes, different species will mate. However, their offspring are sterile—they cannot reproduce.

The Latin names used in classification relate either to the type of animal or plant, or in some cases to the person who discovered it, or the place where it flourishes. The genus name is always printed with a capital letter, and the species name with a small letter. If a proper name is used in a species, it is always Latinized, as for example in the name of Coke's hartebeeste, *Alcephalus cokei*.

The American timber wolf and the European wolf are both varieties of the same animal. They differ only in color and size—just as members of the human race do. A complete classification of the animal is as follows:

Kingdom: *Animalia*
Phylum: *Chordata*
Subphylum: *Vertebrata*
Class: *Mammalia*
Order: *Carnivora*
Family: *Canidae*
Genus: *Canis*
Species: *lupus*

171

ANIMALS: LONGEVITY AND SPECIALIZED NAMES

	Life span (years)	Male	Female	Young	Group
Antelope	10	buck	doe	fawn	herd
Bear	15–50	boar	sow	cub	sleuth
Cat	15	tom	queen	kitten	cluster
Cattle	20	bull	cow	calf	herd
Deer	10–20	buck, hart, stag	doe, hind	fawn	herd
Dog	12–15	dog	bitch	puppy	kennel
Donkey	20	jack	jenny	foal	herd
Duck	10	drake	duck	duckling	team
Elephant	60	bull	cow	calf	herd
Fox	10	dog	vixen	cub	skulk
Giraffe	10–25	bull	cow	calf	herd
Goat	10	billy goat	nanny goat	kid	herd
Goose	25	gander	goose	gosling	skein (when in flight), gaggle
Hippopotamus	30–40	bull	cow	calf	herd
Horse	20–30	stallion	mare	foal	herd
Kangaroo	10–20	buck	doe	joey	mob
Lion	25	lion	lioness	cub	pride
Ostrich	50	cock	hen	chick	flock
Pig	10–15	boar	sow	piglet	drove
Rabbit	5–8	buck	doe	kit	warren
Rhinoceros	25–50	bull	cow	calf	crash
Sheep	10–15	ram	ewe	lamb	flock
Tiger	10–25	tiger	tigress	cub	
Whale	20	bull	cow	calf	school, pod
Zebra	20–25	stallion	mare	foal	herd

PEOPLE AS MAMMALS

Men and women are mammals with the scientific name *Homo sapiens*. This is the only surviving species of several human species that have existed during the last 2,800,000 years. The various living human races are all varieties of *Homo sapiens*.

▼ **A reconstruction** of Steinheim man, an early form of *Homo sapiens*.

HOW LONG SOME ANIMALS TAKE TO DEVELOP

The first five animals in the list are mammals and times given are for periods spent inside the mother. The rest of the animals lay eggs and times given refer to the period between laying and hatching of the eggs.

Animal	Development period
Human being	9 months
Elephant	20–22 months
Dog	8–9 weeks
Cat	9 weeks
Rat	3 weeks
Honeybee	3 days
Salmon	19–80 days depending on the temperature of the water in which the eggs are laid
Giant Salamander	8–12 weeks
Hawk	3–4 weeks
Python	about 2 weeks depending on the temperature

ANIMAL JOURNEYS

Many animals make incredible journeys—migrations—every year, in search of warmer weather or more food.

▼ **The route taken** by the migrating Monarch butterfly—from Canada to Mexico and sometimes out over the Pacific.

▶ **The common eel** is the most famous traveler. It migrates thousands of miles from European rivers to spawning grounds in the Sargasso Sea.

THE PARTS OF A DOG

▼ **The dog is perhaps our favorite animal** and has been an important companion for thousands of years. Dogs appear on ancient Egyptian wall paintings and have even traveled into space. There are more than 100 breeds of domestic dog—*Canis familiaris*. This generalized picture shows the main parts of a typical dog.

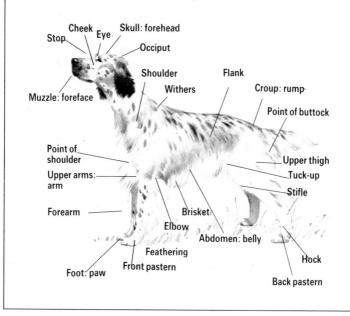

THE PARTS OF A BIRD
A male chaffinch in summer plumage

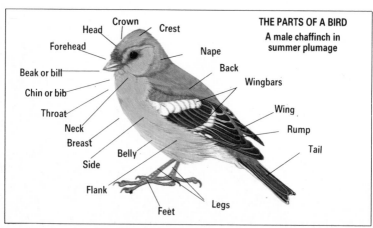

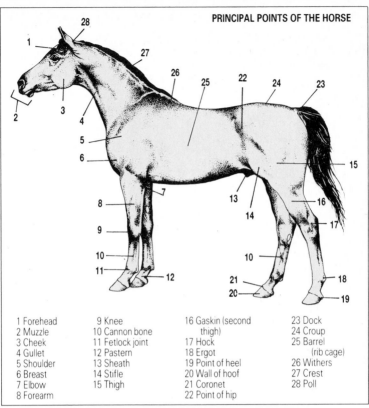

PRINCIPAL POINTS OF THE HORSE

1 Forehead	9 Knee	16 Gaskin (second thigh)	23 Dock
2 Muzzle	10 Cannon bone	17 Hock	24 Croup
3 Cheek	11 Fetlock joint	18 Ergot	25 Barrel (rib cage)
4 Gullet	12 Pastern	19 Point of heel	26 Withers
5 Shoulder	13 Sheath	20 Wall of hoof	27 Crest
6 Breast	14 Stifle	21 Coronet	28 Poll
7 Elbow	15 Thigh	22 Point of hip	
8 Forearm			

THE PARTS OF AN INSECT

▶ **This drawing of a butterfly** shows the main parts of a typical insect's body. There are many groups of insects—three common groups are bees, grasshoppers, and beetles.

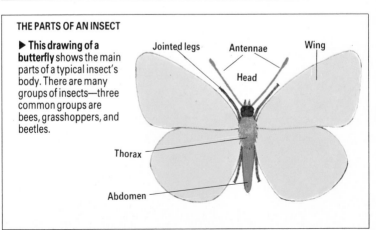

175

THE MAIN PARTS OF A PLANT

Flower: The part of a flowering plant concerned with reproduction. Most flowers have both male and female organs. The male part produces pollen which pollinates the female part (usually of another flower) and leads to the production of a seed—from which a new plant grows.

Leaf: A plant's leaves are its food-making factories, containing chlorophyll, which uses sunlight to make food from carbon dioxide in the air and water in the soil. The veins carry water up from the roots and transport food made in the leaves to the rest of the plant.

Stem: This supports the leaves and flowers. It contains tubes to carry water and food around the plant, and it stores food.

Roots: These anchor the plant to the ground, absorb water and mineral salts from the soil, and in some cases (for example, the carrot) store food. The root cap protects the root as it forces its way down through the soil in search of water; the root hairs actually absorb the water.

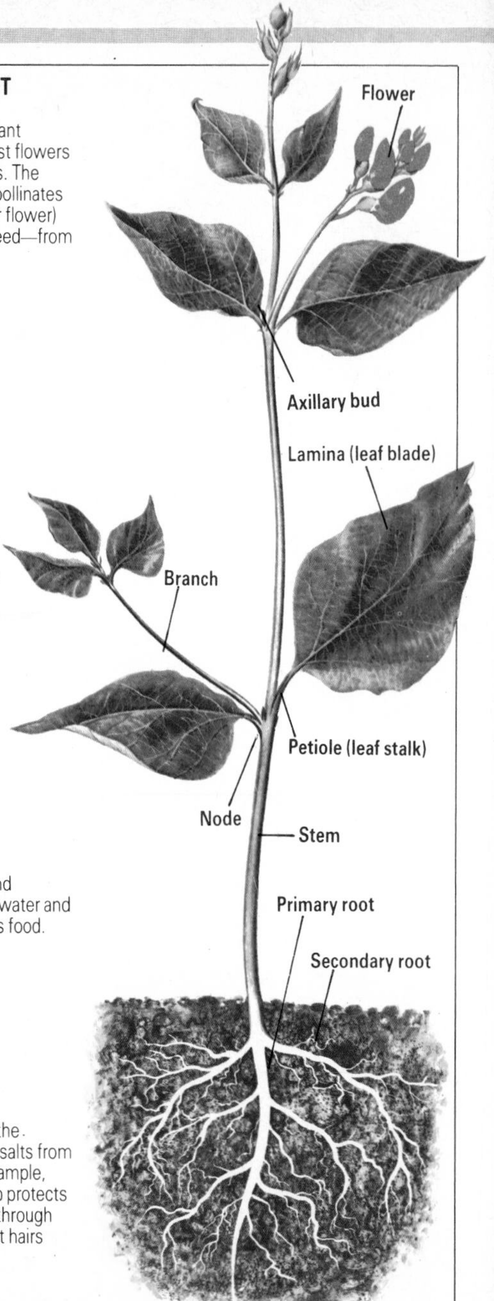

Flower

Axillary bud

Lamina (leaf blade)

Branch

Petiole (leaf stalk)

Node

Stem

Primary root

Secondary root

PARTS OF A TYPICAL FLOWER

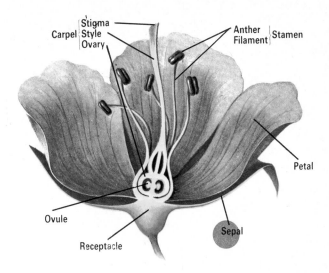

Carpel { Stigma / Style / Ovary

Anther / Filament } Stamen

Petal

Ovule

Sepal

Receptacle

SEED STRUCTURE

These two illustrations show (*top*) a dicotyledon seed (bean), and (*bottom*) a monocotyledon seed (corn). Most of the space in a seed is taken up by its food store—the cotyledons in the bean; the endosperm in the corn.

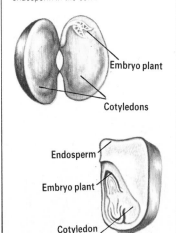

Embryo plant

Cotyledons

Endosperm

Embryo plant

Cotyledon

▲ **In a typical plant,** pollen produced by the anther travels down through the style and into the ovary to fertilize the egg in the ovule. After fertilization, the flower dies and the ovule becomes a seed.

▼ **Botanists believe** that the North American magnolia was one of the first flowering plants.

177

DIFFERENT KINDS OF FRUIT

A fruit is the seed case of a flowering plant. Some fruits have just one seed; most fruits have more. Fruits are usually divided into two main groups—fleshy and dry. Fleshy fruits are soft and juicy and are eaten by animals. The animals then drop the seeds, often some distance from the parent plant. Dry fruits dry out as they ripen. They often have a method of scattering their seeds. For example, the pea pod bursts open, flinging its seeds out, and the winged sycamore "key" is the perfect shape to be carried away by the wind.

FLESHY FRUITS

Drupes
The fruit has a fleshy outer layer, and a hard inner layer (the stone). The actual seed is inside the stone. Blackberries and raspberries consist of several small drupes (drupels) lightly joined together.

Cherries

Peach

Plum

Raspberry

Blackberry

Berries
The entire fruit is fleshy and contains many seeds. It is usually formed from several carpels, each segment of the fruit being formed from one carpel.

Tomato

Orange

Grapes

Gooseberry

Pome
The true fruit, formed from the carpels, is the core. The edible part is the swollen receptacle.

Apple

Pear

DRY FRUITS

Dehiscent
These split open when ripe. Peas and beans have pods, each formed from one carpel. Poppies have capsules formed from several carpels.

Pea

Poppy.

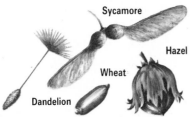

Sycamore

Hazel

Wheat

Dandelion

Indehiscent
Indehiscent fruits do not split open when ripe. They therefore cannot germinate until the ovary wall (the woody or leathery "coat") rots or is broken.

▼ **A cross section** of a tree trunk. The trunk consists mainly of vessels that carry water between the roots and the branches. One year's growth shows as one layer of vessels—an *annual ring*. We can age a tree by counting its rings. In older trees, only the outer rings—the *sapwood*—contain working vessels. Dead vessels in the center form *heartwood*. *Medullary rays* are lines of cells through which food passes between the vessels. Rays often help form the grain of a wood.

▼ **A typical mushroom** or toadstool. These are the reproductive parts of threadlike fungi that exist in soil and trees. Their job is to carry spores above ground where they can be scattered by the wind. **Warning**: do **not** eat mushrooms and toadstools you have picked unless you **know** they are edible—many are poisonous.

Cap

Gills (spores are produced here)

Stem

Ring

Volva

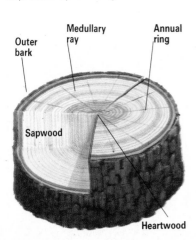

Medullary ray

Annual ring

Outer bark

Sapwood

Heartwood

Natural Record Breakers

ANIMAL SPEED RECORDS

	mph	km/h
Peregrine falcon (in dive)	180	290
Spine-tailed swift	106	170
Sailfish	68	109
Cheetah	65	105
Pronghorn antelope	60	97
Racing pigeon	60	97
Lion	50	80
Gazelle	50	80
Hare	45	72
Zebra	40	64
Racehorse	40	64
Shark	40	64
Greyhound	39	63
Rabbit	35	56
Giraffe	32	51
Grizzly bear	30	48
Cat	30	48
Elephant	26	40
Sealion	25	40
Human	20	32
Black mamba	20	32
Bee	11	18
Pig	11	18
Chicken	9	14
Spider	1.17	1.88
Tortoise	0.5	0.8
Snail	0.03	0.05

Note: These are maximum speeds and are normally achieved only over very short distances.

Insect record holders include the goliath beetles (heaviest), a stick insect (longest), wasps called fairy flies (smallest), springtails (most plentiful), queen termites (longest lived), and cicadas (loudest).

The world's largest flower is produced by the plant *Rafflesia arnoldii*, which is found in the forests of Indonesia. The flower may measure more than 3 ft. (1 meter) across, and its petals are ¾ in. (2 cm) thick. These blooms, with their powerful scent of rotting meat, often weigh as much as 15 lb. (6.8 kg) each.

JOURNEY'S END

Longest bird migration is by the Arctic tern (*Sterna paradisaea*), which leads a life of perpetual summer. It leaves the Arctic as summer ends and flies 11,000 miles (18,000 km) to Antarctica. At the end of the Antarctic summer it flies back to its breeding ground – so making a round trip of 22,000 miles (36,000 km).

Longest mammal migration is by the Alaska fur seal (*Callorhinus ursinus*), which does a round trip of 6,000 miles (9,600 km).

Most traveled butterfly is the Monarch butterfly (*Danaus plexippus*) of North America. This butterfly flies all the way from Hudson Bay to Florida or Mexico. The butterflies that arrive back in Canada the following summer are descendants of those that left the south in the spring! The round trip is 2,500 miles (4,000 km).

FISH RECORDS

The longest bony fish is the beluga (*Huso huso*), a kind of sturgeon found in the U.S.S.R. It has been known to grow up to 28 ft. (8.5 m) in length, and reach a weight of 3,000 lb (1,360 kg).

The heaviest bony fish is the ocean sunfish (*Mola mola*) which can weigh up to 2 tons.

The smallest fish and also the smallest vertebrate is the Dwarf goby, found in fresh water in the Philippines and the Marshall Islands. The maximum size for these tiny fish is ½ in. (1.25,cm).

The largest fish of all is the whale shark (*Rhincodon typus*), which can be up to 46 ft. (14 m) long. Some reports have even mentioned specimens up to 70 ft. (21 m) long and weighing 20 tons!

CAT RECORDS

Largest member of the cat family is the tiger (*Panthera tigris*). Males have been found up to 10½ ft. (3.2 m) in length, standing 3 ft. (1 meter) high at the shoulder.

Rarest of the cats is probably the Javan tiger, a race of *Panthera tigris* which is now only known in one restricted area of the island of Java. About half a dozen are thought to survive.

Longest lived of all big cats is probably the lion (*Panthera leo*), which is known to live up to 30 years in captivity.

RECORD TREES

Tallest are the California coast redwoods, which grow over 330 ft. (100 m) high.

Thickest trunk is that of a Montezuma cypress in Mexico, with a diameter of 40 ft. (12 m).

Oldest are the bristlecone pines of Nevada, California, and Arizona—nearly 5,000 years old.

Earliest surviving species is the maidenhair tree or ginkgo of China; it first appeared about 160 million years ago.

LARGEST, SMALLEST, FASTEST, OLDEST ANIMAL

Largest animal is the blue or sulfur-bottom whale (*Balaenoptera musculus*). Specimens have been caught measuring more than 100 ft. (30 m) long, though blue whales this size have not been seen for many years.

Smallest animals are some of the protozoa—single-celled creatures. Many of them are around 0.00007874 in. (2 μ) long. They can be seen only with a powerful microscope.

Largest animal living on land is the African elephant (*Loxodonta africana*). Bull elephants are about 11½ ft. (3.5 m) tall and weigh up to 7 tons.

Longest living animal is the giant tortoise (*Testudo elephantopus*), known to live up to 177 years.

Fastest animal on land is the cheetah (*Acinonyx jubatus*), which can run at up to 65 mph (105 km/h) over short distances.

Fastest fliers are probably some of the swifts, which can reach 106 mph (170 km/h) in level flight; peregrine falcons (*Falco peregrinus*) can dive at up to 180 mph (290 km/h).

THE EVOLUTION DEBATE

▲ **The French naturalist** Jean Baptiste Lamarck. He was one of the first people to formulate a theory of evolution.

In the 18th and 19th centuries, science began to overturn prevailing religious explanations of how life had evolved. Europeans were bringing plants and animals back from distant lands, naturalists were grouping living things together, and fossils were being discovered. In 1809, Jean Baptiste Lamarck published his *Zoological Philosophy*. This suggested that individual animals and plants adapted to the environment by acquiring new features during their lifetime which they passed on to their offspring. Genetics has since proved this wrong. Then English naturalist Charles Darwin (1809–82) proposed that change—evolution—occurred by natural selection. This is the survival (and reproduction) of life forms best suited to their surroundings. Fellow Englishman Alfred Russell Wallace (1823–1913) came up with the same theory at the same time, but Darwin won the race by publishing *On the Origin of Species* in 1859. Today, evolutionary theory is still based on this book.

Leading Naturalists

Brown, Robert (1773–1858) Scottish botanist who brought back about 4,000 species of plants from Australia in 1805. He amended Linnaeus's classification system, and separated the higher plants into *gymnosperms* (which produce seeds without fruit) and *angiosperms* (flowering plants which produce seeds enclosed in fruits). He recognized the existence of the cell "nucleus" and gave it its name.

Burbank, Luther (1849–1926) American naturalist who worked extensively on breeding new varieties of plants. During his life he produced a new kind of potato and 60 varieties of plum. He also experimented with pineapples, walnuts, almonds, and several species of flowers.

Candolle, Augustin de (1778–1841) Swiss-French botanist who improved Linnaeus's classification of the plants. He invented the word "taxonomy" to describe the science of classification. Most of his classification remains in use today.

Fabre, Jean Henri (1823–1915) French naturalist, sometimes referred to as the "Insect Man." He spent much of his life watching and writing about insects in the south of France. Although he made many fascinating discoveries about insect behavior, he did not always draw the right conclusions from his detailed observations.

Frisch, Karl von (1886–1982) An Austrian biologist who was particularly interested in the behavior of animals and how they communicate with each other. The most celebrated of his many discoveries was that of the "language of the bees"—how the honey bees dance on the combs of the hive to tell each other where to find food.

Fuchs, Leonhard (1501–66) German botanist who prepared the first glossary of botanical terms. He wrote *History of Plants*, which describes many species of

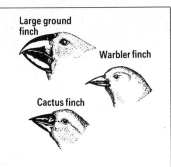

Three of the finch species on the Pacific Galapagos Islands. They probably evolved from one species, their beaks changing as they specialized on different kinds of foods. Darwin visited these islands as naturalist on board the ship HMS *Beagle*. What he saw there shaped much of his later theory of evolution.

▲ **Karl von Linné,** who founded the classification system used today. He even latinized his own name—Carolus Linnaeus.

plants. The genus *Fuchsia* was later named after him.

Linnaeus, Carolus (1707–78) Swedish naturalist and founder of modern taxonomy.

Mendel, Gregor (1822–82) Austrian botanist and monk who discovered the principles of heredity. He studied the inheritance of certain characteristics of pea plants. From his results, he proposed the two basic laws of inheritance. His work was not recognized until 16 years after his death.

Ray, John (*c*.1627–1705) English naturalist who is often called the father of English natural history. He made collections in England and Europe on which to base complete systematic descriptions of animal and vegetable life. His method provided the foundation for the natural system of classifying plants.

Theophrastus (*c*.317–287 B.C.) Greek philosopher and follower of Aristotle.

His works on the history of plants are among the first to attempt a plant classification.

Tinbergen, Nikolaas (born 1907) A Dutch biologist who has made many important contributions to the study of animal behavior. By studying such diverse animals as butterflies, sticklebacks, and gulls, he discovered many of the signals that they use to communicate with each other and to ensure that they do the right things at the right time.

In 1768, Captain James Cook's first landfall in Australia was at a place he originally named Stingray Bay. However, he later changed the name to Botany Bay, in honor of the remarkable plant collections made in the area by Sir Joseph Banks. Banks was a famous naturalist who had volunteered to accompany Cook on the *Endeavour*. Nowadays, Botany Bay is surrounded by the airport and suburbs of Sydney.

183

Sports

Sports are popular all over the world. We love discussing them and flock to major events by the thousands. We can judge the popularity of sports by the amount of space devoted to them in our daily newspapers. Most sports require a combination of physical fitness, mental sharpness, and teamwork. As a hobby, sports provide demanding exercise with a purpose and are a good way to make friends. Both professional and amateur sports are a common ground for people of all ages, backgrounds, and nationalities.

▲ **Competitors in the 110-meter (120-yard) hurdles.** The races of this track event are started from a sprinting position. The hurdles are cleared as part of a run, without breaking stride.

HURDLING

There are 10 hurdles to clear in both the men's and the women's races. The shorter event, the high hurdles, is over 110 m (120 yd.) for men and 100 m (110 yd.) for women. The men's hurdles are 3 ft. 6 in. (1.07 m) high, the women's 2 ft. 9 in. (84 cm). In the 400-m (440-yd.) events, men race over 3-ft. (91-cm) hurdles, women over 2 ft. 6 in. (76-cm) hurdles. All these events are run in lanes, with a staggered start for the 400-m race.

185

ATHLETICS

Ruling body—International Amateur Athletic Federation (IAAF)

Men's World Records

100 meters	9.83 sec	Ben Johnson (Can.)	8-30-87
200 meters	19.72 sec	Pietro Mennea (Italy)	9-12-79
400 meters	43.86 sec	Lee Evans (U.S.A.)	10-18-68
800 meters	1 min 41.73 sec	Sebastian Coe (G.B.)	6-10-81
1,000 meters	2 min 12.18 sec	Sebastian Coe (G.B.)	7-11-81
1,500 meters	3 min 29.46 sec	Saïd Aouita (Morocco)	8-23-85
1 mile	3 min 46.32 sec	Steve Cram (G.B.)	7-27-85
2,000 meters	4 min 50.81 sec	Saïd Aouita (Morocco)	7-16-87
3,000 meters	7 min 32.1 sec	Henry Rono (Kenya)	6-27-78
5,000 meters	12 min. 58.39 sec	Saïd Aouita (Morocco)	7-22-87
10,000 meters	27 min 13.81 sec	Fernando Mamede (Portugal)	7-2-84
Marathon*	2 hr 7 min 12 sec	Carlos Lopes (Portugal)	4-20-85
110 meters hurdles	12.93 sec	Renaldo Nehemiah (U.S.A.)	8-19-81
400 meters hurdles	47.02 sec	Edwin Moses (U.S.A.)	8-31-83
3,000 meters steeplechase	8 min 05.4 sec	Henry Rono (Kenya)	5-13-78
4 × 100 meters relay	37.83 sec	United States	8-11-84
4 × 400 meters relay	2 min 56.16 sec	United States	10-20-68
High jump	7 ft 11¼ in (2.42 m)	Patrik Sjöberg (Sweden)	6-30-87
Pole vault	19 ft 10¼ in (6.05 m)	Sergey Bubka (U.S.S.R.)	6-9-88
Long jump	29 ft 2½ in (8.90 m)	Bob Beamon (U.S.A.)	10-18-68
Triple jump	58 ft 11½ in (17.97 m)	Willie Banks (U.S.A.)	6-16-85
Shot put	75 ft 8 in (23.06 m)	Ulf Timmermann (G.D.R.—East Germany)	5-22-88
Discus throw	243 ft ½ in (74.08 m)	Jürgen Schult (G.D.R.)	6-6-86
Hammer throw	284 ft 7 in (86.74 m)	Yuriy Sedykh (U.S.S.R.)	8-30-86
Javelin throw	287 ft 7 in (87.66 m)	Jan Zelezny (Czechoslovakia)	5-31-87
Decathlon	8,847 points	Daley Thompson (G.B.)	8-8/9-84

*World best time (no official world record because of variation in courses).

◀ **Discus throwing** was very popular in ancient Greece. It has been an Olympic event since the first modern Olympics in 1896.

The discus has the shape of a dinner plate, with a thick center tapering to a thin outer rim. The men's discus weighs 4½ lb (2 kg). The women's is smaller and weighs half as much. The discus is thrown from inside a circular boundary. A wire cage around the boundary protects spectators and competitors from stray throws. The discus is held against the palm of the hand, kept in place by the fingertips. A thrower begins the throw facing backward. He or she then builds up momentum by whirling around for 1½ turns before letting the discus go.

Women's World Records

100 meters	10.76 sec	Evelyn Ashford (U.S.A.)	8-22-84
200 meters	21.71 sec	Marita Koch (G.D.R.—East Germany)	6-10-79
	21.71 sec	Heike Drechsler (G.D.R.)	6-29 & 8-29-86
400 meters	47.60 sec	Marita Koch (G.D.R.)	10-6-85
800 meters	1 min 53.28 sec	Jarmila Kratochvilova (Czech.)	7-26-83
1,500 meters	3 min 52.47 sec	Tatyana Kazankina (U.S.S.R.)	8-13-80
1 mile	4 min 16.71 sec	Mary Slaney (U.S.A.)	8-21-85
3,000 meters	8 min 22.62 sec	Tatyana Kazankina (U.S.S.R.)	8-26-84
5,000 meters	14 min 37.33 sec	Ingrid Kristiansen (Norway)	8-5-86
10,000 meters	30 min 13.74 sec	Ingrid Kristiansen (Norway)	7-5-86
Marathon*	2 hr 21 min 06 sec	Ingrid Kristiansen (Norway)	4-21-85
100 meters hurdles	12.25 sec	Ginka Zagorcheva (Bulgaria)	8-8-87
400 meters hurdles	53.32 sec	Marina Stepanova (U.S.S.R.)	8-30-86
4 × 100 meters relay	41.37 sec	East Germany	10-6-85
4 × 400 meters relay	3 min 15.92 sec	East Germany	6-3-84
High jump	6 ft 10½ in (2.9 m)	Stefka Kostadinova (Bulgaria)	8-30-87
Long jump	24 ft 8¼ in (7.52 m)	Galina Chistyakova (U.S.S.R.)	6-11-88
Shot put	73 ft 11 in (22.53 m)	Natalya Lisovskaya (U.S.S.R.)	5-27-84
Discus throw	244 ft 7½ in (74.56 m)	Zdenka Silhava (Czechoslovakia)	8-26-84
Javelin throw	254 ft ¾ in (77.44m)	Fatima Whitbread (G.B.)	8-28-86
Heptathlon	7,148 points	Jackie Joyner (U.S.A.)	7-6/7-86

*World best time (no official world record because of variation in courses).

STANLEY CUP WINNERS (HOCKEY)

1894	Montreal A.A.A.
1895	Montreal Victorias
1896	Winnipeg Victorias
1897–99	Montreal Victorias
1900	Montreal Shamrocks
1901	Winnipeg Victorias
1902	Montreal A.A.A.
1903–05	Ottawa Silver Seven
1906	Montreal Wanderers
1907	Kenora Thistles[1]
1907	Mont. Wanderers[2]
1908	Montreal Wanderers
1909	Ottawa Senators
1910	Montreal Wanderers
1911	Ottawa Senators
1912–13	Quebec Bulldogs
1914	Toronto
1915	Vancouver Millionaires
1916	Montreal Canadiens
1917	Seattle Metropolitans
1918	Toronto Arenas
1919	No champion
1920–21	Ottawa Senators
1922	Toronto St. Patricks
1923	Ottawa Senators
1924	Montreal Canadiens
1925	Victoria Cougars
1926	Montreal Maroons
1927	Ottawa Senators
1928	N.Y. Rangers
1929	Boston Bruins
1930–31	Montreal Canadiens
1932	Toronto Maple Leafs
1933	N.Y. Rangers
1934	Chicago Black Hawks
1935	Montreal Maroons
1936–37	Detroit Red Wings
1938	Chicago Black Hawks
1939	Boston Bruins
1940	N.Y. Rangers
1941	Boston Bruins
1942	Toronto Maple Leafs
1943	Detroit Red Wings
1944	Montreal Canadiens
1945	Toronto Maple Leafs
1946	Montreal Canadiens
1947–49	Toronto Maple Leafs
1950	Detroit Red Wings
1951	Toronto Maple Leafs
1952	Detroit Red Wings
1953	Montreal Canadiens
1954–55	Detroit Red Wings
1956–60	Montreal Canadiens
1961	Chicago Black Hawks
1962–64	Toronto Maple Leafs
1965–66	Montreal Canadiens
1967	Toronto Maple Leafs
1968–69	Montreal Canadiens
1970	Boston Bruins
1971	Montreal Canadiens
1972	Boston Bruins
1973	Montreal Canadiens
1974–75	Philadelphia Flyers
1976–79	Montreal Canadiens
1980–83	New York Islanders
1984	Edmonton Oilers
1985	Edmonton Oilers
1986	Montreal Canadiens
1987	Edmonton Oilers

[1] January.   [2] March.

BASEBALL

World Series Results

1903	Boston AL 5	Pittsburgh NL ... 3		1946	St. Louis NL 4	Boston AL 3
1904	No series			1947	New York AL 4	Brooklyn NL 3
1905	New York NL 4	Philadelphia AL .. 1		1948	Cleveland AL 4	Boston NL 2
1906	Chicago AL 4	Chicago NL 2		1949	New York AL 4	Brooklyn NL 1
1907	Chicago NL 4	Detroit AL .. 0, 1 tie		1950	New York AL 4	Philadelphia NL .. 0
1908	Chicago NL 4	Detroit AL 1		1951	New York AL 4	New York NL 2
1909	Pittsburgh NL ... 4	Detroit AL 3		1952	New York AL 4	Brooklyn NL 3
1910	Philadelphia AL .. 4	Chicago NL 1		1953	New York AL 4	Brooklyn NL 2
1911	Philadelphia AL .. 4	New York NL 2		1954	New York NL 4	Cleveland AL 0
1912	Boston AL 4	New York NL .. 3, 1 tie		1955	Brooklyn NL 4	New York AL 3
1913	Philadelphia AL .. 4	New York NL 1		1956	New York AL 4	Brooklyn NL 3
1914	Boston NL 4	Philadelphia AL .. 0		1957	Milwaukee NL ... 4	New York AL 3
1915	Boston AL 4	Philadelphia NL .. 1		1958	New York AL 4	Milwaukee NL ... 3
1916	Boston AL 4	Brooklyn NL 1		1959	Los Angeles NL .. 4	Chicago AL 2
1917	Chicago AL 4	New York NL 2		1960	Pittsburgh NL ... 4	New York AL 3
1918	Boston AL 4	Chicago NL 2		1961	New York AL 4	Cincinnati NL 1
1919	Cincinnati NL 5	Chicago AL 3		1962	New York AL 4	San Francisco NL 3
1920	Cleveland AL 5	Brooklyn NL 2		1963	Los Angeles NL .. 4	New York AL 0
1921	New York NL 5	New York AL 3		1964	St. Louis NL 4	New York AL 3
1922	New York NL 4	New York AL .. 0, 1 tie		1965	Los Angeles NL .. 4	Minnesota AL ... 3
1923	New York AL 4	New York NL 2		1966	Baltimore AL 4	Los Angeles NL .. 0
1924	Washington AL .. 4	New York NL 3		1967	St. Louis NL 4	Boston AL 3
1925	Pittsburgh NL ... 4	Washington AL .. 3		1968	Detroit AL 4	St. Louis NL 3
1926	St. Louis NL 4	New York AL 3		1969	New York NL 4	Baltimore AL 1
1927	New York AL 4	Pittsburgh NL ... 0		1970	Baltimore AL 4	Cincinnati NL 1
1928	New York AL 4	St. Louis NL 0		1971	Pittsburgh NL ... 4	Baltimore AL 3
1929	Philadelphia AL .. 4	Chicago NL 1		1972	Oakland AL 4	Cincinnati NL 3
1930	Philadelphia AL .. 4	St. Louis NL 2		1973	Oakland AL 4	New York NL 3
1931	St. Louis NL 4	Philadelphia AL .. 3		1974	Oakland AL 4	Los Angeles NL .. 1
1932	New York AL 4	Chicago NL 0		1975	Cincinnati NL 4	Boston AL 3
1933	New York NL 4	Washington AL .. 1		1976	Cincinnati NL 4	New York AL 0
1934	St. Louis NL 4	Detroit AL 3		1977	New York AL 4	Los Angeles NL .. 2
1935	Detroit AL 4	Chicago NL 2		1978	New York AL 4	Los Angeles NL .. 2
1936	New York AL 4	New York NL 2		1979	Pittsburgh NL ... 4	Baltimore AL 3
1937	New York AL 4	New York NL 1		1980	Philadelphia NL .. 4	Kansas City AL .. 2
1938	New York AL 4	Chicago NL 0		1981	Los Angeles NL .. 4	New York AL 2
1939	New York AL 4	Cincinnati NL 0		1982	St. Louis NL 4	Milwaukee AL ... 3
1940	Cincinnati NL 4	Detroit AL 3		1983	Baltimore AL 4	Philadelphia NL .. 1
1941	New York AL 4	Brooklyn NL 1		1984	Detroit AL 4	San Diego NL 1
1942	St. Louis NL .. 4	New York AL		1985	Kansas City AL ... 4	St. Louis NL 3
1943	New York AL 4	St. Louis NL 1		1986	New York NL 4	Boston AL 3
1944	St. Louis NL 4	St. Louis AL 2		1987	Minnesota Twins AL . 4	St. Louis NL 3
1945	Detroit AL 4	Chicago NL 3				

FOOTBALL

Super Bowl Results

Year	Field	Winner		Loser	
1967	Los Angeles Coliseum	Green Bay Packers	35	Kansas City Chiefs	10
1968	Orange Bowl, Miami	Green Bay Packers	33	Oakland Raiders	14
1969	Orange Bowl, Miami	New York Jets	16	Baltimore Colts	7
1970	Tulane Stadium, New Orleans	Kansas City Chiefs	23	Minnesota Vikings	7
1971	Orange Bowl, Miami	Baltimore Colts	16	Dallas Cowboys	13
1972	Tulane Stadium, New Orleans	Dallas Cowboys	24	Miami Dolphins	3
1973	Los Angeles Coliseum	Miami Dolphins	14	Washington Redskins	7
1974	Rice Stadium, Houston	Miami Dolphins	24	Minnesota Vikings	7
1975	Tulane Stadium, New Orleans	Pittsburgh Steelers	16	Minnesota Vikings	6
1976	Orange Bowl, Miami	Pittsburgh Steelers	21	Dallas Cowboys	17
1977	Rose Bowl, Pasadena	Oakland Raiders	32	Minnesota Vikings	14
1978	Superdome, New Orleans	Dallas Cowboys	27	Denver Broncos	10
1979	Orange Bowl, Miami	Pittsburgh Steelers	35	Dallas Cowboys	31
1980	Rose Bowl, Pasadena	Pittsburgh Steelers	31	Los Angeles Rams	19
1981	Superdome, New Orleans	Oakland Raiders	27	Philadelphia Eagles	10
1982	Silverdome, Pontiac, Michigan	San Francisco 49ers	26	Cincinnati Bengals	21
1983	Rose Bowl, Pasadena	Washington Redskins	27	Miami Dolphins	17
1984	Tampa Stadium	Los Angeles Raiders	38	Washington Redskins	9
1985	Stanford Stadium	San Francisco 49ers	38	Miami Dolphins	16
1986	Superdome, New Orleans	Chicago Bears	46	New England Patriots	10
1987	Rose Bowl, Pasadena	New York Giants	39	Denver Broncos	20
1988	Jack Murphy Stadium, San Diego	Washington Redskins	42	Denver Broncos	10

◀ **Football** is a colorful, rough, and exciting sport. It is hugely popular and is rapidly gaining supporters outside the U.S. There are school, college, and professional teams throughout the United States. The game developed mainly from soccer and the English game of rugby. A form of it was played around 1850 and rules were adopted in 1874 and 1906. The game was greatly advanced by the advent of the forward pass in the 1920s. Canadian football is similar to the United States game.

189

WIMBLEDON CHAMPIONS (since 1946)

	Men	Women
1946	Yvon Petra (France)	Pauline Betz (U.S.A.)
1947	Jack Kramer (U.S.A.)	Margaret Osborne (U.S.A.)
1948	Bob Falkenburg (U.S.A.)	Louise Brough (U.S.A.)
1949	Fred Schroeder (U.S.A.)	Louise Brough (U.S.A.)
1950	Budge Patty (U.S.A.)	Louise Brough (U.S.A.)
1951	Dick Savitt (U.S.A.)	Doris Hart (U.S.A.)
1952	Frank Sedgman (Australia)	Maureen Connolly (U.S.A.)
1953	Victor Seixas (U.S.A.)	Maureen Connolly (U.S.A.)
1954	Jaroslav Drobny (Czech.)	Maureen Connolly (U.S.A.)
1955	Tony Trabert (U.S.A.)	Louise Brough (U.S.A.)
1956	Lew Hoad (Australia)	Shirley Fry (U.S.A.)
1957	Lew Hoad (Australia)	Althea Gibson (U.S.A.)
1958	Ashley Cooper (Australia)	Althea Gibson (U.S.A.)
1959	Alex Olmedeo (Peru)	Maria Bueno (Brazil)
1960	Neale Fraser (Australia)	Maria Bueno (Brazil)
1961	Rod Laver (Australia)	Angela Mortimer (G.B.)
1962	Rod Laver (Australia)	Karen Susman (U.S.A.)
1963	Chuck McKinley (U.S.A.)	Margaret Smith (Australia)
1964	Roy Emerson (Australia)	Maria Bueno (Brazil)
1965	Roy Emerson (Australia)	Margaret Smith (Australia)
1966	Manuel Santana (Spain)	Billie Jean King (U.S.A.)
1967	John Newcombe (Aus.)	Billie Jean King (U.S.A.)
1968	Rod Laver (Australia)	Billie Jean King (U.S.A.)
1969	Rod Laver (Australia)	Ann Jones (G.B.)
1970	John Newcombe (Aus.)	Margaret Court[1] (Australia)
1971	John Newcombe (Aus.)	Evonne Goolagong (Aus.)
1972	Stan Smith (U.S.A.)	Billie Jean King (U.S.A.)
1973	Jan Kodes (Czech.)	Billie Jean King (U.S.A.)
1974	Jimmy Connors (U.S.A.)	Chris Evert (U.S.A.)
1975	Arthur Ashe (U.S.A.)	Billie Jean King (U.S.A.)
1976	Bjorn Borg (Sweden)	Chris Evert (U.S.A.)
1977	Bjorn Borg (Sweden)	Virginia Wade (G.B.)
1978	Bjorn Borg (Sweden)	Martina Navratilova (Czechoslovakia)
1979	Bjorn Borg (Sweden)	Martina Navratilova (Czechoslovakia)
1980	Bjorn Borg (Sweden)	Evonne Cawley[2] (Australia)
1981	John McEnroe (U.S.A.)	Chris Evert-Lloyd (U.S.A.)
1982	Jimmy Connors (U.S.A.)	Martina Navratilova (U.S.A.)
1983	John McEnroe (U.S.A.)	Martina Navratilova (U.S.A.)
1984	John McEnroe (U.S.A.)	Martina Navratilova (U.S.A.)
1985	Boris Becker (W. Ger.)	Martina Navratilova (U.S.A.)
1986	Boris Becker (W. Ger.)	Martina Navratilova (U.S.A.)
1987	Pat Cash (Australia)	Martina Navratilova (U.S.A.)
1988	Stefan Edberg (Sweden)	Steffi Graf (W. Ger.)

1. Née Smith   2. Née Goolagong

▲ **Chris Evert**—an outstanding player whose double-handed backhand has been copied by many other women players.

▼ **In 1985, 17-year-old** Boris Becker became the youngest men's Wimbledon champion. He was also the first unseeded champion.

CRICKET

Cricket Records – Test Matches

Highest innings – 365* G. S. Sobers, W. Indies (v Pakistan, Kingston, 1958).

Most runs in series – 974 D. G. Bradman, Australia (v England, 1930); in career – 10,122 S. Gavaskar, India.

Most hundreds (centuries) – 34 S. Gavaskar, India.

Best bowling in match – 19–90 J. C. Laker, England (v Australia, Old Trafford, 1956); in innings – 10–53 J. C. Laker, England (v Australia, Old Trafford, 1956).

Most wickets in series – 49 S. F. Barnes, England (v S. Africa, 1913–14); in career – 366 I. T. Botham, England.

Highest partnership – 451 (2nd Wkt) W. H. Ponsford (266) and D. G. Bradman (244), Australia (v England, Oval, 1934).

Highest total – 903 (for 7) England (v Australia, Oval, 1938).

Most wicket-keeping dismissals in career – 355 R. W. Marsh, Australia.

Most Test appearances – 125 S. Gavaskar, India.

* not out

Cricket Records – All Matches

Highest innings – 499 Hanif Mohommad, Karachi (v Bahawalpur, 1958–9).

Most runs in season – 3816 D. C. S. Compton, England and Middlesex, 1947; in career – 61,237 J. B. Hobbs, England and Surrey.

Most hundreds (centuries) in career – 197 J. B. Hobbs, England and Surrey.

Most runs in over – 36 G. S. Sobers, Notts (v Glamorgan, Swansea, 1968); R. J. Shastri, Bombay (v Baroda, Bombay, 1985).

Best bowling in innings – 10–10 H. Verity, Yorks (v Notts, Leeds, 1932).

Most wickets in season – 304 A. P. Freeman, England and Kent, 1928; in career – 4187 W. Rhodes, England and Yorks.

Highest partnership – 577 (4th wkt) V. S. Hazare (288) and Gul Mahomed (319), Baroda (v Holkar, Baroda, 1947).

Highest total – 1107 (all out) Victoria (v NSW, Melbourne, 1926).

Most wicket-keeping dismissals in career – 1646 R. W. Taylor, England and Derbyshire.

AUTO RACING

World Champions

1950	Giuseppe Farine (Italy)
1951	Juan Manuel Fangio (Argentina)
1952	Alberto Ascari (Italy)
1953	Alberto Ascari (Italy)
1954	Juan Manuel Fangio (Argentina)
1955	Juan Manuel Fangio (Argentina)
1956	Juan Manuel Fangio (Argentina)
1957	Juan Manuel Fangio (Argentina)
1958	Mike Hawthorn (England)
1959	Jack Brabham (Australia)
1960	Jack Brabham (Australia)
1961	Phil Hill (U.S.A.)
1962	Graham Hill (England)
1963	Jim Clark (Scotland)
1964	John Surtees (England)
1965	Jim Clark (Scotland)
1966	Jack Brabham (Australia)
1967	Denis Hulme (New Zealand)
1968	Graham Hill (England)
1969	Jackie Stewart (Scotland)
1970	Jochen Rindt (Austria)
1971	Jackie Stewart (Scotland)
1972	Emerson Fittipaldi (Brazil)
1973	Jackie Stewart (Scotland)
1974	Emerson Fittipaldi (Brazil)
1975	Niki Lauda (Austria)
1976	James Hunt (England)
1977	Niki Lauda (Austria)
1978	Mario Andretti (U.S.A.)
1979	Jody Scheckter (South Africa)
1980	Alan Jones (Australia)
1981	Nelson Picquet (Brazil)
1982	Keke Rosberg (Finland)
1983	Nelson Picquet (Brazil)
1984	Niki Lauda (Austria)
1985	Alain Prost (France)
1986	Alain Prost (France)

A–Z of Sports

BADMINTON

Court—44 × 20 ft. (13.4 × 6.1 m). Singles—44 × 17 ft. (13.4 × 5.2 m).

Height of net—5ft. 1 in. (1.55 m).

Weight of shuttlecock—0.16–0.19 oz (4.73–5.50 g).

Scoring—best of 3 or 5 15-pt games (best of 3 11-pt games, women's singles)

Ruling body—International Badminton Federation (IBF).

World team championships—Thomas Cup (men); Uber Cup (women).

Major individual competitions—World championships; All-England Championships.

BASEBALL

Pitching distance—60 ft. 6 in. (18.4 m).

Side of diamond—90 ft. (27.4 m).

Max. length of bat—3 ft. 6 in. (1.07 m).

Diameter of ball—2¾ in. (7 cm).

Weight of ball—5¼–5½ oz (149–156 g).

Number per side—9 (substitutes allowed).

Number of innings—9 or more (played to finish).

BASKETBALL

Court—85 × 46 ft. (26 × 14 m).

Height of baskets—10 ft. (3 m).

Diameter of baskets—18 in. (45.7 cm).

Circumference of ball—29½–30½ in (75–78 cm).

Weight of ball—21–23 oz (600–650 g).

Duration—40 min actual play (2 × 20) plus periods of 5 min until result is obtained.

Number per side—5 (up to 5 substitutes).

Ruling body—Fédération Internationale de Basketball Amateur (FIBA).

Major competitions—World championships (men and women) and Olympic Games.

BILLIARDS AND SNOOKER

Table—11½ ft. × 5 ft. 9 in. (3.50 × 1.75 m).

Diameter of balls—2¹⁄₁₆ in. (5.25 cm).

Billiards—red, white, spot white.

Billiards scoring—pot or in-off red 3, white 2; cannon 2.

Snooker balls (value)—black (7), pink (6), blue (5), brown (4), green (3), yellow (2), 15 reds (1 each), white (cue ball).

Ruling body—Billiards and Snooker Control Council.

Major competitions—World championships (for both snooker and billiards, professional and amateur).

BOXING

Professional

Ring—14–20 ft. (4.27–6.10 m) square.

Gloves—6 oz (170 g) fly to welterweight, 8 oz (227 g) light-middleweight and above.

Duration—6, 8, 10, 12 or 15 (title) 3-min rounds.

Ruling body—World Boxing Council (WBC) and others.

Amateur

Ring—12–16 ft. (3.66–4.88 m) square.

Gloves—8 oz (227 g).

Duration—3 3-min rounds (seniors).

Ruling body—Amateur International Boxing Association (AIBA).

Weight Limits

	Professional		Amateur	
Weight	st–lb	kg	st–lb	kg
Light-fly	7–11	49.4	7–07	48
Fly	8–00	50.8	8–00	51
Super-fly	8–03	52.2	–	–
Bantam	8–06	53.5	8–07	54
Super-bantam	8–10	55.3	–	–
Feather	9–00	57.2	9–00	57
Super-feather	9–04	59.0	–	–
Light	9–09	61.2	9–07	60
Light-welter	10–00	63.5	10–00	63.5
Welter	10–07	66.7	10–08	67
Light-middle	11–00	69.9	11–02	71
Middle	11–06	72.6	11–11	75
Light-heavy	12–07	79.4	12–10	81
Cruiser	13–13	88.5	–	–
Heavy	No limit		14–05	91
Super-heavy	–	–	No limit	

Professional limits use st–lb, amateur use kg.

CHESS

Ruling body—International Chess Federation.

World Champions

1866–94	Wilhelm Steinitz (Austria)	
1894–1921	Emanuel Lasker (Germany)	
1921–27	Jose R. Capablanca (Cuba)	
1927–35	Alexander A. Alekhine (U.S.S.R.)[1]	
1935–37	Max Euwe (Netherlands)	
1937–46	Alexander A. Alekhine (U.S.S.R.)[1]	

[1] Took French citizenship.

1948–57	Mikhail Botvinnik (U.S.S.R.)
1957–58	Vassily Smyslov (U.S.S.R.)
1958–59	Mikhail Botvinnik (U.S.S.R.)
1960–61	Mikhail Tal (U.S.S.R.)
1961–63	Mikhail Botvinnik (U.S.S.R.)
1963–69	Tigran Petrosian (U.S.S.R.)
1969–72	Boris Spassky (U.S.S.R.)
1972–75	Bobby Fischer[2] (U.S.A.)
1975–85	Anatoli Karpov (U.S.S.R.)
1985–	Gary Kasparov (U.S.S.R.)

[2] Karpov won title when Fischer defaulted.

CRICKET

Pitch—wicket to wicket 22 yd. (20 m); bowling crease 8 ft. 8 in. (2.64 m).

Stumps—28 in. (71.1 cm) high, 9 in. (22.9 cm) overall width.

Bat (max.)—38 in. (96.5 cm) long, 4¼ in. (10.8 cm) wide.

Ball—circum. 8¹³⁄₁₆–9 in. (22.4–22.9 cm), weight 5½–5¾ oz. (156–163 g).

Number per side—11 (subs. only for fielding).

Ruling body—International Cricket Conference (ICC).

CYCLE RACING

Ruling body—Union Cycliste Internationale.

Major competitions: ROAD RACING—Tour de France, Olympic 62-mile (100-km) race.

TRACK RACING—Olympics and world championships (sprint, pursuit, ½-mile (1-km) time trial, motor-paced).

Other cycle sports—six-day racing, cyclo-cross, cycle speedway, bicycle polo, time trials.

EQUESTRIAN SPORTS

Ruling body—Fédération Equestre International (FEI).

Major competitions: SHOW JUMPING—world championships (men's and women's) every 4 years, alternating with Olympics; President's Cup (world team championship) based on Nations Cup results; 2-yearly European Championships (men's and women's); King George V Gold Cup; Queen Elizabeth II Gold Cup.

THREE-DAY EVENT (1 Dressage, 2 Endurance or Cross-country, 3 Show jumping)—4-yearly world championships and Olympics; 2-yearly European Championships; Badminton Horse Trials.

DRESSAGE—Olympics and world championships.

FENCING

Ruling body—Fédération Internationale d'Escrimé (FIE).

Events—foil, épée, sabre; foil (women).

Major competitions—annual world championships (including Olympics).

Duration of bout—first to 5 hits (or 6 min) men; 4 hits (or 5 min) women.

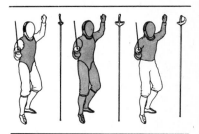

▲ The three weapons used in fencing—the foil (left), the épée (middle), and the saber (right). Women fence only the foil. The target areas are shaded. Fencing was first played as a sport in Egypt around 1360 B.C.

FOOTBALL

Field—360 × 160 ft. (110 × 49 m).

Goals—30 ft. (9 m) high, 18½ ft. (5.6 m) wide, 10 ft. (3 m) off ground for pro., not college game.

Ball—length 11 in. (28 cm), short circum. 21¼ in. (54 cm), weight 14–15 oz (397–425 g).

Duration—60 min (4 × 15) playing time.

Number per side—11 (max. 45 on pro. team).

Scoring—*touchdown* 6 pts, *extra point* 1, *field goal* 3, *safety* 2.

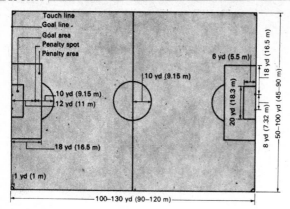

◀ **The layout** of a soccer field.

SOCCER

Ball—circum. 27–28 in. (68–71 cm), weight 14–16 oz. (400–450 g).
Duration of game—90 min (2 × 45) plus 2 × 15 min extra in certain cup games.
Number per side—11 (1 or 2 substitutes, depending on competition).
Ruling body—Fédération Internationale de Football Association (FIFA).

FOOTBALL, AUSTRALIAN RULES

Field—oval 148–202 yd. (135–185 m) by 120–170 yd. (110–155 m).
Goal posts—21 ft. (6.4 m) wide, *behind posts* 6.4 m either side of goal posts.
Ball—short circum. 22½ in. (57.2 cm), weight 16–17 oz. (454–482 g).
Duration—100 min (4 × 25).
Number per side—18 (2 substitutes).
Scoring—*goal* 6 pts, *behind* 1.

GOLF

Ball—max. weight 1.62 oz. (46 g), min. diam. U.K. 1.62 in. (4.11 cm), U.S. 1.68 in. (4.27 cm).
Hole—diam. 4¼ in. (10.8 cm).
Number of clubs carried—14 maximum.
Ruling body—United States Golf Association; Royal and Ancient Golf Club of St. Andrews.
Major competitions: Individual—Open, U.S. Open, U.S. Masters, U.S. PGA.
    Team—World Cup (international teams of 2, annual); Eisenhower Trophy (world amateur, teams of 4, 2-yearly); Ryder Cup (U.S. v Europe, 2-yearly).

GYMNASTICS

Ruling body—Fédération Internationale de Gymnastique.
Events: Men's—floor exercises, rings, parallel bars, pommel horse, vault (lengthwise), horizontal bar; overall; team; women's—floor exercises (to music), vault, uneven parallel bars, beam; overall; team.
Major competitions—World and Olympic championships, alternately every 4 years.

▼ **Nadia Comaneci** of Romania was the first gymnast to score a maximum 10 points—in the 1976 Olympics, where she achieved seven perfect 10s.

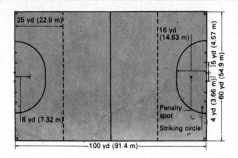

◀ **The layout** of a hockey field.

Field hockey was developed in England. Men's hockey became an Olympic sport in 1908, women's not until 1980.

HOCKEY (FIELD)

Goals—12 ft. (3.66 m) wide, 7 ft. (2.13 m) high.

Ball—circum. 9 in. (23 cm), weight 5½–5¾ oz. (156–163 g), made of cork and twine covered in leather.

Duration of game—70 min (2 × 35).

Number per side—11 (2 subs. in men's game).

Ruling bodies: men's—Fédération Internationale de Hockey (FIH); women's—Women's International Hockey Rules' Board.

Major competitions—Olympic Games and World Cup (4-yearly).

LACROSSE

Field—110 × 60 yd. (100 × 54 m) men; 120 × 70 yd. (110 × 64 m) preferred for women's international matches.

Goals—6 × 6 ft. (1.8 × 1.8 m).

Ball—circum. 7¾–8 in. (19.7–20.3 cm), weight 5–5¼ oz. (141–149 g) men, 4¾–5¼ oz. (135–149 g) women.

Duration—60 min (4 × 15) men, 50 min (2 × 25) women.

Number per side—10.

MODERN PENTATHLON

Order of events—riding, fencing, shooting, swimming, running.

Ruling body—Union Internationale de Pentathlon Moderne et Biathlon.

Major competitions—annual world championships (including Olympics).

MOTORCYCLE RACING

Ruling body—Fédération Internationale Motorcycliste (FIM).

Classes—various, from 80 cc to 500 cc, unlimited, sidecar.

Major competitions—world championships (based on points gained in individual grands prix), Isle of Man TT.

Other motorcycle sports—scrambling (motorcross), trials, grasstrack racing.

AUTO RACING

Ruling body—Fédération Internationale de l'Automobile (FIA).

Major events and competitions: Formula One—World Drivers' Championship (based on points gained in individual grands prix: 9, 6, 4, 3, 2, 1 for first 6).

Sports car racing—Le Mans.

Rally driving—Monte Carlo Rally.

Other motor sports—drag racing, karting, hillclimbing, trials, autocross, rallycross, autotests, stock-car racing, vintage-car racing.

▼ **Emerson Fittipaldi** on the Brands Hatch circuit in a JPS-Ford.

195

◀ **The layout** of a netball court.

| Goal third | Centre third | Goal third |

3 ft (1 m)
32 ft (9.75 m)
50 ft (15.2 m)
100 ft (30.5 m)

NETBALL
Court—100 × 50 ft. (30.5 × 15.2 m).
Net—10 ft. (3.05 m) high; ring diam. 15 in (38 cm).
Ball—as for soccer.
Duration of game—60 min (4 × 15).
Number per side—7 (subs. for injuries).
Ruling body—International Federation of Netball Associations.
World championships—every 4 years.

ROWING
Ruling body—Fédération Internationale des Sociétés d'Aviron (FISA).
International events: men—eights, fours, and pairs (both coxed and coxless), single, double, and quadruple sculls; women—eights, coxed fours, coxless pairs, single, double, and coxed quadruple sculls.
Major competitions—World championships every 4 years, alternating with Olympics; Henley Regatta (including Grand Challenge Cup and Diamond Sculls).
Standard course—men 2,187 yd. (2,000 m), boys 1,640 yd. (1,500 m), women 1,094 yd. (1,000 m).

RUGBY LEAGUE
Field (max.)— 75 yd. (69 m) wide, 110 yd. (100 m) between goals, 6–12 yd. (6–11 m) behind goals.
Goal posts—as for rugby union.
Ball—length 10½–11½ in. (27–29 cm), short circum. 22¾–24 in. (58–61 cm).
Duration of game—80 min (2 × 40).
Number per side—13 (2 substitutes).
Scoring—*try* 3 pts, *conversion* 2, *penalty goal* 2, *dropped goal* 1.
Ruling body—Rugby Football League International Board.
Major competition—World Cup.

RUGBY UNION
Field (max.)—75 yd. (69 m) wide, 110 yd. (100 m) between goals, 25 yd. (22 m) behind goals.
Goal posts—18½ ft. (5.6 m) wide, no height limit, crossbar 10 ft. (3 m) above ground.
Ball—length 11 in. (28 cm), short circum. 22¾–24½ in. (58–62 cm), weight 14–15½ oz. (400–440 g).
Duration of game—80 min (2 × 40).
Number per side—15 (2 subs. for injury only).

▶ **The layout** of a rugby union field.

Rugby began in the 1820s at Rugby school in England when a schoolboy playing a game of football picked up the ball and ran with it.

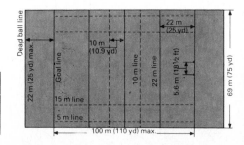

Dead ball line
22 m (25 yd) max.
Goal line
22 m
(25 yd)
10 m
(10.9 yd)
10 m line
22 m line
5.6 m (18½ ft)
69 m (75 yd)
15 m line
5 m line
100 m (110 yd) max.

196

Scoring—*try* 4 pts, *conversion* 2, *penalty goal* 3, *dropped goal* 3.

Ruling body—International Rugby Football Board.

Major competitions—World Cup, Five Nations Championship (England, France, Ireland, Scotland, Wales), Ranfurly Shield (New Zealand), Currie Cup (South Africa).

Touring sides—Lions (G.B.), All Blacks (New Zealand), Springboks (South Africa), Wallabies (Australia), Tricolours (France).

SPEEDWAY

Track—4 laps of 300–450 yd. (274–411 m) surface—red shale or granite dust.

Meeting—20 races, 4 riders in race, each getting 5 rides.

Scoring—1st 3 pts, 2nd 2, 3rd 1.

Machines—Brakeless 500 cc motorcycles.

Ruling body—Fédération Internationale de Motorcycliste (FIM).

Major competitions—World Championship (individual), World Team Cup, World Pairs Championship.

SQUASH

Ball—diam. 1.56–1.63 in. (39.5–41.5 mm), weight 0.82–0.87 oz. (23.3–24.6 g), made of matt surface rubber.

Racket (max.)—length 27 in. (68.6 cm), head 8½ in. (21.6 cm) long by 7¼ in. (18.4 cm) wide.

Scoring—best of 5 9-up games.

Ruling body—International Squash Rackets Federation.

Major competitions—World Open, Women's Open.

SWIMMING AND DIVING

Standard Olympic pool—54.7 yd. (50 m) long, 8 lanes.

Ruling body—Fédération Internationale de Natation Amateur (FINA).

Competitive strokes—freestyle (usually front crawl), backstroke, breaststroke, butterfly; individual medley (butterfly, backstroke, breaststroke, freestyle); medley relay (backstroke, breaststroke, butterfly, freestyle).

Diving events—men's and women's springboard at 9¾ ft. (3 m), highboard at 33 ft. (10 m) (lower boards also used).

Major competitions—Olympics and world championships.

Major long-distance swims—English Channel, Cook Strait (N.Z.), Atlantic City Marathon (U.S.).

TABLE TENNIS

Table—9 × 5 ft. (2.74 × 1.52 m), 2½ ft. (76 cm) off floor.

Net—height 6 in. (15.2 cm), length 6 ft. (1.83 m).

Ball—diam. 1.46–1.50 in. (37–38 mm), weight 0.085–0.089 oz. (2.40–2.53 g), made of celluloid-type plastic, white or yellow.

Bat surface—max. thickness 0.08 in. (2 mm) pimpled rubber or 0.16 in. (4 mm) sandwich rubber.

Scoring—best of 3 or 5 21-pt games.

▶ **Inside a squash court.** One of the side walls has been removed in order to see inside. Both side walls have the same dimensions.

Janangir Khan of Pakistan won five consecutive World Open Squash Championships (1981–85). When he was beaten by Ross Norman (New Zealand) in the 1986 final, it was his first defeat in 5 years, 7 months.

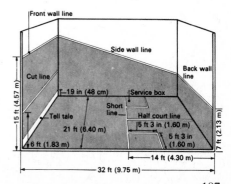

Front wall line
Side wall line
Back wall line
Cut line
19 in (48 cm)
Service box
Short line
Half court line
Tell tale
21 ft (6.40 m)
5 ft 3 in (1.60 m)
5 ft 3 in (1.60 m)
6 ft (1.83 m)
15 ft (4.57 m)
7 ft (2.13 m)
14 ft (4.30 m)
32 ft (9.75 m)

Ruling body—International Table Tennis Federation.

Major competitions—world championships, Swaythling Cup (men's team), Corbillion Cup (women's teams), all 2-yearly.

TENNIS

Ball—diam. 2½–2⅝ in. (6.35–6.67 cm), weight 2–2¹⁄₁₆ oz. (56.7–58.5 g), made of wool-covered rubber, white or yellow.

Rackets—no limits, wood or metal frames, strung with lamb's gut or nylon.

Scoring—best of 3 or 5 6-up sets, with tiebreaker at 6–6 (or first to lead by 2); games of 4 pts (15, 30, 40, game), 40–40 being *deuce* and 2-pt lead required; tiebreaker game usually first to 7 pts with 2-pt lead.

Ruling body—International Lawn Tennis Federation (ILTF).

Major competitions—Wimbledon, Australian Open, U.S. Open, French Open (the four constituting "Grand Slam"), Davis Cup (world team championship), Federation Cup (Women's World Cup), Wightman Cup, Olympics.

VOLLEYBALL

Court—59 × 29½ ft. (18 × 9 m).

Net height—7 ft. 11.7 in. (2.43 m) for men, 7 ft. 3 in. (2.21 m) for women.

Ball—circum. 25.6–26.4 in. (65–67 cm), weight 9–10 oz. (260–280 g).

Number per side—6 (6 substitutes).

Scoring—best of 3 or 5 15-pt sets.

Ruling body—Fédération Internationale de Volleyball (FIV).

Major competitions—Olympics and world championships, alternately every 4 years (men and women).

WATER SKIING

Ruling body—World Water Ski Union.

Events—slalom, jumping, figures (freestyle tricks) and overall title.

World championships—every 2 years.

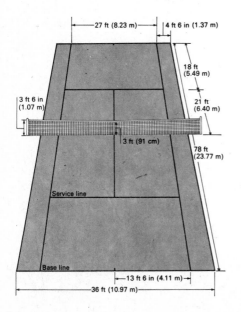

◀ **The layout** of a tennis court. The inner sidelines are used for singles play, the outer ones for doubles. The posts are 3 feet (nearly a meter) from the outer or inner sidelines.

The first rules of tennis were drawn up by the Marylebone Cricket Club in London in 1875, and the first Lawn Tennis Championships were played at the All England Croquet and Lawn Tennis Club at Wimbledon in 1877, with rules very similar to those of today.

WEIGHTLIFTING

Ruling body—International Weightlift.ing Federation (IWF).

Lifts—*Snatch* (bar pulled overhead in one movement) and *clean-and-jerk* (bar raised to shoulders first, then driven aloft. as legs are straightened); (non-Olympic) *bench press, squat, dead lift.*.

World championships—annual (including the Olympics).

Classes—flyweight (52 kg/114½ lb limit), bantam (56 kg/123½ lb), feather (60 kg/132¼ lb), welter (67.5 kg/148¾ lb), middle (75 kg/165¼ lb), light-heavy (82.5 kg/181¾ lb), middle-heavy (90 kg/198½ lb), 1st heavy (100 kg/220½ lb), 2nd heavy (110 kg/242½ lb), super-heavy (over 110 kg/242½ lb).

WINTER SPORTS

Ice Skating

Ruling body—International Skating Union (ISU).

Major competitions—Olympics and world championships (annual).

Figure skating events—men's, women's, pairs, (pairs) dancing (all with compulsory and "free" sections); two sets of marks, for technical merit and artistic impression.

Speed skating events (on oval 440-yd./400-m circuits)—men's 500, 1,000, 1,500, 5,000 and 10,000 m; women's 500, 1,000, 1,500 and 3,000 m; overall titles in world and international events.

Ice Hockey

Rink—max. 200 × 100 ft. (61 × 30.5 m).

Surround—max. 4 ft. (1.22 m) high boards.

Goals—6 × 4 ft. (1.83 × 1.22 m).

Puck—diam. 3 in. (7.6 cm), thickness 1 in. (2.5 cm), weight 5½–6 oz. (156–170 g), made of vulcanized rubber or similar material.

Duration—60 min (3 × 20) playing time.

Number per side—6 (max. 17 on team).

Ruling body—International Ice Hockey Federation.

Major competitions (amateur)—Olympics, annual world championships.

Cresta Run

Course—unique to St. Moritz, 1,213 m (1,326.6 yd.); agg. time for 3 descents.

Event—single seater, ridden face down.

Ruling body—St. Moritz Tobogganing Club.

Major competitions—Grand National (full course, from Top), Curzon Cup (from Junction, 888 m/971 yd.); Olympic event (full course) in 1928 and 1948.

Alpine Ski Racing

Events—downhill, slalom, giant slalom, and combined.

Downhill—vert. drop 800–1,000 m (2,625–3,281 ft.) men; 500–700 m (1,640–2,297 ft.) women.

Slalom—55–75 gates men, 50–60 gates women; alternate gates (pairs of poles 13–16 ft. 4–5 m, apart) have blue or red flags.

Giant Slalom—min. 30 gates 13–26 ft. (4–8 m) wide, at least 33 ft. (10 m) apart.

Ruling body—Fédération Internationale de Ski (FIS).

Major competitions—2-yearly world championships (including Olympics, which has no combined title), annual World Cup (men's and women's, individuals scoring in 15 of 21 top international events, first 10 scoring 25, 20, 15, 11, 8, 6, 4, 3, 2, 1 pts), annual Arlberg-Kandahar.

▼ **Taking a gate** in the slalom—an event which involves weaving a zigzag path around upright markers.

199.

The Olympics

The first recorded Olympic Games took place in 776 B.C., at Olympia, in southwest Greece. The Games were revived in 1896 by Baron de Coubertin.

1896 Athens, Greece
1900 Paris, France
1904 St. Louis, United States
1906 Athens, Greece
1908 London, England
1912 Stockholm, Sweden
1920 Antwerp, Belgium
1924 Paris, France
1928 Amsterdam, Netherlands
1932 Los Angeles, United States
1936 Berlin, Germany
1948 London, England
1952 Helsinki, Finland
1956 Melbourne, Australia
1960 Rome, Italy
1964 Tokyo, Japan
1968 Mexico City, Mexico
1972 Munich, West Germany
1976 Montreal, Canada
1980 Moscow, U.S.S.R.
1984 Los Angeles, United States
1988 Seoul, South Korea*
1992 Barcelona, Spain

*Some events in N. Korea

WINTER OLYMPICS
1924 Chamonix, France
1928 St. Moritz, Switzerland
1932 Lake Placid, United States
1936 Garmisch, Germany
1948 St. Moritz, Switzerland
1952 Oslo, Norway
1956 Cortina, Italy
1960 Squaw Valley, United States
1964 Innsbruck, Austria
1968 Grenoble, France
1972 Sapporo, Japan
1976 Innsbruck, Austria
1980 Lake Placid, United States
1984 Sarajevo, Yugoslavia
1988 Calgary, Canada
1992 Albertville, France

COMMONWEALTH GAMES
1930 Hamilton, Canada
1934 London, England
1938 Sydney, Australia
1950 Auckland, New Zealand
1954 Vancouver, Canada
1958 Cardiff, Wales
1962 Perth, Australia
1966 Kingston, Jamaica
1970 Edinburgh, Scotland
1974 Christchurch, New Zealand
1978 Edmonton, Canada
1982 Brisbane, Australia
1986 Edinburgh, Scotland
1990 Auckland, New Zealand

The outstanding competitor of the 1972 Olympic Games was the American swimmer Mark Spitz, who created an all-time record by winning 7 gold medals, 4 individual and 3 relay.

Jesse Owens was a famous, record-breaking American athlete who won four gold medals at the 1936 Olympic Games. Hitler was furious because this black athlete had disproved his theory of the superiority of the white race.

▼ **The Olympic torch** being carried at the opening ceremony of the 1984 Games by Jesse Owens' granddaughter, Gina Hemphill.

SPORTS AND HISTORY

◀ **Boxing as a sport** was included in the ancient Olympic Games of 688 B.C. Prizefighting without gloves, shown here, began in 18th-century London. Today boxing is governed by the "Queensberry rules," laid down by the Marquis of Queensberry in the 1860s.

◀ **Women, dressed in cumbersome** full-length dresses, playing tennis at Wimbledon in the 1880s. Tennis is derived from the game "real tennis," which was first played in France during the 1300s.

◀ **Ancient Greeks** playing a game similar to hockey. At first, the ancient Olympics featured only foot races. Later, discus and javelin throwing, wrestling and jumping, and boxing and chariot racing were added.

◀ **A game of cricket** in 1743. Notice that the wicket keeper has taken his wig off. You can also see that the bat is curved. The word "cricket" is thought to come from *cricc*, an old English word for "crook." The game is believed to have originated in the sheep country of southeastern England, as early as the 1300s. The straight bat was adopted in 1770.

◀ **These "football" players** of 1600 are blowing up their ball ready for play. It is made of a pig's bladder, covered in leather. Soccer became distinct from rugby football when supporters of the handling game withdrew from the newly formed Football Association in 1863.

Transportation

Every day, thousands of people rely on complex transportation networks to take them back and forth on their daily business. Supertankers carry millions of tons of goods across the sea just as giant container trucks speed them along our freeways. Airliners cross the world in a few hours and hovercraft skim across vast swamps and marshes, opening up unexplored areas. These forms of transportation are relatively recent. For thousands of years, transportation meant horses, horse-drawn carts or carriages, and boats and ships powered only by oars or sails. The building of the canal systems that began in Europe in the 1700s helped to trigger the transportation revolution of the nineteenth century. The nineteenth century was the great age of steam—railroads and steamships. By 1913, the invention of the automobile had begun mass production by great names such as Henry Ford. The twentieth century has seen us constantly refining the transportation we already have. It has also seen transportation take us beyond our planet. What will our next step be?

TRACK RECORDS

- **World's widest gauge:** 5½ ft (1.676 m) in the Indian sub-continent, Chile and Argentina.
- **World's narrowest gauge:** 1¼ ft (0.381 m); 10¼ in (260 mm) is used on the Wells Harbor and the Wells–Walsingham Railway in Norfolk, England.
- **World's longest line:** 5,800 miles (9,334 km) across Siberia, from Moscow to Nakhodka, U.S.S.R., with 97 stops.
- **World's longest straight line:** 297 miles (478 km) across Nullarbor Plain, Western and South Australia.
- **World's highest standard gauge:** 15,800 ft (4,817 m) above sea level on the Morococha Branch at La Cima of Peruvian State Railways, South America.

◀ *Top:* **The world's fastest passenger train**—the bullet train or *Hikari Express*—speeds between Tokyo and Osaka with Mount Fuji in the background. *Bottom:* A more traditional form of transportation, but a very efficient one for crossing desert areas. A caravan of camels passes by the magnificent pyramids at el-Gizeh, Egypt.

Milestones in Transportation

B.C.

c. **3500** First wheeled vehicles, including early form of war chariot, used in Sumeria.

1850 A canal built by King Sesostris III in Egypt.

1800 War chariots developed by the Hittites. Horses used to draw vehicles.

312 Romans construct the Appian Way, which ran 162 miles from Rome to Capua.

▲ **A Babylonian sled,** about 2000 B.C. The wheel was common at this time, but sleds traveled better over rough ground.

A.D.

c. **1100** Magnetic compass developed.

1400s Advent of versatile three-masted ship.

1662 First omnibus (horse-drawn), invented by Blaise Pascal (France).

1769 First steam-powered road vehicles, built by Nicolas Cugnot.

1783 First human ascent in hot-air balloon by J. F. Pilâtre.
First successful experiment with steamboats.

1804 Construction of the first successful steam locomotive by Richard Trevithick.

1819 Macadam paving for roads developed by John L. McAdam.
First ship employing steam power—the *Savannah*—crossed the Atlantic Ocean.

1822 First iron paddle steamer.

1825 Stockton and Darlington Railway opened.

1839 First pedal-driven bicycle, invented by Kirkpatrick Macmillan (G.B.).

1852 First airship, or dirigible (France).

1863 First underground railway opened in London.

1869 Opening of the Suez Canal.
Completion of the first transcontinental railroad in the United States.

1876 Nikolaus Otto improves the four-stroke internal-combustion engine.

▲ **Caravel, around 1490.** These small ships had broad bows, triangular sails, and a high, narrow deck above the stern. Portuguese explorers sailed south in caravels to explore the African coast.

▼ **The first underground** railway in the world—the Metropolitan line, London, 1863.

1885	Gottlieb Daimler and Carl Benz market the first gasoline engine automobiles.
1890	First electric underground railway.
1894	First ships driven by steam turbine.
1897	First diesel engine built.
1903	First successful powered airplane flight by Wilbur and Orville Wright.
1909	First Model-T Ford.
1914	Completion of Panama Canal.
1919	First nonstop transatlantic flight made by John Alcock and Arthur Brown.
1921	First diesel locomotive in regular service (Tunisian Railways).
1930	Design for a jet aircraft patented by Frank Whittle.
1937	Prototype helicopter (the FW61) successfully tested.
1939	Construction and flight of the first jet aircraft by the Heinkel Company of Germany.
1949	The De Havilland *Comet* was the first commercial jet airliner.
1952	First commercial jet airline service.
1954	The submarine *Nautilus*, the world's first atomic-powered ship, launched by the U.S. Navy.
1959	First air-cushion vehicle.
1962	First nuclear-powered merchant ship.
1968	First supersonic airliner.
1970	First jumbo jet.
1984	First woman captains Boeing 747 across Atlantic.

▲ **Electric streetcar,** 1890. Streetcars, originally horse-drawn, were the first cheap, reliable form of transportation in towns and cities.

▼ **The hydrofoil** is perfect for taking people over short stretches of calm water. It travels very fast because the hull lifts out of the water, supported by struts. The first hydrofoil was built in 1906. Alexander Graham Bell built one that could travel at 71 mph.

◀ **American Chuck Yeager** broke the sound barrier in 1947. Twenty years later the world's first international supersonic airliner— *Concorde*, shown here—took to the skies. Developed by the French and the British and named after this co-operation, it travels at twice the speed of sound.

205

Travel by Sea

B.C.

pre-8000 Old Stone Age people using form of dugout canoe.

c. **7250** Earliest form of seafaring trade in Mediterranean between Melos and Greek mainland.

c. **3000** First known ships: Egyptian galleys.

c. **1000** Phoenicians develop bireme, galley with two rows of oars on each side.

c. **200** Romans build huge galleys, with as many as 200 oars.

A.D.

1100 Sailors in the Mediterranean and in the China Seas navigating by means of magnetic compass.

1400s Portuguese develop three-masted ship; facilitates sailing against wind.

1500s Age of the galleon.

1624 Dutch scientist Cornelius van Drebbel demonstrates "submarine," a leather-covered row boat, in England.

1783 Steam propulsion first achieved, by Marquis Jouffroy d'Abbans (France), with 180-ton paddle-steamer *Pyroscaphe* on the Saône, near Lyons.

1790s Sailing ships built with iron hulls.

1800 Robert Fulton (U.S.A.) tests 21-foot copper-covered submarine *Nautilus*.

1801 First successful power-driven vessel the *Charlotte Dundas*, a Clyde canal tug, built by William Symington (G.B.).

1807 Robert Fulton (U.S.A.) builds the *Clermont*, first regular passenger steamer; plies Hudson River, New York to Albany.

1822 First iron-built paddle steamer, the *Aaron Manby*; also first prefabricated ship. Made on Thames River for service in France.

1839 British steamer *Archimedes* first to use screw propeller successfully.

1845 *Rainbow* (U.S.A.), first true clipper ship.

1897 Charles Parsons (G.B.) dramatically demonstrates first turbine-driven ship, *Turbinia*, at Spithead in front of Queen Victoria.

1912 First ocean-going diesel-driven ships.

1954 First nuclear-powered submarine, *Nautilus* (U.S.A.).

1959 First air-cushion vehicle, SR-N1, invented by Christopher Cockerell (G.B.).

First nuclear-powered surface ship, Russian ice-breaker *Lenin*.

1962 *Savannah* (U.S.A.) goes into service as first nuclear-powered merchant ship.

First public air-cushion vehicle service, inaugurated in Britain.

1979 First helicopter-carrying patrol vessel in operation with Danish Fisheries Protection.

1985 Wreckage of the *Titanic* found by U.S./French research team.

▲ **Under full sail,** the windjammer *Preussen* presented more than one acre of canvas to the wind. She was the only five-masted square-sail ship ever built.

OVER THE TOP

● The world's fastest air-cushion vehicle is a U.S. Navy test vehicle which reached 91.9 knots in 1980. It is 78 ft long and weighs approximately 100 tons. The largest civil air-cushion vehicle is the SRN4 Mk III, weighing 305 tons. It carries 418 passengers and 60 cars.

● The world's fastest hydrofoil is the Canadian Navy's *Bras d'Or*, weighing 183 tons and with a top speed of 61 knots. The world's largest is the 1965 Lockheed *Plainview*, 213 ft long, 314 tons fully loaded, and with a speed of 50 knots.

DISASTERS AT SEA

Birkenhead (1852), British troopship, broke in two on rocks off Port Elizabeth (S. Africa); 455 perished, 193 survived.
Sultana (1865), Mississippi river steamer, blew up (boiler explosion); 1,450 died.
Mary Celeste (1872), American half-brig, found abandoned in Atlantic with no sign of life; great mystery of the sea.
General Slocum (1904), an excursion steamer, burned in New York harbor; 1,021 died.
Titanic (1912), British liner, struck iceberg in N. Atlantic; about 1,500 died, 705 survived.
Empress of Ireland (1914), Canadian steamer, sank after collision in St. Lawrence River; 1,024 died.
Thetis (1939), British submarine, sank in Liverpool Bay; 99 perished.
Curacao (1942), British cruiser, sank after collision with liner *Queen Mary*; 335 died.
Toya Maru (1954), Japanese ferry, sank in Tsugaru Strait; 1,172 died.
Andrea Doria (1956), Italian liner, collided with Swedish liner *Stockholm* off Nantucket (MA) in fog, 51 died, about 1,655 rescued.
Thresher (1963), American nuclear submarine, sank in N. Atlantic; 129 died.
Scorpion (1968), American nuclear submarine, sank in N. Atlantic; 99 died.
Tamponas II (1981), Indonesian passenger ship caught fire and sank in Java Sea; 580 died.
Herald of Free Enterprise (1987), Townsend Thoresen passenger and car ferry sank on leaving Zeebrugge Harbor in Belgium. At time of going to press, 188 died, 354 survivors.

GIANTS OF THE SEA

● The world's largest submarines are of the U.S.S.R. Typhoon class, code-named "Oscar." They are believed to weigh 30,000 tons and measure 558 ft in length.

● The world's largest passenger liner is the *Norway*: 70,000 tons, 1,036 ft long, and built in 1961.

● The world's largest aircraft carrier is the U.S.S. *Nimitz*: 92,800 tons, 1,089 ft long. The U.S.S. *Enterprise* is longer but of less tonnage.

● The world's largest battleship is the U.S.S. *New Jersey*: 59,900 tons, 885 ft long.

● The world's largest dry cargo ship is the Liberian *World Gala*: 282,462 tons, 1,109 ft long.

● The world's largest ship of any kind is the *Seawise Giant*: 564,739 tons, 1,503 ft, which was completed in 1979.

Travel by Rail

1801 Richard Trevithick (G.B.) makes full-size steam carriage.

1803 First public freight railway: Surrey Iron Railway, engineered by William Jessop and James Outram (G.B.).

Trevithick builds very first steam locomotive.

1804 Trevithick constructs second steam locomotive, which successfully pulls much more than a horse —a 10-ton load—from Pen-y-darran to Glamorganshire Canal.

1807 World's first passenger railway opened from Swansea to Oystermouth, South Wales. (Horse-drawn, later steam.)

1812 World's first steam railroad began at the Middleton coal mine, Yorkshire, using locomotives designed by John Blenkinsop.

1813 William Hedley (G.B.) builds two smooth-wheeled engines, *Puffing Billy* and *Wylam Billy*.

1814 George Stephenson (G.B.) designs his first locomotive— *Blücher*.

1825 Opening of Stockton & Darlington Railway (Sept. 27) first regularly operated steam railroad in world.

1829 Stephenson's *Rocket* impressively wins Rainhill Trials, Liverpool.

First steam locomotive in America, the British-built train *Stourbridge Lion*, ran at Honesdale, Pennsylvania.

1830 Opening of Liverpool & Manchester Railway (Sept. 15), first regular public passenger service.

South Carolina Railroad opened, first in United States.

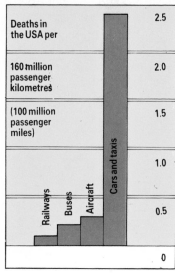

▲ **This chart** of recent statistics shows that travel by rail is very safe.

1863 Opening of world's first underground railroad, in London.

1867 First elevated railroad, experimental overhead track in New York City.

1869 Completion of Pacific Railroad, coast-to-coast across the U.S.A..

STEAM RECORDS

● **1893:** First recorded run of 100 mph made by *Empire State Express* of New York Central and Hudson River Railroad.

● **March 1935:** World record of 108 mph reached by Pacific *Papyrus* of the LNER in Britain.

● **May 1936:** A German 4–6–4 clocked 124.6 mph pulling about 200 tons on almost level track.

● **July 1938:** Britain's Pacific A4 class *Mallard* of LNER pulled 7 carriages weighing about 245 tons down 1-in-200 gradient at 126 mph. This is the official all-time speed record for steam trains.

1879 First electric railroad opened, 274-meter electric tramway, in Berlin.

1885 Canadian Pacific line completed.

1890 First electric underground (subway) railroad, in London.

1893 World's first "official" 100 mph run, by *Locomotive 999*, Grimesville, N.Y.

First electric traction overhead railroad in Liverpool, England.

1895 First mainline electrification, in a tunnel under Baltimore, Maryland.

1921 First diesel-electric locomotive in service; Tunisian Railways.

1932 German State Railways introduces the diesel-electric train—the *Flying Hamburger*.

1948 First gas-turbine electric locomotive tested.

1955 World's first 200 mph run, achieved by French locomotive: 205 mph (330 km/h).

1966 Japanese National Railways open New Tokaido Line with average speed of 101 mph (163 km/h).

1974 World rail speed record of 254.7 mph (410 km/h) set up on August 14 over 6.2 miles (9.97 km) of test track in Colorado by U.S. Federal Railroad.

1976 British Rail starts daily high-speed train service. It covers 94 miles (151.2 km) in 50 minutes, 31 seconds.

1983 World speed record for passenger trains is set in France when the Paris–to–Lyons run is made in just two hours at an average speed of 132 mph (212 km/h).

1984 The last link of a new trans-Siberian railroad is completed.

GOING UNDER

● The world's most extensive public underground railway system is in London, with a route total of 252 miles (405 km). Its greatest depth is 221 ft (67.3 m); its longest route without a change of trains is 34 miles (54.8 km) between Epping and West Ruislip.

● The world's busiest underground railway is the New York City subway with a route total of 237 miles (381 km) and well over two billion passengers a year. Its 475 stations are set closer together than London's 278.

● London's Victoria Line can carry 50,000 people an hour in trains spaced at 2-minute intervals.

RAIL DISASTERS

● **April 20, 1966:** Locomotive explosion, Lumding Junction, India, 55 dead.

● **June 6, 1967:** Collision with fuel truck, Langenweddingin, E. Germany, 82 dead.

● **July 15, 1969:** Collision near Jaipur, India, 85 dead.

● **Feb. 16, 1970:** Crash, North Nigeria, 150 dead.

● **June 17, 1972:** Tunnel crash, Soissons, France, 107 dead.

● **Feb. 28, 1975:** Underground crash in London, England, 41 dead.

● **August 8, 1980:** Passenger and freight train collision near Torun, Poland, 62 dead.

● **June 6, 1981:** Crowded train fell off bridge into river in Bihar State, India, 268 dead.

● **Feb. 8, 1986:** Collision of freight and passenger trains in Canadian Rockies, 50 dead.

Travel by Air

1783 First human ascent, made in a Montgolfier hot-air balloon (which was tied to the ground) by J. F. Pilâtre, in Paris.
First flight in a hydrogen balloon, made by J. A. C. Charles and M. Roberts.

1785 First air crossing of the English Channel, in a hydrogen balloon, by J. P. Blanchard and J. Jeffries.

1852 First (steam) powered airship, flown by Henri Giffard over Paris.

1853 First successful airplane (glider), built by Sir George Cayley.

1890s First successful glider flights, made by Otto Lilienthal of Germany.

1903 First controlled flight in a heavier-than-air machine, by Wilbur and Orville Wright at Kitty Hawk, NC.

1909 First airplane crossing of the English Channel, by Louis Blériot of France in his *Blériot XI* monoplane.

1910 First commercial airline service by airships, established by Count Ferdinand von Zeppelin of Germany.

1919 First transatlantic flight by flying-boat made by Lieut-Cdr Albert C. Read, of the United States.
First nonstop transatlantic airplane flight, made by Capt. J. Alcock and Lieut A. W. Brown of Britain.

1923 First autogiro (model C4) flown by Juan de la Cierva (Spain) at Gatafe, Spain.

1927 First nonstop transatlantic solo flight, made by Charles Lindbergh in his *Spirit of St. Louis*.

AIRLINERS—THE BIG FOUR

Boeing 747: In service 1970; range 6,477 miles (10,424 km); speed 608 mph (978 km/h); seats up to 500.

Douglas DC-10: In service 1971; range 3,580 miles (5,760 km); speed 599 mph (964 km/h); seats 270–400.

Lockheed L-1011 TriStar: In service 1972; range 3,580 miles (5,760 km); speed 588 mph (946 km/h); seats 256–400.

Airbus Industrie A300: In service 1974; range 2,648 miles (4,261 km); speed 415 mph (668 km/h); seats 220–336.

▼ **A biplane**, built by the Wright brothers, flying at Kitty Hawk.

1928 First transatlantic passenger flight, by a German airship.

1930 First patented design for jet aircraft engine, by Frank Whittle in Britain.

Amy Johnson becomes first woman to fly solo from England to Australia.

1933 First solo around-the-world flight, made by Wiley Post in his *Vega* monoplane.

1939 First heavier-than-air transatlantic passenger service, begun by Pan American Airways.

First jet-propelled airplane, built by the Heinkel Company in Germany.

First flight of a single-rotor helicopter, made by Igor Sikorsky.

1947 First supersonic flight, made by Capt. Charles Yeager in a rocket-powered Bell XS-1.

1949 First nonstop around-the-world flight, made by Capt. James Gallagher and crew in a Boeing *Superfortress* bomber.

1952 First jet airliner in regular service, the De Havilland *Comet* on a British Overseas Airways Corporation route.

1965 First conventional aircraft to fly at more than 2,000 mph (3,200 km/h), a U.S. Lockheed YF-12A.

1968 Russian TU-144 is first supersonic airliner to fly (Dec. 31).

1969 World's largest airliner and the first "jumbo" jet, a Boeing 747, makes maiden flight.

Anglo-French supersonic aircraft —*Concorde*—makes short maiden flights in France and England.

1970 British *Concorde* 002 makes its first supersonic flight, reaching 700 mph (1,127 km/h).

The "jumbo" Boeing 747 enters regular service, carrying up to 500 passengers.

1976 First supersonic airliner to begin international flight, the BAC-Aérospatiale *Concorde*.

1986 In December, Dick Rutan and Jeana Yeager (U.S.) pilot the first nonstop around-the-world flight without refueling. *Voyager* completes the trip in 9 days, 3 minutes, and 44 seconds.

Busiest airport is Chicago International Airport (O'Hare), which has an aircraft movement every 45 seconds on average. London's Heathrow handles more international flights than any other airport.

RECORDS IN THE AIR

Aircraft

Speed: 2,193.167 mph (3,529.46 km/h), Capt. Eldon W. Joersz & Maj. George T. Morgan Jr (U.S.A.F.), Lockheed SR-71A, Calif., U.S.A., 7.28.76.

Altitude: 23.39 miles (37.64 km), Alexandr Fedotov (U.S.S.R.), Mikoyan E-266M (MiG-25), 8.31.77.

Gliders

Speed: 121.35 mph (195.3 km/h) over triangular 62-mile (100-km) course, Ingo Renner (Australia), 12.14.82.

Altitude: 46,267 ft (14,102 m), Paul Bikle Jr (U.S.A.), Schweizer SGS 123E, Calif., U.S.A., 2.25.61.

Distance: 907.7 miles (1,460.8 km), Hans-Werner Grosse (W. Germ.), ASW-12, Lübeck-Biarritz, 4.25.72.

Balloons

Distance: 5,208.68 miles (8,382.3 km), B. L. Abruzzo, L. M. Newman (U.S.A.), Ron Clark, Rocky Aoki (Japan), Nagashima, Japan to Covello, Calif., 11.9–12.81.

Duration: 137 hours, 5 minutes, 50 seconds, B. L. Abruzzo, M. L. Anderson, L. M. Newman (U.S.A.), Presque Isle (U.S.A.) to Miserey (France), 8.12–17.78.

Airline Carriers

Aer Lingus
(Republic of
Ireland)

Aeroflot
(Soviet Union)

Air Canada
(Canada)

Air France
(France)

Air-India
(India)

Air Malta
(Malta)

Air New Zealand
(New Zealand)

Alitalia
(Italy)

British Airways
(United Kingdom)

British Caledonian
(United Kingdom)

Cathay Pacific
(Hong Kong)

CSA
(Czechoslovakia)

El Al
(Israel)

Gulf Air
(Oman)

Iberia
(Spain)

Interflug
(East Germany)

212

**Iraqi Airways
(Iraq)**

**Japan Air Lines
(Japan)**

**KLM
(Netherlands)**

**Korean Air
(S. Korea)**

**LOT
(Poland)**

**Lufthansa
(West Germany)**

**Olympic Airways
(Greece)**

**Pan Am
(United States)**

**Qantas
(Australia)**

**Sabena
(Belgium)**

**SAS
(Denmark, Norway,
Sweden)**

**Saudia
(Saudi Arabia)**

**Singapore Airlines
(Singapore)**

**Swissair
(Switzerland)**

**TWA
(United States)**

**Varig
(Brazil)**

213

NATIONAL CIVIL AIRCRAFT MARKINGS

AP	Pakistan	J7	Dominica	V2	Antigua
A2	Botswana	J8	St. Vincent	V3	Belize
A3	Tonga	LN	Norway	V8	Brunei
A40	Oman	LV	Argentina	XA/B/C	Mexico
A5	Bhutan	LX	Luxembourg	XT	Burkina Faso
A6	United Arab	LZ	Bulgaria	XU	Kampuchea
	Emirates	MI	Marshall Is.	XY	Burma
A7	Qatar	MONGOL/		YA	Afghanistan
A9C	Bahrain	HMAY	Mongolia	YI	Iraq
B	China	N	U.S.A.	YJ	Vanuatu
	(People's Republic)	OB	Peru	YK	Syria
B	China/Taiwan	OD	Lebanon	YN	Nicaragua
C	Canada	OE	Austria	YR	Romania
CC	Chile	OH	Finland	YS	El Salvador
CCCP	Soviet Union	OK	Czechoslovakia	YU	Yugoslavia
CN	Morocco	OO	Belgium	YV	Venezuela
CP	Bolivia	OY	Denmark	Z	Zimbabwe
CR/CS	Portugal	P	N. Korea (D.P.R.K.)	ZA	Albania
CU	Cuba	PH	Netherlands	ZK/L/M	New Zealand
CX	Uruguay	PJ	Netherlands	ZP	Paraguay
C2	Nauru		Antilles	ZS/T/U	South Africa
C3	Andorra	PK	Indonesia	3A	Monaco
C5	Gambia	PP/PT	Brazil	3B	Mauritius
C6	Bahamas	PZ	Suriname	3C	Equatorial Guinea
C9	Mozambique	P2	Papua New	3D	Swaziland
D	Federal Republic		Guinea	3X	Guinea
	of Germany	RDPL	Laos	4R	Sri Lanka
DDR	German	RP	Philippines	4W	Yemen Arab
	Democratic	SE	Sweden		Republic
	Republic	SP	Poland	4X	Israel
DQ	Fiji	ST	Sudan	5A	Libya
D2	Angola	SU	Egypt	5B	Cyprus
D4	Cape Verde Rep.	SX	Greece	5H	Tanzania
D6	Comoro Rep.	S2	Bangladesh	5N	Nigeria
EC	Spain	S7	Seychelles	5R	Madagascar
EI	Eire (Ireland)	S9	São Tomé	5T	Mauritania
EL	Liberia	TC	Turkey	5U	Niger
EP	Iran	TF	Iceland	5V	Togo
ET	Ethiopia	TG	Guatemala	5W	Western Samoa
F	France	TI	Costa Rica	5X	Uganda
F-O	French Ov. Depts	TJ	Cameroon	5Y	Kenya
G	United Kingdom &	TL	Central African	6O	Somalia
	Channel Isles		Republic	6V	Senegal
HA	Hungary	TN	Congo	6Y	Jamaica
HB	Switzerland &	TR	Gabon	7O	People's Dem.
	Liechtenstein	TS	Tunisia		Rep. of Yemen
HC	Ecuador	TT	Chad	7P	Lesotho
HH	Haiti	TU	Ivory Coast	7Q	Malawi
HI	Dominican Rep.	TY	Benin	7T	Algeria
HK	Colombia	TZ	Mali	8P	Barbados
HL	Republic of	T3	Kiribati	8Q	Maldives Rep.
	Korea (S. Korea)	VH	Australia	8R	Guyana
HP	Panama	VN	Vietnam	9G	Ghana
HR	Honduras	VP-F	Falkland Is.	9H	Malta
HS	Thailand	VP-LKA/LZ	St. Kitts-Nevis	9J	Zambia
HZ	Saudi Arabia	VP-LMA/LUZ	Montserrat	9K	Kuwait
H4	Solomon Is.	VP-LVA/ZZ	British Virgin Is.	9L	Sierra Leone
I	Italy	VQ-H	St. Helena	9M	Malaysia
JA	Japan	VQ-T	Turks & Caicos Is.	9N	Nepal
JY	Jordan	VR-B	Bermuda	9Q	Zaire
J2	Djibouti	VR-C	Cayman Is.	9U	Burundi
J3	Grenada	VT-G	Gibraltar	9V	Singapore
J5	Guinea-Bissau	VR-H	Hong Kong	9XR	Rwanda
J6	St. Lucia	VT	India	9Y	Trinidad & Tobago

AIR DISASTERS

Date		Deaths
4-4-33	*Akron* dirigible (U.S.) crashed, New Jersey coast	73
5-6-37	*Hindenburg* zeppelin (Ger.) burned at mooring, Lakehurst, N.J.	36
8-23-44	U.S. Air Force B-24 hit school, Freckelton, England	76
6-24-50	DC-4 airliner (U.S.) exploded in storm over Lake Michigan	58
12-20-52	U.S. Air Force C-124 fell and burned, Washington	87
6-18-53	U.S. Air Force C-124 crashed and burned near Tokyo	129
6-30-56	Super-Constellation and DC-7 airliners collided over Grand Canyon	128
2-6-58	Elizabethan airliner (G.B.) crashed on take-off at Munich, W. Germany	23
12-16-60	DC-8 and Super-Constellation airliners collided over New York	134
2-15-61	Boeing 707 (Belgian) crashed near Brussels	73
6-3-62	Boeing 707 (French) crashed on take-off, Paris	130
6-22-62	Boeing 707 (French) crashed in storm, Guadeloupe	113
5-20-65	Boeing 720B (Pak.) crashed at Cairo airport	121
1-24-66	Boeing 707 (Indian) crashed on Mont Blanc (France)	117
2-4-66	Boeing 727 (Jap.) plunged into Tokyo Bay	133
3-5-66	Boeing 707 (G.B.) crashed on Mt. Fuji (Japan)	124
4-20-67	Britannia turboprop (Swiss) crashed at Nicosia (Cyprus)	126
3-16-69	DC-9 (Venez.) crashed on take-off, Maracaibo	155
7-30-71	Boeing 727 (Jap.) collided with F-86 fighter, Japan	162
8-14-72	Ilyushin-62 (E. Ger.) crashed on take-off, Berlin	156
10-13-72	Ilyushin-62 (U.S.S.R.) crashed near Moscow	176
12-4-72	Spanish charter jet airliner crashed on take-off, Canary Is.	155
1-22-73	Boeing 707 (chartered) crashed on landing at Kano, Nigeria	176
3-3-74	DC-10 (Turk.) crashed in forest, Ermenonville, France	346
9-10-76	British Trident 3 and Yugoslavian DC-9 collided in midair near Zagreb (Yug.)	176
3-27-77	Two Boeing 747s (American and Dutch) collided on ground at Tenerife Los Rodeos airport (Canary Islands)	582
1-1-78	Boeing 747 (Indian) crashed into the sea off Bombay (India)	213
11-15-78	DC-8 (Iceland) crashed while attempting to land, Sri Lanka	262
3-14-79	Trident (China) crashed near Beijing (Peking)	200
5-24-79	DC-10 (U.S.) crashed near Chicago	273
11-29-79	Air New Zealand DC-10 crashed, Mt. Erebus, Antarctica	257
4-25-80	British chartered Boeing 727 crashed in Canary Islands	146
7-7-80	Airliner (U.S.S.R.; type unspecified) crashed on take-off, Alma-Ata	163
8-19-80	Lockheed Tristar (Saudi) destroyed by fire after emergency landing, Riyadh	301
12-1-81	DC-9 (Yugoslav.) crashed in Corsica	174
1-13-82	Boeing 737 (U.S.) crashed into Potomac River after take-off	78
7-9-82	Boeing 727 (U.S.) crashed after take-off in Kenner, La.	153
9-11-82	CH-47 Chinook helicopter (U.S. Army) crashed at airshow, Mannheim, W. Ger.	46
9-1-83	Boeing 747 (S. Korea) shot down over Soviet airspace	269
11-27-83	Boeing 747 (Colomb.) crashed near Barajas airport, Madrid	183
2-19-85	Spanish Boeing 727 crashed into Mt. Oiz, Spain	148
6-23-85	Boeing 747 (India) crashed into sea off Ireland	329
8-2-85	Delta jumbo jet (U.S.) crashed at Dallas-Fort Worth Airport	133
8-12-85	Japanese Boeing 747 crashed into Mt. Ogura, Japan	520
8-22-85	British Airtours Boeing 737 burst into flames on runway before take-off at Manchester Airport, England	55
12-12-85	Arrow Air DC-8 (U.S.) crashed after take-off at Gander, Newfoundland	256
3-31-86	Mexican Boeing 727 crashed into mountain in Mexico	166
8-31-86	Mexican DC-9 collided with Piper PA-28 over Los Angeles	67
5-9-87	Polish Ilyushin 62 airliner crashed into forest outside Warsaw	183

Travel by Car

1862 J. J. Lenoir (Belg.) builds first car with internal-combustion engine, in Paris. It is gas fueled.

1875 Siegfried Marcus (Austrian) builds better gasoline-engine car.

1876 Nikolaus Otto (Ger.) builds first successful four-stroke internal-combustion engine, gas fueled.

1885 Karl Benz (Ger.) produces first commercially successful car.

1888 Benz produces first car to be advertised and sold as standard model.

1901 A car with front-wheel drive, the Korn & Latil Voiturette, is built in France.

A car fitted with a speedometer is made in London.

1902 The Belgian-made Dechamps car is built with a standard electric self-starter.

A 9 hp Napier car is built in London with an all-metal body.

A Pan-American automobile is built in the United States with a silencer.

1904 The first car to travel at over 100 mph, at Ostend, Belgium, driven by Louis Rignolly.

1909 First Model-T Ford.

1916 The first automatic windshield wipers are fitted to a Willys Knight car in the U.S.A.

1919 The first servo-assisted four-wheel brakes (power brakes) are fitted to the H6 Hispano-Suiza.

1920 The Duesenberg Model A car is built with hydraulic brakes in the U.S.A.

1926 Safety-glass windshields are fitted as standard to Stutz and Ricken-backer cars in the U.S.A.

Power-steering is fitted to a Pierce Arrow car in the U.S.A.

1950 The first gas-turbine private car is built in Britain for a Rover two-seater.

1967 The rotary Wankel-engine car is built in Germany.

1985 Fastest steam-driven car, *Steamin' Demon*, travels at 145.6 mph.

EARLY RECORDS

● The first races were as much a test of endurance as speed. Many failed to complete the course, or even to start. Over 100 cars entered the first Reliability Trial, of 1894, but only 19 actually started.

● The winner of the first real race, from Paris to Bordeaux and back, in 1895, was Emil Levassor. He earned an all-time record for the longest racing drive—48 hours and 48 minutes with hardly a break.

● Early racers were beset by many problems. The races were held on ordinary roads which were often rough and threw up clouds of blinding dust, and animals sometimes attacked the cars.

● The most deadly of all early races was the 1903 Paris–to–Madrid race. Spectators crowded onto the course. Dust filled the air, and drivers unable to see the road had to follow the tops of telegraph poles and trees. So many people were killed that the race, known as the Race of Death, was stopped.

1899 Renault

U.S.A.	Number	Per 1,000 people
Passenger cars (1985)	130,000,000	544
Commercial vehicles (1985)	39,000,000	163
Nigeria		
Passenger cars (1981)	262,000	2.9
Commercial vehicles (1981)	90,000	0.9

▼ **Four common car shapes.** Sedans and station wagons make spacious family cars. A convertible has a roof that can be lowered in fine weather. Small hatchbacks are very popular today—ideal for running errands in towns and cities.

Saloon

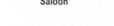

Convertible

Estate

Hatchback

WORLD SPEED BEATERS

	mph	km/h
1898 Jeantaud electric car	39.24	63.15
1899 Jenatzy's *La Jamais Contente*	65.79	105.88
1902 Serpollet steam car	75.06	120.80
1903 Gobron-Brillé	84.73	136.36
1904 Ford 999 (driven by Henry Ford)	91.37	147.05
1905 Napier	109.64	176.45
1906 Stanley steamer, the *Beetle*	121.57	195.65
1922 Sunbeam	133.75	215.25
1925 Sunbeam (M. Campbell)	150.87	242.80
1926 Sunbeam (Henry Segrave)	152.33	245.15
1927 Thomas Special	171.02	275.23
1927 Sunbeam (Henry Segrave)	203.79	327.97
1928 White-Triplex (R. Keech)	207.56	334.02
1929 *Golden Arrow* (Henry Segrave)	231.45	372.47
1931 Napier-Campbell (M. Campbell)	246.09	396.04
·1932 Napier-Campbell (M. Campbell)	253.98	408.73
1935 Campbell Special (M. Campbell)	304.32	489.74
1937 *Thunderbolt* (G. Eyston)	312.00	502.12
1938 *Thunderbolt* (G. Eyston)	357.51	575.34
1939 Railton (J. R. Cobb)	369.71	594.97
1947 Railton (J. R. Cobb)	394.21	634.40

The following were jet- or rocket-powered cars:

1963 *Spirit of America* (C. Breedlove)	407.46	655.73
1964 *Green Monster* (A. Arfons)	536.72	863.75
1965 *Spirit of America* – Sonic 1	614.00	988.12
1970 *Blue Flame* (G. Gabelich)	631.38	1,016.09
1983 *Thrust 2* (R. Nobel)	633.67	1,019.76

▼ **Cars that sum up their eras**—the elegant 1930s, the exciting 1960s, and the practical 1980s.

1935 Hispano Suiza

1961 E-Type Jaguar

1981 Ford Fiesta

217

SOME MOTORING FIRSTS

● Citroën introduced front-wheel drive and unit construction (body and chassis in one unit) as early as 1934.

● White lines running down the middle of the road were first used in Trenton, Michigan, in 1911.

● The first parking meter appeared in 1935 (in Oklahoma City, Oklahoma), and in the same year the first factory-fitted windshield washers (on a Triumph). It was also the year of the world's longest marathon car run. Driving 19 hours every day from June 23, 1935, to July 22, 1936, François Lecot covered 250,000 miles at an average speed of 40 mph.

● The first car fitted with a back-up signal was a Wills Sainte Claire (U.S.A.), in 1921.

● In 1924 the world's first expressway was opened. It ran from Milan to Varese in Italy. Germany's first (1935) was from Damstadt to Frankfurt. America's first dual-carriageway turnpike (the Pennsylvania Turnpike) opened in 1940, and Britain's first expressway (the Preston Bypass) opened in 1958.

● Russia made her first private car, the Niami 1, in 1926. "The People's Car," China's first, appeared in 1951.

● The world's first motor show was held in the Champs Elysées, Paris, in 1894. There were just nine exhibitors.

● The first motor race took place in 1895, in France. The winner averaged 15 mph over the 730-mile course from Paris to Bordeaux and back, and drove through the night with the help of candles and oil lamps.

● 1896 was the year of the first electric starter, the first four-cylinder car engine (a Panhard-Levassor), and of Henry Ford's first car. It was the only car in his home town of Detroit, Michigan, and for security he chained it to a lamppost when he left it unattended.

● 1898 was the year of the first fully enclosed car, a Renault.

● Early car heaters were "Motor Hot Water Bottles." The first heater using heat from the engine appeared in the U.S.A. in 1926.

● Traffic lights first appeared in Detroit in 1919. Britain introduced them in 1928.

● Synchromesh gears first appeared in a standard production car in the U.S., in a 1929 Cadillac. Vauxhall and Rolls-Royce followed in Britain in 1932.

● In 1922 Ford became the first firm to build over a million cars in one year. This was equaled by Volkswagen in 1962, and by British Leyland in 1968.

● 1936 was the year of the first diesel-engine private car, a Mercedes-Benz. Diesels are cheaper to run and more reliable than gasoline engines. However, diesel engines cost more, are noisier, and have less acceleration.

MOTOR CAR INTERNATIONAL IDENTIFICATION LETTERS

A	Austria	**GCA**	Guatemala	**RCH**	Chile
ADN	Yemen PDR	**GH**	Ghana	**RH**	Haiti
AFG	Afghanistan	**GR**	Greece	**RI**	Indonesia*
AL	Albania	**GUY**	Guyana*	**RIM**	Mauritania
AND	Andorra	**H**	Hungary	**RL**	Lebanon
AUS	Australia*	**HK**	Hong Kong*	**RM**	Madagascar
B	Belgium	**HKJ**	Jordan		(Malagasy Rep.)
BD	Bangladesh*	**I**	Italy	**RMM**	Mali
BDS	Barbados*	**IL**	Israel	**RN**	Niger
BG	Bulgaria	**IND**	India*	**RO**	Romania
BH	Belize	**IR**	Iran	**ROK**	South Korea
BR	Brazil	**IRL**	Ireland,	**ROU**	Uruguay
BRN	Bahrain		Republic of*	**RP**	Philippines
BRU	Brunei*	**IRQ**	Iraq	**RSM**	San Marino
BS	Bahamas*	**IS**	Iceland	**RU**	Burundi
BUR	Burma	**J**	Japan	**RWA**	Rwanda
C	Cuba	**JA**	Jamaica*	**S**	Sweden
CDN	Canada	**K**	Kampuchea	**SD**	Swaziland*
CH	Switzerland	**KWT**	Kuwait	**SF**	Finland
CI	Ivory Coast	**L**	Luxembourg	**SGP**	Singapore*
CL	Sri Lanka*	**LAO**	Laos	**SME**	Suriname*
CO	Colombia	**LAR**	Libya	**SN**	Senegal
CR	Costa Rica	**LB**	Liberia	**SU**	U.S.S.R.
CS	Czechoslovakia	**LS**	Lesotho*	**SWA**	
CY	Cyprus*	**M**	Malta*	**or**	Namibia*
D	West Germany	**MA**	Morocco	**ZA**	
DDR	East Germany	**MAL**	Malaysia*	**SY**	Seychelles*
DK	Denmark	**MC**	Monaco	**SYR**	Syria
DOM	Dominican Rep.	**MEX**	Mexico	**T**	Thailand*
DY	Benin	**MS**	Mauritius*	**TG**	Togo
DZ	Algeria	**MW**	Malawi*	**TN**	Tunisia
E	Spain	**N**	Norway	**TR**	Turkey
EAK	Kenya*	**NA**	Netherlands	**TT**	Trinidad and
EAT or	Tanzania*		Antilles		Tobago*
EAZ		**NIC**	Nicaragua	**USA**	United States
EAU	Uganda*	**NL**	Netherlands	**V**	Vatican City
EC	Ecuador	**NZ**	New Zealand*	**VN**	Vietnam
ES	El Salvador	**P**	Portugal	**WAG**	Gambia
ET	Egypt	**PA**	Panama	**WAL**	Sierra Leone
ETH	Ethiopia	**PAK**	Pakistan*	**WAN**	Nigeria
F	France	**PE**	Peru	**WD**	Dominica*
FJI	Fiji*	**PL**	Poland	**WG**	Grenada*
FL	Liechtenstein	**PNG**	Papua	**WL**	St. Lucia
FR	Faroe Islands		New Guinea*	**WS**	Western Samoa
GB	Great Britain &	**PY**	Paraguay	**WV**	St. Vincent*
	Northern Ireland*	**RA**	Argentina	**YU**	Yugoslavia
GBA	Alderney	**RB**	Botswana*	**YV**	Venezuela
GBG	Guernsey	Channel	**RC**	Taiwan	**Z**	Zambia*
GBJ	Jersey	Islands	**RCA**	Central African	**ZA**	South Africa*
GBM	Isle of Man*		Rep.	**ZRE**	Zaire
GBZ	Gibraltar	**RCB**	Congo	**ZW**	Zimbabwe*

* Drive on the left, otherwise drive on the right.

219

CAR INSIGNIA

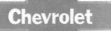

Chevrolet

Fiat

Rover

Lancia

Peugeot

Renault

Vauxhall

Cadillac

Audi

Ford

Mercedes-Benz

Volvo

Aston Martin

Rolls-Royce

Saab

M.G.

Porsche

Volkswagen

Motorcycles

1869 A steam engine is fitted to a Michaux bicycle. Other steam bikes followed.

1876 German Nicolaus Otto patents a four-stroke internal-combustion engine that uses coal gas.

1885 The first gasoline-driven motorcycle, a single-cylinder four-stroke engine machine, built by Gottlieb Daimler in Germany, is patented.

1887 Englishman Edward Butler patents a two-stroke, gasoline-driven tricycle.

In France, Felix Millet has built first multi-cylinder motorcycle.

1894 The first commercially produced motorcycle (twin-cylinder four-stroke) is manufactured in Munich, Germany, by Hildebrand and Wolfmüller.

1896 The first motorcycle race, held by the Automobile Club de France, runs from Paris to Nantes.

1902 The first motorscooter appears in France.

1907 The first Isle of Man TT race is held in May, and won by Charles Collier on a Matchless, averaging 38.33 mph (61.68 km/h).

1914 The motorscooter is manufactured in France by Georges Gauthier.

1923 The first motorcycle speedway race is organized in Australia.

JAPANESE MANUFACTURERS

Honda, the best established Japanese manufacturer, was set up in 1948. The first Suzuki was made in 1952, the first Yamaha in 1954, and the name Kawasaki first appeared on a gasoline tank in 1961. The first world-beating Japanese bike was the 50 cc Honda Super Club. Over 24,000 were made in its first year. By 1965, 15 years after Honda produced their first bike, Japanese motorcycle production had passed two million each year. About a quarter of these machines were exported.

▼ **This bike** is accepted as the world's first motorcycle. It had no brakes, lights, suspension, or gears, and its wooden frame made it very slow and awkward.

Daimler 1885

▼ **Japanese Kawasaki manufacturers** say that their GP21000RX is the world's fastest production streetbike. It can reach around 161 mph (260 km/h). Its power comes from a transverse four-cylinder unit, and it has a six-speed gearbox. Its performance is improved by a light frame and aerodynamic styling.

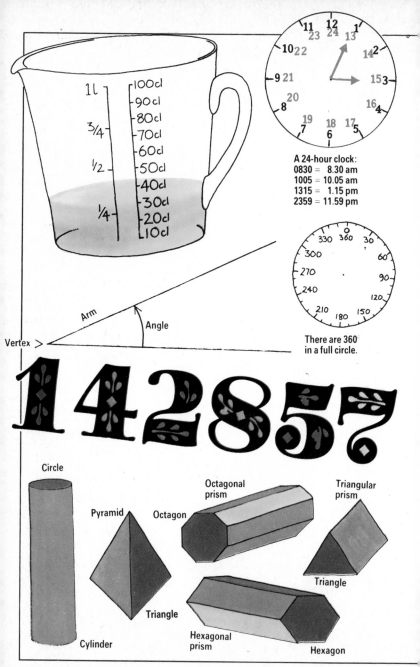

1 l
3/4
1/2
1/4

100cl
90cl
80cl
70cl
60cl
50cl
40cl
30cl
20cl
10cl

11 23
12 24
1 13
10 22
2 14
9 21
3 15
8 20
4 16
7 19
6 18
5 17

A 24-hour clock:
0830 = 8.30 am
1005 = 10.05 am
1315 = 1.15 pm
2359 = 11.59 pm

0 360
330
30
300
60
270
90
240
120
210
180
150

There are 360
in a full circle.

Arm

Angle

Vertex >

1 4 2 8 5 7

Circle

Pyramid

Octagon

Octagonal prism

Triangular prism

Triangle

Triangle

Cylinder

Hexagonal prism

Hexagon

Useful Facts and Figures

How many square links in a square rod, or level tablespoons of flour in an ounce? How many sheets of paper in a ream or firkins of beer in a hogshead? What system of measurement did the ancient Egyptians use? The answers to these questions are here, together with other valuable information and followed by an index for the whole book.

◀ **Assorted facts and figures.** The number halfway down the page—142857—has been called a "roundabout" number because of its special properties. For example, if you multiply it by the number 2, you get 285714—the same numbers, in the same order, except that the number 2 now leads. The same happens if you multiply it by 3, 4, 5, or 6, or divide it by 2 or 5—you still get the same numbers in the same order but with a different number leading the rest. Also, see what happens when you add it, or multiply it, seven times.

BIRTHSTONES		
Month	**Hebrew (Biblical)**	**Present Day**
January	garnet	garnet
February	amethyst	amethyst
March	jasper	aquamarine bloodstone
April	sapphire	diamond
May	chalcedony carnelian agate	emerald chrysoprase
June	emerald	pearl moonstone alexandrite
July	onyx	ruby carnelian
August	carnelian	peridot sardonyx
September	chrysolite	sapphire lapis luzuli
October	aquamarine beryl	opal tourmaline
November	topaz	topaz
December	ruby	turquoise zircon

TRADITIONAL ANNIVERSARY NAMES	
Year	**Name**
1	paper
2	cotton
3	leather
4	fruit, flowers
5	wood
6	iron, sugar
7	wool, copper
8	bronze
9	pottery
10	tin, aluminum
11	steel
12	silk, fine linen
13	lace
14	ivory
15	crystal
20	china
25	silver
30	pearl
35	coral
40	ruby
45	sapphire
50	golden
55	emerald
60	diamond
75	diamond

Weights and Measures

WEIGHT

Metric units
milligram (mg)
1,000 mg=1 gram (g)
1,000 g=1 kilogram (kg)
100 kg=1 quintal (q)
1,000 kg=1 metric ton, or tonne (t)

Imperial units (Avoirdupois)
grain (gr); dram (dr)
7,000 gr=1 pound (lb)
16 dr=1 ounce (oz)
16 oz=1 lb
14 lb=1 stone
28 lb=1 quarter
112 lb=1 hundredweight (cwt)
20 cwt=1 (long) ton=2240 lb
2,000 lb=1 short ton (U.S.)

Troy
24 gr=1 pennyweight (dwt)
20 dwt=1 (Troy) ounce=480 gr
12 (Troy) oz=1 (Troy) lb (U.S.)=5760 gr

Apothecaries' weight
20 gr=1 scruple
3 scruples=1 dram
8 drams=1 (apoth.) ounce=480 gr
12 (apoth.) oz=1 (apoth.) pound=0.82 lb

AREA

Metric units
square millimeter (mm^2)
100 mm^2=1 square centimeter (cm^2)
10,000 cm^2=1 square meter (m^2)
100 m^2=1 are (a)=1 square decameter
100 a=1 hectare (ha)=1 square hectometer
100 ha=1 square kilometer (km^2)

Imperial units
square inch (in^2)
144 in^2=1 square foot (ft^2)
9 ft^2=1 square yard (yd^2)
4,840 yd^2=1 acre
640 acres=1 square mile (mile^2)

625 square links=1 square rod
16 square rods=1 square chain
10 square chains=1 acre
36 square miles=1 township (U.S.)

CAPACITY

Metric units
milliliter (ml)
1,000 ml=1 liter (l)
100 l=1 hectoliter (hl)

Imperial units
gill
4 gills=1 pint
2 pints=1 quart
4 quarts=1 gallon=277.274 in^3

Dry
2 gallons=1 peck
4 pecks=1 bushel
8 bushels=1 quarter
36 bushels=1 chaldron

Apothecaries' fluid
minim (min)
60 min=1 fluid dram (fl. dr)
8 fl. dr=1 fluid ounce (fl. oz)
5 fl. oz=1 gill
20 fl. oz=1 pint

U.S. units
1 U.S. gallon (liquid)=0.8327 gallon (imp.)
1 U.S. gallon (dry)=0.9689 gallon (imp.)
60 minims (U.S.)=1 fluid dram (U.S.)
8 fluid drams (U.S.)=1 fluid ounce (U.S.)
1 fluid oz (U.S.)=1.0408 fl. oz (apoth.)

VOLUME

Metric units
cubic millimeter (mm^3)
1,000 mm^3=1 cubic centimeter (cm^3)
1,000 cm^3=1 cubic decimeter (dm^3)=1 litre
1,000 dm^3=1 cubic meter (m^3)
1,000,000,000 m^3=1 cubic kilometer (km^3)

Imperial units
cubic inch (in^3)
1,728 in^3=1 cubic foot (ft^3)
27 ft^3=1 cubic yard (yd^3)
5,451,776,000 yd^3=1 cubic mile (mile^3)

LENGTH

Metric units
millimeter (mm)
10 mm=1 centimeter (cm)
100 cm=1 meter (m)
1,000 m=1 kilometer (km)

1 micron (μ)=10^{-6} m (i.e. 1 micrometer)
1 millimicron (mμ)=10^{-9} m (i.e. 1 nanometer)
1 angstrom (Å)=10^{-10} m (i.e. 100 picometers)

Imperial units
inch (in)
12 in=1 foot (ft)
3 ft=1 yard (yd)
1,760 yd=1 mile=5,280 ft

1 mil=$\frac{1}{1000}$ in
12 lines=1 in
1 link=7.92 in
100 links=1 chain=22 yd
1 rod, pole or perch=5½ yd
4 rods=1 chain
10 chains=1 furlong=220 yd
8 furlongs=1 mile
3 miles=1 league (statute)

USEFUL MEASURES

Imperial
2 teaspoons	=	1 dessertspoon
2 dessertspoons	=	1 tablespoon
16 tablespoons	=	1 cup
2 cups	=	1 pint
1 pint	=	20 fl. oz

American
1 Amer. pint	=	16 fl. oz
1 Amer. cup	=	8 fl. oz

Metric (working) equivalents
1 teaspoon	=	5 ml
1 Amer. teaspoon	=	4 ml
1 pint	=	½ litre (approx.)
1 litre	=	1¾ pints (approx.)
1 lb	=	½ kilo (approx.)

Level tablespoons per oz (approx.)
Breadcrumbs (dry)	3–4
Cheese (grated)	3–4
Flour	2
Gelatin	2
Raisins, etc.	2
Rice	2
Sugar (granulated)	1

MISCELLANEOUS MEASURES

Nautical
1 span=9 in
8 spans=1 fathom=6 ft
1 cable's length=$\frac{1}{10}$ nautical mile
1 nautical mile (old)=6,080 ft
1 nautical mile (international)=6,076.1 ft=
   1.151 statute mile (=1,852 meters)
60 nautical miles=1 degree
3 nautical miles=1 league (nautical)
1 knot=1 nautical mile per hour
1 ton (shipping, U.K.)=42 cubic feet
1 ton (displacement)=35 cubic feet
1 ton (register)=100 cubic feet

Crude oil (petroleum)
1 barrel=35 imperial gallons
   =42 U.S. gallons

Timber
1,000 millisteres=1 stere=1 m^3
1 board foot=144 in^3 (12×12×1 in)
1 cord foot=16 ft^3

1 cord=8 cord feet
1 hoppus foot=4/π ft^3 (round timber)
1 Petrograd standard=165 ft^3

Paper (writing)
24 sheets=1 quire
20 quires=1 ream=480 sheets

Printing
1 point=$\frac{1}{72}$ in
1 pica=$\frac{1}{6}$ in=12 points

Cloth
1 ell=45 in
1 bolt=120 ft=32 ells

Brewing
9 gallons=1 firkin
4 firkins=1 barrel=36 gallons
6 firkins=1 hogshead=54 gallons
4 hogsheads=1 tun

225

CONVERSION FACTORS

1 acre=0.4047 hectares
1 bushel (imp.)=36.369 liters
1 centimeter=0.3937 inch
1 chain=20.1168 meters
1 cord=3.62456 cubic meters
1 cubic centimeter=0.0610 cubic inch
1 cubic decimeter=61.024 cubic inches
1 cubic foot=0.0283 cubic meter
1 cubic inch=16.387 cubic centimeters
1 cubic meter=35.3146 cubic feet=1.3079
  cubic yards
1 cubic yard=0.7646 cubic meter
1 fathom=1.8288 meters
1 fluid oz (apoth.)=28.4131 milliliters
1 fluid oz (U.S.)=29.5735 milliliters
1 foot=0.3048 meter=30.48 centimeters
1 foot per second=0.6818 mph=1.097
  km/h
1 gallon (imperial)=4.5461 liters
1 gallon (U.S. liquid)=3.7854 liters
1 gill=0.142 liter
1 gram=0.0353 ounce=0.002205 pound=
  15.43 grains=0.0321 ounce (Troy)
1 hectare=2.4710 acres
1 hundredweight=50.80 kilograms
1 inch=2.54 centimeters
1 kilogram=2.2046 pounds
1 kilometer=0.6214 mile=1,093.6 yards
1 knot (international)=0.5144 meters/sec=
  1.852 km/h
1 liter=0.220 gallon (imperial)=0.2642
  gallon (U.S.)=1.7598 pints (imperial)=
  0.8799 quarts
1 meter=39.3701 in=3.2808 ft=1.0936 yd
1 metric ton=0.9842 long ton=1.1023 short
  ton
1 mile (statute)=1.6093 kilometers
1 mile (nautical)=1.852 kilometers
1 millimeter=0.03937 inch
1 ounce=28.350 grams
1 peck (imperial)=9.0922 liters
1 pennyweight=1.555 grams
1 pica (printer's)=4.2175 millimeters
1 pint (imperial)=0.5683 liter
1 pound=0.4536 kilogram
1 quart (imperial)=1.1365 liters
1 square centimeter=0.1550 square inch
1 square foot=0.0929 square meter
1 square inch=6.4516 square centimeters
1 square kilometer=0.3860 square mile
1 square meter=10.7639 square feet=
  1.1960 square yards
1 square mile=2.5900 square kilometers
1 square yard=0.8361 square meter
1 ton (long)=1.0160 metric tons (tonnes)
1 ton (short)=0.9072 metric ton (tonne)
1 yard=0.9144 meter

ANGLE

second (")
60"=1 minute (')
60'=1 degree (°)
90°=1 quadrant, or right angle
4 quadrants=1 circle=360°
1 radian=57.2958°=57°17'44.8"
2π radians=1 circle=360°
1°=0.017453 radian

TIME

second (s or sec)
60 s=1 minute (min)
60 min=1 hour (h or hr)
24 h=1 day (d)
7 days=1 week
365¼ days=1 year
10 years=1 decade
100 years=1 century
1,000 years=1 millennium
1 mean solar day=24 h 3 min 56.555 s
1 sidereal day=23 h 56 min 4.091 s
1 solar, tropical, or equinoctial year=
  365.2422 d (365 d 5 h 48 min 46 s)
1 sidereal year=365.2564 d
  (365 d 6 h 9 min 9.5 s)
1 synodic (lunar) month=29.5306 d
1 sidereal month=27.3217 d
1 lunar year=354 d=12 synodic months

INTERNATIONAL PAPER SIZES*

	mm	inches
A0	841×1189	33.11×46.81
A1	594×841	23.39×33.11
A2	420×594	16.54×23.39
A3	297×420	11.69×16.54
A4	210×297	8.27×11.69
A5	148×210	5.83×8.27
A6	105×148	4.13×5.83
A7	74×105	2.91×4.13
A8	52×74	2.05×2.91
A9	37×52	1.46×2.05
A10	26×37	1.02×1.46

* The sizes are based on a rectangle of area
1 sq meter (A0), with sides in the ratio
$1 : \sqrt{2}$.

HISTORICAL UNITS

Where used	Current equivalent inches and cm	

Cubit (elbow to fingertip)

Egypt (2650 B.C.)	20.6 in	52.4 cm
Babylon (1500 B.C.)	20.9 in	53.0 cm
Assyria (700 B.C.)	21.6 in	54.9 cm
Jerusalem (A.D. 1)	20.6 in	52.3 cm
Druid England (A.D. 1)	20.4 in	51.8 cm
Black Cubit (Arabia A.D. 800s)	21.3 in	54.1 cm
Mexico (Aztec)	20.7 in	52.5 cm
Ancient China	20.9 in	53.2 cm
Ancient Greece	18.2 in	46.3 cm
England	18.0 in	45.7 cm
Northern Cubit (c. 3000 B.C.–A.D. 1800s)	26.6 in	67.6 cm

Foot (length of foot)

Athens	12.44 in	31.4 cm
Aegina	12.36 in	31.4 cm
Miletus	12.52 in	31.8 cm
Olympia	12.64 in	32.1 cm
Etruria	12.44 in	31.6 cm
Rome	11.66 in	29.6 cm
Northern	13.19 in	33.5 cm
England (Medieval)	13.19 in	33.5 cm
France	12.79 in	32.5 cm
Moscow	13.15 in	33.4 cm

Ancient Greece
1 digit (=1.84 cm=0.72 in)
100 digits=1 orguia (about 6 ft)
10 orguias=1 amma (about 20 yd)
10 ammas=1 stadion (=184 m=about 200 yd)

Ancient Rome
1 digitus (=1.85 cm=0.73 in)
3 digiti=1 palmus (=7.4 cm=2.9 in)
4 palmi=1 pes (=29.6 cm=11.7 in)
5 pes=1 passus (=1.48 m=4.86 ft)
125 passus=1 stadium (=185 m=202.3 yd)
8 stadia=1 milliar (=1480 m=0.92 mile)

TEMPERATURE

°Fahrenheit		°Centigrade
212	– Boiling Pt. –	100
194		90
176		80
158		70
140		60
122		50
104		40
86		30
68		20
50		10
32	– Freezing Pt. –	0
14		−10
−4		−20
−22		−30
−40		−40
−58		−50

To convert Fahrenheit to Centigrade: subtract 32, multiply by 5, divide by 9. To convert Centigrade (or Celsius) to Fahrenheit: multiply by 9, divide by 5, and add 32.

▼ **Ancient systems** of measurement were often based on the body. The ancient Egyptians used a span (across the hand) and a cubit (from fingertip to elbow) to measure length.

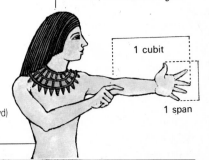

1 cubit

1 span

The metric system was devised in 1790 when the French Revolutionary government decided that the meter should be one ten-millionth of the distance between the equator and the pole on a meridian passing through Paris. Later the meter was defined as the distance between two fine lines engraved on a bar of platinum-iridium alloy when the bar was at a temperature of melting ice, with the bar resting on two rollers 0.571 meter (1 ft 10½ in) apart. The meter is now defined as 1,650,763.73 wavelengths of the orange-red light given off by krypton 86, a rare gas found in the atmosphere.

NUMERATION

Arabic	Roman	Binary*
1	I	1
2	II	10
3	III	11
4	IV	100
5	V	101
6	VI	110
7	VII	111
8	VIII	1000
9	IX	1001
10	X	1010
11	XI	1011
12	XII	1100
13	XIII	1101
14	XIV	1110
15	XV	1111
16	XVI	10000
17	XVII	10001
18	XVIII	10010
19	XIX	10011
20	XX	10100
21	XXI	10101
29	XXIX	11101
30	XXX	11110
32	XXXII	100000
40	XL	101000
50	L	110010
60	LX	111100
64	LXIV	1000000
90	XC	1011010
99	XCIX	1100011
100	C	1100100
128	CXXVIII	10000000
200	CC	11001000
256	CCLVI	100000000
300	CCC	100101100
400	CD	110010000
500	D	111110100
512	DXII	1000000000
600	DC	1001011000
900	CM	1110000100
1,000	M	1111101000
1,024	MXXIV	10000000000
1,500	MD	10111011100
2,000	MM	11111010000
4,000	MV̄	111110100000
5,000	V̄	1001110001000
10,000	X̄	10011100010000
20,000	X̄X̄	100111000100000
100,000	C̄	11000011010100000

* NB: In the binary system, there are just two symbols, 0 and 1. The base of the system is 2 (written 10), just as 10 is the base of the decimal system. And just as 10^3 (10 to the power of 3) is written in the decimal system by a one followed by three zeros, so 2^3 is written 1000 in the binary system. In other words, 8 (which is 2^3) is written 1000. To write a number in the binary system, you break it up into powers of 2. For example, 13=8+4+1, i.e. $\mathbf{1} \times 2^3$, $\mathbf{1} \times 2^2$, $\mathbf{0} \times 2^1$, $\mathbf{1} \times 2^0$; it is written 1101. If you want to double a number in the binary system (i.e. raise it to the power of 2, or the power of "10" in the binary system), just add a zero on the right.

MATHEMATICAL FORMULAS*

* r=radius, h=height.

Circumference

Circle	$2\pi r$

Area

Circle	πr^2
Surface of sphere	$4\pi r^2$
Ellipse, semi-axes a, b	πab
Triangle, base b	$\frac{1}{2}bh$
Rectangle, sides a, b	ab
Trapezoid, parallel sides a, c	$\frac{1}{2}h(a+c)$
Regular pentagon, side a	$1.721a^2$
Regular hexagon, side a	$2.598a^2$
Regular octagon, side a	$4.828a^2$

Volume

Sphere	$\frac{4}{3}\pi r^3$
Cylinder	$h\pi r^2$
Cone	$\frac{1}{3}h\pi r^2$
Rectangular prism, sides a, b, c	abc
Pyramid, base area b	$\frac{1}{3}hb$

Algebraic

$a^2 - b^2 = (a+b)(a-b)$
$a^2 + 2ab + b^2 = (a+b)^2$
$a^2 - 2ab + b^2 = (a-b)^2$

For quadratic equation $ax^2 + bx + c = 0$,

$$x = \frac{-b \pm \sqrt{b^2 - 4ac}}{2a}$$

ellipse

CALORIC VALUE OF FOODS

Average portion	Calories
Apple (1) 5 oz (142 g)	70
Bacon (fried) 2 oz (57 g)	250–320
Banana (1) 5 oz (142 g)	110
Beans, green (boiled) 4 oz (113 g)	10
Beef (roast) 3 oz (85 g)	325
Beef steak (grilled) 6 oz (170 g)	520
Beer (ale) 1 pint (0.56 l)	180
Bread (white, 1 slice) 1 oz (28 g)	73
Bread (whole wheat, 1 slice) 1 oz (28 g)	65
Butter ½ oz (14 g)	110
Cabbage (boiled) 5 oz (142 g)	15
Carrots (boiled) 4 oz (113 g)	24
Celery (raw) 4 oz (113 g)	8
Cheese (cheddar) 1 oz (28 g)	112
Cheese (cottage) 1 oz (28 g)	29
Chicken (roast) 4 oz (113 g)	220
Chocolate (milk) 2 oz (57 g)	300
Cod (grilled) 4 oz (113 g)	170
Coffee (cream, no sugar) 6 fl oz (170 ml)	25
Corn flakes 1 oz (28 g)	100
Cream (double) ½ oz (14 g)	64
Egg (boiled, 1) 2 oz (57 g)	90
Grapefruit (½) 7 oz (198 g)	42
Honey ½ oz (14 g)	41
Lamb (roast) 3 oz (85 g)	250
Lettuce 2 oz (57 g)	5
Margarine ½ oz (14 g)	110
Melon (1 slice) 5 oz (142 g)	30
Milk (cup) 6 fl oz (170 ml)	110
Orange (1) 6 oz (170 g)	60
Peanuts 2 oz (57 g)	330
Potatoes (fried) 4 oz (113 g)	270
(boiled, baked) 4 oz (113 g)	90
Rice (boiled) 6 oz (170 g)	600
Sardines (tinned) 3 oz (85 g)	240
Sausages (pork, 2) 4 oz (113 g)	400
Spinach (boiled) 1½ oz (43 g)	10
Spirits (measure) 1 fl oz (8 ml)	63
Strawberries 5 oz (142 g)	35
Sugar 2 oz (57 g)	215
1 teaspoon	25
Tea (cup, no sugar) 6 fl oz (170 ml)	15
Tomato (1) 3 oz (85 g)	12
Wine, dry (glass) 4 fl oz (114 ml)	84
sweet (glass) 4 fl oz (114 ml)	128

APPROXIMATE OVEN TEMPERATURES

Description	Electric		Gas
	°F	°C	
very cool	225°	107°	240°
	250°	121°	265°
cool	275°	135°	290°
	300°	149°	310°
warm	325°	163°	335°
moderate	350°	177°	355°
fairly hot	375°	191°	375°
	400°	204°	400°
hot	425°	218°	425°
very hot	450°	232°	450°
	475°	246°	470°

DERIVATION OF DAYS AND MONTHS

Day, month	Named after
Sunday	the Sun
Monday	the Moon
Tuesday	Tiu, Norse god of war
Wednesday	Woden, Anglo-Saxon chief of gods
Thursday	Thor, Norse god of thunder
Friday	Frigga, Norse goddess
Saturday	Saturn, Roman god of harvests
January	Janus, Roman god of doors and gates
February	Februa, Roman period of purification
March	Mars, Roman god of war
April	aperire, Latin for "to open"
May*	Maia, Roman goddess of spring and growth
June*	Juno, Roman goddess of marriage
July	Julius Caesar
August	Augustus, first emperor of Rome
September	septem, Latin for "seven"
October	octo, Latin for "eight"
November	novem, Latin for "nine"
December	decem, Latin for "ten"

◀ **An ellipse** is a regular oval or flattened circle shape. The diagram shows that it is an angled section of a cone. The planets of the solar system move in elliptical curves.

* According to some scholars, May comes from *majores* (older men), June from *juniores* (young men), to whom months were held to be sacred.

229

Flags of the World

Afghanistan

Albania

Algeria

Andorra

Angola

Antigua and Barbuda

Argentina

Australia

Austria

Bahamas

Bahrain

Bangladesh

Barbados

Belgium

Belize

Benin

Bhutan

Bolivia

Botswana

Brazil

Brunei

Bulgaria

Burkina Faso

Burma

Burundi

Cambodia

Cameroon

Canada

Central African Republic

Chad

Chile

China

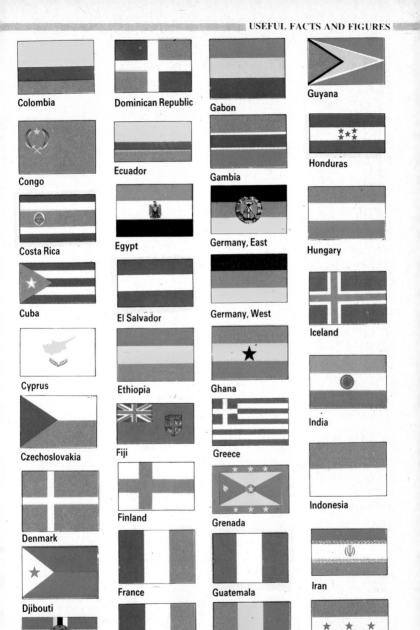

Colombia

Dominican Republic

Gabon

Guyana

Congo

Ecuador

Gambia

Honduras

Costa Rica

Egypt

Germany, East

Hungary

Cuba

El Salvador

Germany, West

Cyprus

Ethiopia

Ghana

Iceland

Czechoslovakia

Fiji

Greece

India

Denmark

Finland

Grenada

Indonesia

Djibouti

France

Guatemala

Iran

Dominica

French Guiana

Guinea

Iraq

231

Ireland

Israel

Italy

Ivory Coast

Jamaica

Japan

Jordan

Kenya

Kiribati

Korea, North

Korea, South

Kuwait

Laos

Lebanon

Lesotho

Liberia

Libya

Luxembourg

Madagascar

Malawi

Malaysia

Maldives

Mali

Malta

Mauritania

Mexico

Monaco

Mongolia

Morocco

Mozambique

Nauru

Nepal

Netherlands

New Zealand

Nicaragua

Niger

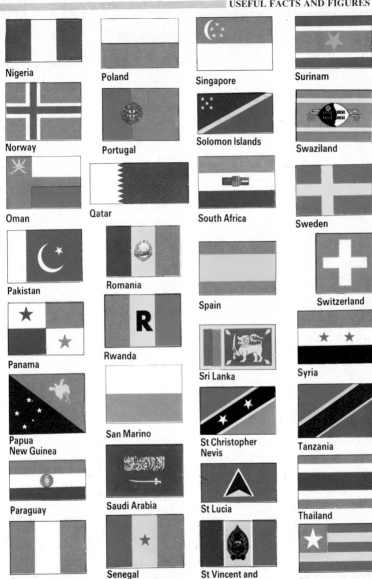

Nigeria

Poland

Singapore

Surinam

Norway

Portugal

Solomon Islands

Swaziland

Oman

Qatar

South Africa

Sweden

Pakistan

Romania

Spain

Switzerland

Panama

Rwanda

Sri Lanka

Syria

Papua
New Guinea

San Marino

St Christopher
Nevis

Tanzania

Paraguay

Saudi Arabia

St Lucia

Thailand

Peru

Senegal

St Vincent and
Grenadines

Togo

Philippines

Sierra Leone

Sudan

Tonga

233

Trinidad and Tobago

Uganda

Vatican City

Yemen PDR

Tunisia

United Kingdom

Yugoslavia

Uruguay

Venezuela

Turkey

Vietnam

Zaire

Tuvalu

USA

USSR

Western Samoa

Zambia

UAE
(United Arab Emirates)

Vanuatu

Yemen AR

Zimbabwe

NOBEL PEACE PRIZE

1901 Henri Dunant (Swiss) & Frédéric Passy (French)	**1911** Tobias Asser (Dutch) & Alfred Fried (Austrian)
1902 Elie Ducommun and Albert Gobat (Swiss)	**1912** Elihu Root (American)
1903 Sir William Cremer (British)	**1913** Henri La Fontaine (Belgian)
1904 Institute of International Law	**1914–16** *No award*
1905 Baroness Bertha von Suttner (Austrian)	**1917** International Red Cross
1906 Theodore Roosevelt (American)	**1918** *No award*
1907 Ernesto Moneta (Italian) & Louis Renault (French)	**1919** Woodrow Wilson (American)
1908 Klas Arnoldson (Swedish) & Fredrik Bajer (Danish)	**1920** Léon Bourgeois (French)
1909 Auguste Beernaert (Belgian) & Paul d'Estournelles (French)	**1921** Karl Branting (Swedish) & Christian Lange (Norwegian)
1910 Permanent International Peace Bureau	**1922** Fridtjof Nansen (Norwegian)
	1923–24 *No award*
	1925 Sir Austen Chamberlain (British) & Charles Dawes (American)
	1926 Aristide Briand (French) & Gustav Stresemann (German)

1927	Ferdinand Buisson (French) & Ludwig Quidde (German)
1928	*No award*
1929	Frank Kellog (American)
1930	Nathan Söderblom (Swedish)
1931	Jane Addams & Nicholas Butler (American)
1932	*No award*
1933	Sir Norman Angell (British)
1934	Arthur Henderson (British)
1935	Carl von Ossietzky (German)
1936	Carlos de Saavedra Lamas (Argentinian)
1937	Viscount Cecil of Chelwood (British)
1938	Nansen International Office for Refugees
1939–43	*No award*
1944	International Red Cross
1945	Cordell Hull (American)
1946	Emily Balch & John Mott (American)
1947	Friends Service Council (British) & American Friends Service Committee
1948	*No award*
1949	Lord John Boyd Orr (British)
1950	Ralph Bunche (American)
1951	Léon Jouhaux (French)
1952	Albert Schweitzer (Alsatian)
1953	George C. Marshall (American)
1954	Office of the U.N. High Commissioner for Refugees
1955–56	*No award*
1957	Lester Pearson (Canadian)
1958	Dominique Georges Pire (Belgian)
1959	Philip Noel-Baker (British)
1960	Albert Luthuli (South African)
1961	Dag Hammarskjöld (Swedish)
1962	Linus Pauling (American)
1963	International Red Cross & League of Red Cross Societies
1964	Martin Luther King, Jr. (American)
1965	UNICEF (U.N. Children's Fund)
1966–67	*No award*
1968	René Cassin (French)
1969	International Labor Organization
1970	Norman Borlaug (American)
1971	Willy Brandt (West German)
1972	*No award*
1973	Henry Kissinger (American); Le Duc Tho (North Vietnamese) – declined

1974	Sean MacBride (Irish) & Eisaku Sato (Japanese)
1975	Andrei Sakharov (Russian)
1976	Betty Williamś & Mairead Corrigan (British–N. Ireland)
1977	Amnesty International
1978	Mohammed Anwar El Sadat (Egyptian) & Menachem Begin (Israeli)
1979	Mother Teresa of Calcutta (Indian)
1980	Adolfo Perez Esquival (Argentinian)
1981	Office of the U.N. High Commissioner for Refugees
1982	Alva Myrdal (Swedish) & Alfonso Garcia Robles (Mexican)
1983	Lech Welesa (Polish)
1984	Bishop Desmond Tutu (South African)
1985	International Physicians for the Prevention of Nuclear War (American)
1986	Elie Wiesel (American)
1987	Oscar Arias (Costa Rica)

▼ **Willy Brandt,** chancellor of West Germany from 1969 to 1974 and winner of the 1971 Nobel Peace Prize.

Index

This index is only very general, as a more detailed one would be repeating the whole book!
Page numbers in *italics* refer to illustrations.
Page numbers preceded by an *m* refer to maps.

W–Z

ACKNOWLEDGMENTS

The publishers wish to thank the following for kindly supplying photographs for this book.

Page 1 *left* Michael Chinery, *middle* Neil Lorrimer, *right* Fotomas Index; 3 *top* Frank Driggs Collection, *bottom* Colorsport; 10 Space Frontiers; 11 Saul Levy; 15 RTHPL; 16 British Museum; 17 Royal Astronomical Society; 18 Mansell Collection; 19 NASA; 20 NASA; 24 Hawaiian Travel Centre; 26 Zefa; 32 French Tourist Office; 33 New Zealand House; 34/35 Zefa; 38 J. Allan Cash Photo Library; 40 Dave Collins; 43 Dev O'Neill/US Congress; 45 Satour; 52/53 Zefa; 54 *top* Novosti, *bottom* Barbara Taylor; 57 United Nations; 60 Investors Chronicle; 61 Spink & Son; 65 Ver Brauchor Bank Ag Hamburg; 66/67 Michael Holford; 71 Palace Museum Taiwan; 73 R. David; 74 Scala; 77 Popperfoto; 78/79 National Maritime Museum; 82 Zefa; 87 Robert Harding; 89 Dave Collins; 93 Keystone; 97 Popperfoto; 98 Bibliotheque National, Paris; 101 *left* BBC Hulton, *right* Picture Point; 103 Sonia Halliday; 104 Mansell Collection; 105 Popperfoto; 106 Dr Duncan Thompson; 109 British Museum; 112/113 Science Photo Library; 115 Mansell Collection; 117 Picture Point; 124 Kodak Museum; 128 top & bottom Mansell Collection; 131 Popperfoto; 134 Imitor; 135 Italian Tourist Office; 136 Geological Museum; 139 Zefa; 140/141 National Museum Vincent Van Gogh, Amsterdam; 145 *top* Mansell Collection, *bottom* Royal College of Music; 146 Frank Driggs Collection, *bottom* Syndication International; 147 BBC Hulton; 148 *left* Jesse Davis, *right* Zoe Dominic; 153 Lotusfilms; 156 Tate Gallery; 158 Philadelphia Museum of Art/Purchased by W P Wistach Collection; 159 Maurithuis, Hague; 162 National Portrait Gallery; 164/165 Heather Angel; 182 Imitor; 183 Mansell Collection; 184/185, 186 Colorsport; 189 Zefa; 190 *top* Allsport/Steve Powell, *bottom* Colorsport; 194 S & G Press Agency; 195, 199 & 200 Colorsport; 202 top & bottom Zefa; 207 P & O Lines; 210 & 221 Mansell Collection; 235 German Embassy.

Picture Research Penny Warn.